RED
LEGS
and
BLACK
SOX

RED LEGS and BLACK SOX

EDD ROUSH AND THE UNTOLD STORY
OF THE 1919 WORLD SERIES

SUSAN DELLINGER, PHD

emmis
books

For further information, contact the publisher at

Emmis Books
1700 Madison Road
Cincinnati, OH 45206
www.emmisbooks.com

LIBRARY OF CONGRESS CATALOGING-IN-PUBLICATION DATA

Dellinger, Susan.
Red legs and black sox : Edd Roush and the untold story of the 1919
World Series / by Susan Dellinger.
p. cm.
ISBN-13: 978-1-57860-229-2
ISBN-10: 1-57860-229-7
1. Roush, Edd, 1893- 2. Baseball players--United States--Biography.
3. Cincinnati Reds (Baseball team). 4. Chicago White Sox (Baseball
team). 5. World Series (Baseball) (1919) I. Title.
GV865.R65D45 2005
796.357092--dc22

2005030206

COVER PHOTO CREDITS
Edd Roush in Cincinnati Reds uniform sweater, 1938.SDN-065275
Action photos of 1919 World series,
SDN-061908; SDN-061955; SDN-061909.
All *Chicago Daily News* negatives collection,
Courtesy of the Chicago Historical Society

Note: All interior images not otherwise credited are from the
ROUSH FAMILY COLLECTION.

COVER & INTERIOR DESIGNED BY STEVE SULLIVAN
EDITED BY JACK HEFFRON

DISTRIBUTED BY PUBLISHERS GROUP WEST

DEDICATION

To Essie Mae Swallow Roush

This book is lovingly dedicated to my dear departed grandmother without whose willingness to tell the story through her letters and faithful collection of memorabilia, this book could never have been written.

TABLE OF CONTENTS

EDD J. ROUSH
CHICAGO A.L. 1913
NEW YORK N.L. 1916, 1927 TO 1930
CINCINNATI N.L. 1916 TO 1926, 1931

LEADING N.L. BATTER IN 1917 AND 1919
BATTED .352 IN 1921, .352 IN 1922, .351
IN 1923, .348 IN 1924. BATTED OVER
.300-13 SEASONS. LIFETIME BATTING
AVERAGE OF .323. MOST OUTFIELD
PUTOUTS, 410 IN 1920. F.L. 1914-1915.

ROUSH PLAQUE IN BASEBALL HALL OF FAME,
COOPERSTOWN, NEW YORK

INTRODUCTION

"It comes out to a bit over one percent of the thirteen thousand odd
men who have ever played major league ball…we know they are there,
tucked away up-country and in the back of our minds: old men,
and younger ones on the way, who prove and sustain the elegance
of our baseball dreams."

– Roger Angell. "Up at the Hall." **The New Yorker** *(8/31/87)*

I n today's world of ESPN and multi-million-dollar athletes,
sport is omnipresent. A modern fan pushes a button to view
a ballgame, hear experts debate a controversial play, or listen to gossip about the most private details of an athlete's life.
An aging superstar can sit in the fully equipped theater room
of his mansion and watch himself on a life-size screen. He can
enjoy hundreds of replays of his glory years.

But there was another time, a time before television, a time
before radio. Football was in its infancy and basketball was a
game played in schools. Baseball was king. Every town had a
team, and every little boy aspired to play. Fans learned game
scores from party-line telephone calls, telegraph operators, and

the local postman. The names of heroes were displayed on barns in fields of grain.

The baseball stars of the early twentieth century were no less talented than those of today, but all that is left of these past heroes is oral history and shared memory preserved in print. This is the story of one such hero. From 1913 to 1931 he strode that diamond-shaped stage. Fans in Cincinnati and New York chanted his name as he approached the plate, *"Roush...Roush...Roush!"*

He was also the last eyewitness to the 1919 World Series, known as the "Black Sox" Series. In this book the story of the most infamous moment in baseball history is told, for the most part, through the eyes of a man who was on the field. He was the star of the Cincinnati Reds, and so for the first time this iconic tale is told from the perspective of Reds players, managers, and the people of Cincinnati.

This book could never have been written without the help of numerous baseball historians and scholars both living and dead. Most particularly, I am indebted to the Society of American Baseball Researchers (SABR) for its very existence. With a membership of 7,000 worldwide, this association's charter is to research and record the important events in the history of the game of baseball. Without the assistance of numerous members, this granddaughter could never have written the baseball story that under girds the life of her grandfather, Edd J. Roush.

Certain individuals deserve special plaudits here. First and foremost I wish to thank three people who served as "readers" on this journey. Over a period of eight months, these men edited every single page of this book. My sincere thanks to: **Mike Lackey, Robert Schaefer,** and **Bill Marshall.**

The following people made specific and invaluable contributions to this book:

- **Gene Carney** was a continual sounding board and source of information regarding the finer points of the Black Sox Scandal and 1919 Series. His web site www.baseball1.com/carney and the 1919 Black Sox Yahoo Group continue to inspire and provoke baseball research.
- **Jim Sandoval** provided the tip that led to the discovery of Detective Cal Crim and his report on the 1919 Scandal.
- **Mike Nola** provided perspective on the White Sox and colorized the front cover photo.

Certain members of SABR provided expert advice in specialty areas of baseball research.
- **1919 World Series**
~ William Cook, Rod Nelson, David Karickhoff, and Maxwell Kates
- **Cincinnati Reds**
~ Eric Sallee, Pete Cava, Dan Nathan, and Greg Rhodes
- **Early Career**
~ Dan O'Brien, Bob Hoie, and David Johnson

I am also indebted to staff members at various institutions for research including the Cincinnati Historical Society, the Willard Library in Evansville, Indiana, and the Chicago Historical Society. In particular I wish to thank **Tim Wiles**, Director of Research and **Jeff Arnett**, Director of Public Programs at the Baseball Hall of Fame Museum and Library in Cooperstown.

I am thankful to family members and friends of persons appearing in this book who were willing to be interviewed both in person and by phone:

Jimmy and Betty Widmeyer

Jonathan Slater and Marilyn Smith

Barbara Trautman

Claude Hinds and Randy Hollenbaugh

Robert Manley

Joe Kanzler
Tom and Connie Bressler
Tom Rariden
Jamie McKechnie and Carol Matchett
Dan Murphy and Christophe Trautman
Nita Walter Bigelow
Jack O'Mara
Loveren Sharp
Quina and Bari Schmidlapp

Thanks to personal friends and family who assisted in reading, research, and support for this author.
Alma Shufflebarger
Ellen Kimmel
Bev and Bert Quinlan

I thank **Richard Hunt** and the entire staff at Emmis Books for their creative work on behalf of this book. In particular, I owe a large debt of gratitude to my patient editor, **Jack Heffron**, without whom this book would never have been written. And special thanks to **Steve Sullivan** for creating a smashing book cover and to **Connie Springer** for her research assistance.

Finally (and most importantly) I thank my immediate family for their patience and support during the months of writing.
Dr. Robert Dellinger
Jade Roush Dellinger
Cathy Sowell
George, Greg, Kim and Matt Meinberg
Mumford and Essie Dellinger

PART I

EDD ROUSH ON THE ROAD
TO GREATNESS

1

Her Ten-Thousand-Dollar Beauty

"He loved to play baseball; even more than all that sweet stuff
he used to bring and leave at my house. He worked in a confectionery
shop and used to hang around and walk me home from the picture show
every night I worked there. To me, he was just one of those Roush kids.
He and Fred were always in some kind of mischief."

– Essie Mae (Swallow) Roush (1909)

It was an Indiana autumn evening in 1909. Standing at the
piano situated between picture screen and audience, a girl,
plainly dressed with hair in a shapeless bun, gathered her
sheet music. As the remainder of the moviegoers departed, she
placed the pieces in their somewhat irregular box (originally
meant to carry her sister's hi-top shoes). The gestures were
mechanical; she repeated them every night after completing her
work as the theater's accompanist. But tonight she was still lost
in the fantasy world of the movies.[1]

She imagined she was Mary Pickford calmly feigning indifference to her screen suitor, Douglas Fairbanks. She moved
from behind the piano bench and flipped her wrist as if pitching a white feather boa over the left shoulder of her brown,
homemade dress. She tilted her chin upward, and then slowly
lowered it in disdain at an empty chair in the front row. After

two or three seconds she moved to her imaginary suitor in flowing, chest-first strides.

She stopped abruptly, pushing one side of her hair back in an authentic Pickford gesture, and said (*avec hauteur*), "I shan't accompany you to the summer house this year, Virgil. I should die of ennui." And giving him a last glimpse of her flashing beauty, she made a quick exit. She smiled to herself as she shed her imaginary boa and resumed her real life.

Essie Mae Swallow, at eighteen, was like the family butter churn. She was fairly plain to look at, a sturdy southern Indiana girl with white skin, direct blue eyes, a thin persevering mouth, and regally thin hands. The long finger branches appeared to entwine the piano keys when she played. Her outer appearance was calm, but inside was a fiery determination to make butter of a life that predicted only milk.

Before her sister left, that goal seemed possible. For years Tina Swallow had been the driving force in Essie Mae's life. Six years Essie Mae's senior, Tina was her predecessor at the Baldwin piano in the Amuzu picture show (formerly known as the Theatorium.) She sang the numbered songs with such verve that often people came only to hear her. Although from a poor background, she dreamed of a better life, and her beauty, voice, and fiber guaranteed her ascent among the local elite.

Essie Mae's first exposure to "the finer things" was through Tina, who had been accepted into the society of wealthy coal-mining people who invaded Oakland City, Indiana, to drill for oil and natural gas in 1908. Though Essie Mae was still invited to these affairs, it was no fun without Tina. Seated across from one another, they were separated by the Ingles' Haviland and Fostoria, objects that never adorned the Swallow table. The girls could sneak secret glances. Whenever Essie Mae said "the right thing," Tina was there with a wink to show her approval.

Now Tina was gone.

As Essie Mae ascended the aisle to leave, she imagined she heard Will Parson's cornet as it blared through the theater on that night five months earlier when Tina left. The Amuzu was packed. All of Oakland City had come to see the "Boomerang Artist" in Will and Ray Hutchison's show. Will's wife, Meg, sang a medley of tunes to open the evening. Tina was the show's piano accompanist. After the medley and a blast on Will's cornet, Ray appeared in green tights and a sequined shirt, bending in unbelievable gyrations. Ray Hutchison was a contortionist—one of the best on the Pantages circuit. But his initial appearance disappointed the audience. The boomerang "thing" he carried was nothing but a bent piece of wood. However, excitement grew as the audience watched the boomerang fly time after time above their heads and away from their grabbing hands to return to its owner.

As Essie Mae stood in the shadows of the now empty theater, she felt the same goose pimples she had felt that night as the voices of townspeople rose and fell with the movement of the boomerang. But then it was over, and her big sister left forever, to travel the circuit and be Ray's wife. To travel the world! To make her name! To die years later in Florida, a bloated, blond

AMUZU THEATER AND MAIN ST. OF OAKLAND CITY, 1910

showgirl fresh out of dreams.

Essie Mae stayed and played in her sister's shadow.

Jarring herself from the memories, Essie Mae left the theater. As she passed through the double doors she said good night to the manager, Paul Ellis. Then she saw Edd—that silly kid who spelled his name wrong[2]—waiting in his usual spot under the darkened marquee. As always, she tested her feelings. There was no tingle, no rush of adrenalin, just the usual pleasure of seeing the familiar face and knowing she would not walk home alone.

She greeted him with a smile but felt a twinge of guilt. Why was she allowing him to waste his time with her when she really had no feelings for him? He should be with his own crowd and not with a "has-been" two years older than he. But she had told him that many times. She had asked him, "Why don't you go with those girls in your group?" He never answered. He just continued to wait for her at the picture show and walk her home.

Edd offered her some of the taffy globules in his candy box. He worked at Doug's Confectionery across the street from the theater and would sometimes get off early and catch the remainder of a movie. He always took home the last of the taffy after cleaning the machine. Essie Mae took a piece of taffy as they began their accustomed eight-block trek to the Swallow home on Dale Street. For a block they walked without speaking, chewing taffy and lost in their own thoughts. The only sound was the squeaking of Edd's corduroy pants.

Both Edd and Essie Mae were loners. They enjoyed their respective private worlds—Edd's baseball, Essie's vaudeville. Both dreamed of life far beyond the confines of Oakland City, of a glittering world of glass chandeliers, furs, vest pocket watches, marble floors, and elegant meals.

Edd was a handsome boy at sixteen: tall, very dark, with a well-toned muscular body. He inherited his big frame from both parents, Will and Laura. Laura Harrington Roush was a large woman of German descent. It was rumored that she was part Indian. Indeed, she looked it. She was a true farmer's wife and was proud to have won the recent Gibson County Hog-Calling Contest.

Essie felt that Laura favored Edd's twin brother, Fred. Fred had no job and far fewer chores on the Roush farm than did Edd. It was easy to differentiate Fred, "the baby," from Edd because they were not identical twins. Fred was heavier and had a round, child-like face that contrasted with the lean, firm-jawed Edd. He also tended toward laziness. Though Edd and Fred were very different, they were close and remained close throughout their lives, passing away within weeks of each other at age 94.

After milking the cows at four in the morning, Edd would join Fred and their father, Will, in the milk wagon headed for town. When the boys were younger, they would have to take the milk to the customer's door and ladle it out for them. In these more progressive times, they delivered newfangled cans with spigots on the top. Will eased the wagon down the center of the road as Fred carried the milk to the houses on the left side and Edd covered the right.

Edd and Fred enjoyed racing up Broadway Street (being careful not to spill the milk). There were more houses on the right side, so Edd took the handicap since he was larger and faster than Fred. If the milk wagon bell did not awaken the customers, they were stirred by the laughter of the boys racing back to the moving wagon. Daisy, the horse, never stopped her slow trot. She knew the daily route very well.

Will enjoyed his sons, but was a bit partial to Edd. Edd was much like his father—athletic, good-humored, quiet, a man of strong convictions with a good head for business.

The Roush men were in a particular hurry on the Saturday

ROUSH FARM, 1910. EDD, FRED, WILL,
GRANDPA HARRINGTON AND DAISY

milk run because all three played baseball in the afternoon—on different teams. But then, so did almost every able-bodied man in the surrounding southern Indiana countryside. In the harsh winter, young men played basketball at the local college gym. All summer and as long as the weather held into the fall, there was rarely an open field to be found on weekend afternoons. Players were of all ages, judged only by their ability to catch, throw, and bat.

As Essie walked with Edd, she finally turned to him and said, "I'll go along then now. It's not far. You go on home."

Edd's face drooped, but sensing her determination, he said, "I'll see you at Christian Endeavor tomorrow night?"

"Sure," she said. "Bye." She hurried the remaining five blocks home.

Sunday dawned clear and sunny, much like the day that had preceded it. A perfect September morning. Edd had moved through his morning chores mechanically, lost in thought. He wondered why Essie Mae had left the church with Eloise Whitman so quickly last night, particularly after he had been elected president of Christian Endeavor. Didn't she even want to congratulate him?

Then he shifted his focus to baseball. Today was the big game. The Oakland City WalkOvers (uniforms provided by the WalkOver Shoe Company) were composed of the town's best players. They had only lost two games this summer, trouncing Washington, Petersburg, Mount Carmel, New Harmony, and even one of the Vincennes teams. The only team to beat them was their number one rival, Princeton.

Competition was vicious between these little towns, and often fights broke out after the games. With a population of 6,448 in the 1910 census, Princeton, the Gibson County seat, was twice the size of Oakland City. Over 90 percent of the people in the towns worked on farms or coal mines. These tough men and women labored long hours all week, and Sunday was their big day. After church they lined up to pay their five cents for the best entertainment in town—the local baseball game.

As was the custom in Oakland City, the townspeople gathered at the railroad station after church awaiting the arrival of the weekly train from Indianapolis. Essie Mae was there with Eloise and her younger sister, Eva. She had become much closer to Eva since Tina left. Today she looked almost attractive in her Sunday garb, a blue dress with matching parasol. It had been Tina's.

After greeting the train, the crowd moved east two blocks to the WalkOvers' field to cheer their team. Edd and Fred didn't meet the train after church. They ran home to change clothes. After the big game, the younger men would play ball on the same field until dark, hoping that some of the crowd would stay to watch.

Edd changed quickly and ran the mile to the field. When he arrived, he found that the Princeton Cubs had arrived early and were ready to play, but the WalkOvers were missing their right fielder, Charley Farmer. As Edd drew close to the players,

Horace Whitman (older brother of Eloise) shouted, "Here comes that Roush kid. Let's put him in for Charley!"

The pitcher, Frank Bryant, attested to Edd's ability to catch, and Willard Wilkey, a friend of Edd's father, said he was "far and away the best young hitter he'd seen around." Manager Claude Trusler made a quick decision. "If Charley doesn't show in five minutes, Roush, you're in!"

Edd prayed that Charley Farmer wouldn't show. He hadn't been at church either. Maybe he was sick today. Oh please, God, let Charley be sick---just for one day!

Someone yelled, "Let's play ball!" and Edd found himself in right field with heart pounding. The innings flew. Edd concentrated on the game and was oblivious to the fans surrounding the field, as he would be in Cincinnati and New York years later.

In the bottom of the fourth with a tied score and a man on second, Edd hit a double down the first base line. The Oakland City crowd cheered wildly and taunted the Princeton rooters. On second base, Edd stifled an urge to steal third. This game was too important for him to take a chance that might be costly. After all, this wasn't a battle between eighteen men; it was a struggle between two towns, each hoping to uphold its pride through the prowess of its athletes.

In the sixth inning, Edd hit another double straight up the middle, and he scored on Ott Barker's single two batters later. As Edd flew into home, his stride resembled that of his granddad Harrington, who had been a runner for the Union in the Civil War.

The score was now 8 to 6 with the WalkOvers in the lead. Though Edd did not get another hit, he made a difficult catch in the top of the eighth. Thrusting his 160 pounds skyward, he grabbed the ball with the fingertips of his left hand. The many hours of throwing the ball over the roof of the barn and running around to the other side to catch it paid off.

Oakland City won the game 10 to 7, and from that day on Edd was a member of the team. As he walked off the field he spotted Essie Mae's blue dress. He went toward her carrying his pride as if it were a trophy he could present to her.

"You were great!" she said. "Dad says you're a fine ball player. Everyone thinks so. Will they let you play again?"

He put his hand on her arm indicating that they should walk toward town. It was the first time he had ever purposefully touched her. As he did, she felt an electricity that surprised her. He sensed her reaction and quickly withdrew his hand. But when he looked at her, she smiled, and he knew that he had done what was natural and needn't be ashamed.

Essie talked of the game on the way back to town: what people said, how she felt, how "scared" Edd must have been. Edd confided something then that he had kept to himself for a long time.

EDD AND ESSIE WALKING DOWN A COUNTRY LANE, CIRCA 1911

"I'm going to try and make the big leagues."

After some thought, Essie Mae said, "I think you can do it, Edd. I know you can. Why, I read where Ty Cobb makes ten thousand dollars a year playing baseball."

"So will I," he boasted.

Essie Mae laughed and said, "You'll be my ten-thousand-dollar beauty!"

Neither ever forgot this conversation. Edd decided to pursue a career in baseball on that day in 1909. For years Essie affectionately called him her $10,000 Beauty—until it finally came true in 1919.

HIGH PROMISE

It was the beginning of hunting season in November 1913. Essie saw the familiar glint in Edd's eyes. With a sigh, she said, "So, when are you leaving?"

Edd was lost in thought as he continued to polish the barrel of the Wesson rifle lying across his lap. It was his treasure given to him by his grandfather Joseph, who died when he was eight.[3] He wiped it with reverence, with respect, with muscle memory of the feel of it in the crook of his arm.

Essie was worried about him. He had been a different person since he got home from Lincoln, Nebraska. He was sullen, quiet, depressed. Any forays into a discussion of what happened in Chicago and Lincoln were met with utter silence.

It had taken Edd four long years to get to this point—four years, five cities, five "debuts." According to sportswriters in varying locales, it was not a single ball player who had made this journey but rather five different baseball players had passed through their respective towns from 1911 to 1913.

In 1910, a fellow named "Edd Roush" played for the Oakland City Walk-Overs. He started in 1909 at age sixteen as a shortshop. Later he moved to first and second base, ending up in right field. In 1911, "Eddie Rouch" played second base and left field for the Princeton Rexalls. At the tail end of this season, a guy named "Ed Rousch" played eleven games for the Henderson

(Kentucky) Hens.[4] He was an infielder.

In 1912, the Evansville (Indiana) Yankees debuted "Ed Rausch." When this team moved up to Class B in the Central League the next year, "Eddie Roush" played right field.

In 1913, a "Mr. Edward Rausch" was signed late in the season as an outfielder for the Chicago White Sox. After one month, he was farmed out to the Lincoln Links. The Links claimed to have a utility outfielder named "Ed Roushe."

He had been called "Ed," "Ed J," "Eddie," and "Double D". He was " the Roach," "Rooch," "Rowshee," "Roashay," and "Roosh." It had been ages since he'd heard his name pronounced correctly—"Rowwsh."

No wonder Edd was confused. Was he the same guy they had called the Central League "phenom" and the Chicago "marvel"? He was hitting over .400 in Evansville when the big-time scouts came to see this hot shot for themselves. They tapped him for the Big Show, but they didn't play him. He sat seething on the White Sox bench for four weeks until they'd sent him down for a miserable month in that awful little Nebraska farm town.

The beginning of Edd's ascension into national fame is properly placed in 1913, when he was called up to the Chicago White Sox. However, in the preceding years he had experienced the struggles of a young athlete seeking his place in history. From 1909 through 1912, Claude Trusler was the manager of the Oakland City Walk-Overs. Claude would remember the Roush twins, Edd and Fred: "If you took one of them on, you could expect to fight them both; they were tough farm kids." Edd was chosen first, and Fred joined the team later when they needed a catcher. Edd began at shortstop, then moved to first base. When he noticed that the 6'3" second baseman, Henry Geise, let too many zingers through his legs, he suggested they switch positions. Henry agreed and Edd settled in at second base.

As the WalkOvers beat every opponent within fifty miles,

ROUSH & LOWE ON
WALK-OVERS TEAM

Edd and pitcher Pete Lowe were the stars of the team. They were each paid a dollar every Sunday to perform. After the game, the younger players liked to walk over to Doug Campbell's confectionary shop[5] for ice cream.

After the game on July 4, 1911, an event occurred that changed the way Edd thought about baseball. The Walk-Overs beat the Rexalls handily that day, as usual. As the players headed for the confectionary shop, the Princeton manager called Edd and Pete to the side for a chat.

"How much are they paying you fellas to play for Oakland?" the manager asked.

Pete spoke up quickly: "We get a buck a game." His pudgy, freckled face beamed with pride.

The manager smiled. "I guess you know that some of the players on your team get five bucks a game." He waited. "And they're not a good as you two are."

Until that moment, it had never occurred to Edd that some players made more money than others on the same team. He saw red.

The manager moved in to close the deal. "I'll give you both five dollars a game if you play for Princeton."

Five dollars was a king's ransom to Edd's family, and he was still smarting from the unfair treatment on his own team. He said, "You've got a deal." Pete declined. The manager had just stolen the best player from his competitor. He walked away with a smile.[6]

Edd debuted with the Princeton Rexalls on July 16, 1911. Princeton beat Oakland City. Although the hometown fans booed the turncoat mercilessly, Edd's performance was stellar with two doubles and one home run.

Edd began the 1912 season with Princeton, but his tenure there was short. With a .455 batting average and a 1.074 slugging percentage, he was tearing up the league, when he was recruited by the Evansville Yankees. Edd liked Evansville and he enjoyed almost two years of playing there. Edd would later say that, next to Cincinnati, Evansville had the most loyal fans. It was also a step up. In 1912, Evansville was a Class D team in the K.I.T. "Kitty" League.

Evansville was a natural choice for a young southern Indiana athlete. It was the biggest town within a hundred miles and drew folks from many nearby smaller towns. It held a regal position on a curve of the Ohio River linking Indiana, Illinois, and Kentucky. The closest big cities—Indianapolis, Nashville, and Cincinnati—were almost a day's train ride away. Many young Hoosiers sought their fortunes in Evansville as clerks, salesmen, and plant workers. In 1912 the city was abuzz with the process of changing from gaslight to electricity. The lovely Vendome Hotel graced the downtown, and the Masonic Lodge that would soon become an important part of Edd's life was not far away. The Germania Mannerchor singing club on Fulton Street hosted dances, concerts, and billiard games for its thriving membership.

In a few years, Evansville would be the site for the first free-standing Sears store, where you could order your new Ford or even the new $2,485 Cole "Sixty"—a car that started by "simply pressing a Delco electric button." In this city D. C. Stephenson would rule over citizens with an evil grip as the Grand Dragon of Indiana's Ku Klux Klan.[7] The *Evansville Courier* was the major mouthpiece of the news for several counties around.

Edd debuted as a Yank on July 26, 1912. Manager Barton called him the "hittin' kid" who was famous for "dropping Texas leaguers into left and right field." The local scribe gave a positive review of his performance.

> Fresh from the lots around Princeton the new outfielder jumped into the game like an old head and did much toward landing a regular job. In his first appearance at the plate, he picked off a neat single and proceeded to get Red Basham's goat by stealing second....He stole second again in the eighth inning and handled three chances in left field gracefully. –*Evansville Courier*

The same sports section included an interesting article about a boxer charging that he had been "doped" before a match. His name was Abe Attell. This boxer's life would impact the life of Edd and many others in 1919, with unpleasant consequences.

During the 1913 season, the Evansville team was upgraded to Class C in the Central League. They played in a pasture off Louisiana Street in Coal Mine Park, which was renamed Ohio Valley Park. Their new manager was an Evansville native, Charles "Punch" Knoll. In his honor they dropped the Yankee moniker and became known as the Punchers. Knoll, eleven years older than Roush at 31, had been in professional baseball since 1901. His career would eventually span thirty years as a minor league player/manager and include one season with the Washington Senators. He played next to Edd in the outfield and taught him how to move around on different hitters.

Edd was one of three players Knoll kept from the 1912 squad. He gave Edd a ten-dollar-a-month raise and made sure he signed his contract on time.

The season opener was played on April 23 in front of five hundred fans. The opponent was the Grand Rapids Black Sox. With an ominous foreshadowing of 1919, the Black Sox won the game, 4-1, but Edd was the Evansville star.

Throughout the beginning weeks of the season, Edd was playing great ball as the Punchers outfielder and cleanup hitter. During this time Edd learned to love the outfield. He played both right and center but preferred center, where he could see all the action happening in front of him like his own private play. He learned that most batters take their hard swing on the first pitch, so this was when he stayed deep. If they failed, he moved up. Before the last pitch he became almost invisible to the fans because he was half-squatting behind the second baseman. This pattern usually worked, but Edd also studied each batter. He knew the ones who wouldn't shrink from the taking the full swing on the last pitch too. He played deep for them.

On Saturdays, all manner of humanity descended on Evansville from surrounding towns, arriving by foot, by wagon, by train, by horse, and a few by car. Some came in the coal-fired electric train they called a "doodle bug." Princeton rooters came on a similar train called "The Plug." The trains spurted and smoked all the way there. On May 11, 1913, the Punchers were scheduled to play the Springfield (Ohio) Reapers. Edd's friends and neighbors chose this game to turn out in his honor.

Essie and her friends prepared white satin ribbons that everyone wore pinned to their shirts while they sat in the stands that day. In large block print, the six-inch ribbon read "ROUSH ROOTERS from Oakland City." Edd's parents and brother filled the milk wagon with a picnic lunch and directed Daisy onto the road south. They left at 8 a.m. after the farm chores were done. On the way they passed friends and neighbors, some of whom were walking the thirty miles to Evansville.

1913 EVANSVILLE PUNCHERS
FRONT ROW: OSMAN, GOSLIN, BARTON, TURNER, KENNEY, THOMPSON
MIDDLE ROW: STORCH, CARTWRIGHT
BACK ROW: GOSSAGE, KLACHBUSH, GOSNEL, SMITH, HICKS, ROUSH

When Edd took the field, he saw more than two hundred white ribbons dancing in the wind with his name on them. They were worn by people he had known from the time he was a little boy. He was overwhelmed with pride in these simple folk who had come here for him.

And then his nerves took hold. For the first time that season he didn't get a hit in the game.

THE SCOUTS COME TO TOWN

Major league scouts began to notice Edd. In those days, the newspapers published the batting averages of the top players in all the leagues. Scouts saw the name Roush at the top of President Louis Heilbroner's list for the Central League. After more than a month of play, Edd was far and away the top hitter in America—easily eclipsing veterans like Ty Cobb and Tris Speaker.

Scouts for Connie Mack, John McGraw, Charles Comiskey, and Garry Herrmann made plans to visit Evansville. At the same time a series of communiqués passed between owners and managers. Letters and telegrams carrying the name Roush flew swiftly down the wood-paneled corridors of several executive offices. Several came to Evansville owner Harry Stahlhefer from Cincinnati Reds owner Garry Herrmann.

On May 24, Herrmann wrote requesting the opportunity to bid on this "inexperienced" youth. On his way to his office downtown that morning, he stopped at a newsstand on 4th and Vine to pick up a copy of the *Cincinnati Post*. He liked the newsboy there. Herrmann didn't bother to learn his name, but he would become familiar with the name Jimmy Widmeyer in 1919.

In the meantime, another scout was in the stands in Evansville. His name was Kid Gleason. He had come down from Chicago.

Mr. Aug. Herrmann   June 1, 1913
Cincinnati, Ohio

Dear Sir,

Your letter of May 24, was received today, upon my return home with the club, and in reply will say, that I have sold player Roush, to Chicago Americans for $3,000 Cash. On May 24th, Mr. Comiskey made me the offer of $3,000 and I accepted it, as I thought it was as good an offer as I would receive from any other club.

At the time I disposed of this player, I had not received your letter asking for a chance to bid on him.

Trusting that you will think as I do, that I did the proper thing in disposing of this player, when I received the price that I had expected to realize from his sale.

With Best Wishes for yourself and club, I remain

Yours Very Truly
Harry W. Stahlhefer

Windy City - 1, Queen City - 0. In truth, the Sox needed help. They were getting creamed on their eastern run in Philly and were locked with Boston for fourth place in the American League. However, Garry Herrmann would not forget that Harry Stahlhefer had sold Edd Roush out from under him. He would continue to pursue this player for the Reds. Three years later, in 1916, his goal would be realized.

On May 28, Harry Stahlhefer went to bed a happy man. He was delighted with the windfall sale of this "hot property." He had increased the Evansville coffers by $3,000 ($300,000+ in 2006 dollars). Further, the deal allowed him to keep his player through the end of the season. As owner of a small team, he had been treated with respect by three owners of major league clubs, although he didn't deal with Comiskey directly. Instead, the final paperwork was handled by a little bookkeeper with a lisp named Harry Grabiner.[8]

What Stahlhefer missed was the fact that, had he waited a few days, he could have sparked a bidding war for Edd Roush between three teams—the Sox, the Giants, and the Reds. What no one could know then was that Edd Roush would eventually wear the uniforms of all three teams in his career.

CHICAGO, AUGUST 15, 1913

If the thirty-mile trip to Evansville seemed far from home to Edd, then the four hundred miles to Chicago was like going to a foreign country. He remembered the pride on the faces of his dad and Fred as they waved goodbye at the Princeton train station. Now, as he walked up to the former city dump turned into the grand Comiskey park, he wondered if he would be worthy of their pride. The uniform they gave him was a little tight in the shoulders, but that was all right. He had both his right- and left-hand gloves and that was what mattered.

Edd reported on a Friday morning while the Sox were in the middle of practice. "Old Roman" Comiskey, the owner, wasn't present because he was preparing for his birthday celebration that night. But, there they were—the guys he'd read about in the newspapers. The pitchers were tossing balls around and laughing about some "prissy" sportswriter who had just written an article about the evils of ballplayers drinking alcohol.[9] The writer's name was Hugh Fullerton. The Sox would hear his name again in just a few years, but then they wouldn't be laughing.

As Edd looked around, the first players he recognized were Ed "Knuckles" Cicotte and Ray "Cracker" Schalk. Schalk stood up just then to throw the ball and Edd was surprised. He really was a little guy! He was also a very nice guy as Edd would soon learn. Schalk took a liking to this young rookie and showed him the ropes in the first few days. Edd would remember Schalk's kindness toward him when they met again on the field in 1919 as opponents.

Edd also recognized "Prince" Hal Chase and "Death Valley" Jim Scott. There was a young guy hitting fungoes that Edd didn't recognize but would come to know as George "Buck" Weaver. Then Manager Jimmy Callahan walked over and shook his hand. He told Edd to go chase some fly balls.

As Edd walked to the outfield, he saw the players who held the positions that he most coveted—Frank "Ping" Bodie and "Chink" Mattick. He would be filling in for Shano Collins. He went directly to right field and shot a few back with his left hand. Pretty soon he moved over to left field, threw one glove down and picked up another and threw the ball with his right hand. He shot it in on a line, just as he had from right field. The pitchers stopped laughing. Everyone gaped at the ambidextrous new kid they'd heard about.

Another "kid" ran into the infield and yelled, "Roush,

come over here!" It was the assistant manager, Kid Gleason. The rookie trotted in.

Gleason barked, "Are you a right- or left-hand thrower?"

"Don't make no difference to me. When I play right, I throw with my left. When I'm in left, I throw with my right."

"Don't make any difference to you?" Gleason was incredulous.

"Nope. But I always bat left-handed."

Gleason walked away scratching his stomach under his belt. But he watched Edd closely the rest of the morning.

The next day, the headlines trumpeted the arrival of the rookie:

> ## ROUSH A MARVEL TO CHICAGO, MAKES KID GLEASON WONDER
> Eddie has the entire White Sox team looking on with mouths open when he pulls the ambidextrous stuff—Bill Bailey says he fields and throws well. – *Chicago Tribune*

Another newspaper ran the story of an interview with Callahan. He was quoted as saying that he "had an idea that throwing with his left hand is the natural way [for Rausch]." He said that he would "probably insist that the youngster throw that way." He also quelled the qrowing rumors that the Sox intended to turn Edd into an ambidextrous pitcher and ended his commentary with the old saw, "he looks like a good prospect."

Edd was assigned to be the roommate of another Sox rookie who showed great promise that year, a pitcher named Reb Russell. When they got into their room after the long day, Edd was exhausted. All he wanted to do was go to bed, but Reb had a different idea. After a bit of talk, he pulled out a special letter that had arrived for him that day from his girlfriend in

Mississippi. He was eager to know what was in the letter, but he couldn't read it. Edd gave up an hour of sleep that night to read the letter to Reb again and again.

Callahan and Gleason agreed that Edd had speed and connected with some good hits in batting practice. They gave their new addition a try against the Red Sox. He batted against Fred Anderson and grounded out three times. He played the field well—with both arms. He played in center field replacing Bodie for two games, and then Callahan told him to take his gloves off and return to the bench.

Callahan did want to give Roush an honest try-out. He developed a plan to take out Chase, who had an injured ankle, put Collins on first, and Roush in the outfield for a couple games. According to Martin Kohout in his biography of Chase,[10] Chase refused the idea saying he could "stick to the bag for a while longer." This ruined Edd's chances to show his ability. It was not the last time that Hal Chase would "steal" from Roush.[11]

Finally, Edd played again on September 11, in Philadelphia, batting for Jim Scott.

He smacked a single to right off of Chief Bender, his one hit in three weeks with the American League. His AL batting average would go in the history books as a miserable .100. Edd would later say with pride, "I got my first hit in the majors off of Chief Bender." But it was too late; Callahan had already made up his mind.

On September 14, I. E. Sanborn wrote the story that many thought would chronicle the end of Edd's career.

> Outfielder Rousch was sent west tonight with instructions to report to the Lincoln team of the Western league for the rest of the season. He has not been given enough work yet to show that he

will not yet fill the bill, as he has not shown sufficient experience to get the job of any of the
present gardeners. Manager Callahan thinks the
youngster has sufficient promise to bear watching, however, in spite of his ambidexterity.

Edd's roommate, Reb, wished him well that last day at
Griffith Stadium (the team was on their eastern swing).
Callahan put him on the train in Washington, D.C. and assured
him that his trunk with his personal belongings would be sent
from Chicago the next day. It didn't arrive for two weeks. Since
Edd had directed the club to send his check home to his family, he had only ten dollars in his pocket and one change of
clothes in his small satchel. Most of all he missed Essie's letters
that were in the inside pocket of his missing trunk.

It was a lonely and miserable two weeks in Lincoln. As he
sat in his little room alone, he missed Oakland City. If only he
had Essie's letters to read; that would help.

There was no public phone in the hotel, and he didn't want
to cause any "fuss" on his behalf.

After all, he was now a "failed" baseball player. If only
they'd given him a couple more chances and let him hit a few
more times. Why did Chase have to make so much fun of him?
Reb tried to protect him, but he was no match against the wily
"Prince." What did they care that he used two gloves? It was
none of their damn business!

The weather in Lincoln was windy and gelid as the fall season
took hold on the Plains. His daily routine became perfunctory.
He put on his uniform and jacket and went out on the field. He
parried any attempt at friendliness from fellow players. He
spoke to no one. They called him "the dummy," and he didn't
care. He fell into a batting slump, and the fans booed. They
booed every time he came up to bat.

Finally two letters came—one from Essie and one from his mother. They were both full of anger and encouragement. He had gotten "a raw deal" in Chicago. Essie's ten-thousand-dollar beauty would prove himself again.

When the trunk finally arrived, Edd packed his things and skipped town. He didn't tell anyone, just got on a train to Des Moines heading for Indiana. He left Lincoln in shame, determined never to return. He would still be Lincoln property, and luckily there were no repercussions.

Although Edd left with feelings of failure, a few days later a sportswriter had the following to say:

> One of the great ball players of modern times—Eddie Roushe [sic] is the chap I have in mind—has hung up his glove and declared himself down and out as an exponent of the national pastime....Believe it or not, bleacher critics razzed Eddie off the Lincoln club. ...Tumbling into a batting slump, Roush was given the Bronx cheer by the bleacher bugs. The experience got under his hide.
> – Cy Sherman, *Lincoln Nebraska Star*

As Edd stood at the front desk of the Lincoln hotel waiting for the clerk, he browsed the sports page of the local newspaper. He noticed an article about the new Federal League appointing someone named James A. Gilmore from Chicago as its new president. This new league was called the "Outlaw League" for raiding the American and National Leagues of their best players and managers. Somehow it made him feel even more insignificant.

Just then the clerk returned and, as Edd checked out of the hotel, he made a decision.

He pushed the old right-hand glove that had plagued him for years across the counter and gave it to the hotel clerk on duty that afternoon.[12]

And, at that moment, Edd decided from now on he was going to throw with his natural arm—if he ever played baseball again.

---

[1] Author's Note: Entire chapter taken directly from taped interviews with Essie Roush, 1978. Physical locations of buildings and streets in 1909 Oakland City compliments of Bill Marshall, resident and friend of family.

[2] As the family story goes, Edd's father, Will, spelled his name with two "d's" to make sure he would never be called Edward or Edwin. Today staffers at the Baseball Hall of Fame refer to Roush as "old double d."

[3] The middle initial "J" was given to both Edd and Fred to symbolize their grandfathers, Joseph and Jerry.

[4] Eddie Sisson paid Roush $70 a month to play eleven games (.222 BA) with the Henderson Kentucky "Hens" (August 17-27, 1911). He returned to finish the season with Princeton because he didn't like Henderson; it was too far from home (50 miles).

[5] Grandma Harrington would later buy this confectionary shop with her "widow money." Laura Roush would inherit it, and at her death she would will it to Edd's brother, Fred.

[6] The Princeton manager had another reason to smile. Roush's reputation in Princeton went beyond baseball. After a game on June 22, Edd and John Pierce were walking along the Wabash river when they noticed a fellow in the river splaying water and calling for help. The fisherman had fallen from his boat, which was drifting away in the currents. Edd dove in, baseball cleats and all, and pulled Roy Westfall, age 23, back into the boat. The next day the local paper ran the headline: Eddie Roush Saves Drowning Man. The people of Princeton admired Roush.

[7] At the height of Klan influence in the American Midwest, many ballplayers were rumored to have been members. Edd Roush had memories of conflicts within the Cincinnati Reds between Catholics and Protestants.

[8] Grabiner was the assistant to Charles Fredericks, Comiskey's nephew and club secretary. Grabiner would take on the duties of club Business/General Manager and spend years in service to the White Sox as Comiskey's most trusted and loyal lieutenant. Bob Hoie, SABR researcher, 2005.

9   Hugh Fullerton. "Booze the Enemy of Ball Players," Lincoln Daily Star (reprint from Farm and Fireside)

10 Martin Kohout. *Hal Chase*. McFarland & Company, 2001.

11 Roush and Chase would be teammates on the Reds in 1916-18.

12 Years later a Roush "game-used" glove would sell at an internet auction for a mere $86. Could it have been that no one believed the great-grandson of the Nebraska hotel clerk when he "guaranteed" its authenticity? After all, all the expert bidders knew that Edd Roush was a "lefty." What would he be doing playing with a righty glove?

2

Hiding in the Bushes

"If the Federal League didn't do anything else, it brought out Edd
Roush one of the great players of the game."
– *James Crusinberry,* **Baseball Magazine,** *June, 1952*

JANUARY 1914

INDIANAPOLIS, INDIANA

N one of the passengers took much notice as the train from
Evansville slowed into the station. Princeton was one of
the many little towns they would see along the half-day
journey to Indianapolis. They would clank through fields of
hibernating corn over softly rolling hills in southern Indiana. With
every tenth click of the train tracks, a little woods would appear
and break the monotony. Passengers who knew the area knew
about the secret stash hidden in those intermittent woods. They
envisioned themselves tromping through the wet, dewy under-
brush on an April morning seeking the prize buried beneath rot-
ting leaves and around the fallen branches and stumps. They
could smell again the crinkly morel mushrooms bursting their
flavor into the freshly churned butter in the black iron skillet of
the farmhouse. Mushroom hunting was a spring sport in southern Indiana.

As a few passengers glanced out the windows, they saw two

men standing on the platform, one holding a small valise. One looked like a younger version of the other—father and son, no doubt. The younger of the two, hardly out of boyhood, wore what appeared to be a borrowed suit. It didn't fit his sprouting frame. His shoulders and upper arms strained against the home-sewn seams. The older man in his brown coat, white wrinkled shirt, and suspenders looked

ROOKIE CRACKERJACK CARD OF EDD ROUSCH [SIC][1]

like a farmer. Both wore serious expressions, as if the trip on which they were embarking was of great importance.

As he and his father took their seats on the train, Edd Roush was, indeed, nervous. After his failure in Lincoln last September, Edd had come home to stay. He thought he was washed up in baseball. His father had said it simply: "They didn't know what they had."

Then November 10 arrived and quail-hunting season began. The Roush men and many of the other locals would hunt every day except Sunday. Their two best bird dogs would join them. Edd's favorite was "Bud." By the end of November, Will Roush was thirsting for bigger game. He invited Edd to join him on a fortnight expedition to hunt pheasant. Fred stayed home to take care of the farm with his mother. Maybe it was the fresh fall Kentucky air or maybe it was the perfect silence of the wooded slopping hills, but for whatever reason, Edd came home a changed man. He realized he *had* to play baseball.

After two months at home with the usual routine of waking up for 4 a.m. milkings, he knew he had to get away from those damnable cows. He had endured the stern pleasure on his mother's face and the clear disappointment on the faces of Will and Essie long enough. He hated the smell of the polluted air from the coal mines that surrounded the town. He missed the grassy smell of the baseball field; the feel of the bat in his hands and the anticipation of the hit; the fun of staring out beneath the bill of his cap and trying to outguess the pitcher; the taste of the dirt in his mouth when he slid into home plate; the long drive to center field that he could turn his back on, then run with all his might and turn around just in time to catch. These were his thoughts as he flanked his father walking silently through the woods in search of quail and pheasant.

On that simple hunting trip Edd began to take responsibility

for his life. He had lived a couple lifetimes in the last few years, but he had been sleepwalking through them. One thought crystallized that would become a truism throughout his life: "There is no way to earn money that is easier than playing baseball." So, as he walked into the cozy farmhouse of his youth, he was looking for the next locker room to call home.

EDD IN FULL HUNTING GEAR

In the first few days of December, Edd sat down at his mother's secretary and wrote the letters. He chose three Midwestern teams that fit his criteria—close to home. He guessed that if the major leagues had rejected him, maybe the Federal League would consider him. There was publicity about good players joining this league. Walter Johnson had already "jumped" (although he would come home for more money later), and there was even talk that Ty Cobb and Tris Speaker might do the same. Uncomfortable in dealing with the "money men," he wrote to the managers.

One letter went to Joe Tinker in Chicago, one to Mordecai "Three Finger" Brown in St. Louis, and one to "Whoa" Bill Phillips in Indianapolis. Then he waited. He told no one about the letters, not even Essie. Better not to risk more disappointment for them.

He heard from Mordecai Brown first. Mordecai was a fellow Hoosier who was born just up the the southwestern border of Indiana in Nyesville. The St. Louis outfield was solid, so Brown didn't need anyone. But...he would pass the word along on Edd's behalf. He never heard from Tinker.[2] And then, in the week after Christmas, the telephone call from Indianapolis came. Phillips was interested. He had seen Edd play in Evansville. He already had three outfielders—Benny Kauff, Jappie Scheer, and Vin Campbell—but he needed a good man in the back-up spot. Could Edd come up to Indianapolis in early January? He'd pay expenses.

Edd savored every word. His heart beat fast. Maybe, just maybe, he'd play baseball again. When everyone gathered for dinner that night, some of the unspoken feelings that had been brewing beneath the surface within the Roush family emerged. Laura, the matriarch, had the most to lose. First, she was loath to accept that one of her sons might make a career of "playing" some game. Although she enjoyed the extra money, she had always resented Edd's time away from the really important work—the upkeep of the family dairy farm.

From the time they were small, the twins had learned to obey their mother. Laura was a woman who lived in absolutes—it was right or it was wrong. She lacked the social graces to endear herself to others. Her personality was serious, and she lacked the saving grace of humor. She worked hard every day of her life and expected no less from others.

It was common knowledge that Edd took after his father. From an early age, Edd had great respect for his dad and proceeded to emulate him. Will loved to hunt, fish, and play baseball. So did Edd. Will was a religious man. So was Edd. Will loved his Laura and allowed her to dominate his home life. Edd's life with Essie would be a carbon copy. Will's personality was quiet and somewhat shy. He wasn't a talker, but after a few beers his gregarious side would emerge and he could be downright sociable. He was slow to anger, but when he got enough—Katy bar the door!

Like Will, Edd was calm and controlled in most circumstances, but below the surface burned a rage that could be unleashed quickly with violent results. More than one infielder would feel the lash of his spikes. More than one umpire would feel the lash of his tongue. More than one baseball team would do without him, the holdout, until after the season began. And, above all, Will and Edd shared a love of baseball. Will would have loved the opportunities that were coming to Edd. He lived vicariously through his son.

WILL ROUSH IN BASEBALL
UNIFORM, 1895

At dinner that evening, the Roush family engaged in a heated discussion about Edd's baseball career. Finally, against all of Laura's objections, Will laid down the law. Edd *would* go to Indianapolis, and, God willing, he *would* make a living playing baseball.

Will won, but Laura would not forget. She would punish Edd for this decision for years to come. Soon she would be able to extract her pound of flesh from a new family member, making Essie's life miserable for the next thirty years.

One more decision was made that night. Because Edd was underage, his father would accompany him on the trip.

And so they sat on the train speeding toward the capital city of Indiana. Somewhere between Bloomington and Greencastle, Will said, "Son, have you decided what salary you want them to pay you up there? It being a new league and all."

The question hit Edd out of the blue. "I haven't thought about it. What do you think?"

Will paused a moment. He had seldom had such a serious conversation with his son. "Well, I think you should name *your* price. You should think about baseball as a business, just like our farm is a business. We have a product, and our customers pay us a fair price for it."

Edd said, "But everyone knows that milk is two cents a jug. That's different."

"I'm not so sure it is that different. You have something to offer those city folks. You're a damned good ball player. They know that, and they'll have to pay for your services, just like anything else. You have to decide how much you're worth, then stick to it. Don't let them bamboozle you."

They sat in silence for a few minutes.

Finally Edd spoke, "I was getting a hundred and twenty-five a month in Chicago. Essie told me she read in the paper that Ty Cobb makes ten thousand to play baseball in Detroit." Edd paused for effect, then added, "But I'm not Ty Cobb."

"Remember how mad you got when you found out that some of the fellas on the WalkOvers were getting five dollars a game and you were getting a dollar?"

Edd nodded.

"What would you say is a fair price for your services?"

Edd shrugged.

"If you don't know, you'll take about anything they'll give you then, huh?"

"Okay, if I'm making a hundred and twenty-five a month, that's about six hundred for the season. Should I ask for more? Maybe a thousand?"

"How does two thousand sound to you?" Will had given this some thought.

"Sounds mighty fine," Edd said. "But will they pay it?"

"They're putting together a new team up there, and that owner, guy by the name of Krause, has some money."

Edd sat silent.

Finally, Will said, ""So, are we agreed now? We're going to ask for two thousand. If they won't pay it, we'll just get back on the train and come home. Nothing ventured, nothing gained. Agreed?"

Edd nodded and then smiled. All he could think of was how proud Essie would be.[3]

As the train pulled into the station, Will made his final comment: "Look here. If they don't treat you right, you come home. No questions asked."

Edd nodded again.

Will finished with, "It's a hard thing you're doing. We're all proud of you."

Edd pushed back the tears of a well-loved child. He knew that his father spoke from his heart. If only he'd known that it wouldn't be long before Will was gone forever, he would have turned around right then and gone home.

Will and Edd took a streetcar to Greenlawn Park on west Washington Street and Kentucky Avenue. The park was bordered by a set of railroad tracks on the north, and the White River on the west. The railroad tracks reminded Edd of Comiskey Park, but he would learn that this new park was built over a graveyard. The "Hoofeds," as they would become known, often joked about the ghosts that haunted their park. But right now the park was still under construction, preparing for the season debut in April.

They found their way to the office of player/manager "Whoa Bill Phillips. (According to legend, he got his nickname from a close call he had when trying to break a wild horse.) He was a stocky man with a square jaw but kind eyes. Although the little office was cold on that January day, Phillips's handshake was warm. Edd felt an immediate affinity with the man.

Phillips got right down to business and laid out his situation. The team president, Eddy Krause, had given him full reign to put together a team. As he'd said on the phone, he needed a good outfielder to back-up his starters. He'd heard "good things" about Eddie from Punch Knoll and Nixey Callahan. He'd seen Eddie play in Evansville and had thought for some time that he had great potential. Perhaps Eddie was his man.

He had already discussed this matter with their "money man," Bill Watkins, and they'd drawn up a contract for Edd to sign today. In one abrupt movement, he pushed a prepared contract across the desk in front of Edd. Edd pushed it in front of his dad. Will then explained that his son was underage, so he had come along to do the business. No one spoke as Will read the important information. He saw immediately that the offer of $1,500 was insufficient.

Will laid the contract back down on the desk and said, "We been thinking that my son here should have a salary of $2,000. If you can't pay it, we need him back on the farm. We'll get back on the train and go home to Oakland City." He turned pointedly to Edd and received a somewhat hesitant but confirming nod.

Bill Phillips was a good coach but extremely uncomfortable with the business end of his job. He looked hard at the father and son in front of him and decided that no amount of "dickering" was going to change their minds. He'd had his eye on Eddie and wasn't about to lose him over $500. He knew the team had had paid three times this for the highly touted Benny Kauff, but something within him whispered that Roush would prove to be a better player.

He said, "Okay, I'll pay it. I don't know why, but I'll pay it."

It was over, just like that. It would be the quickest and easiest salary negotiation in Edd's career. Edd signed his name, and his father signed under it.

There was some final discussion. Bill had to be sure that Lincoln would release Edd from their contract. He didn't mention that Watkins had talked to Hugh Jones earlier that day and Lincoln was amenable.[4] (Roush was the "unreliable" kid who had jumped out on them before the season ended last September.) Edd was to report to Texas in March for spring training.

The entire meeting took less than one half hour. As the Roush men boarded the train back to Oakland, Edd thought of a million questions he hadn't asked. Where would he live? What was the schedule? How many road trips were on it? He hadn't even asked to see the field—snow covered as it was. He thought about how if his Dad hadn't been with him he would have accepted Phillips' first offer of $1,500 in a heartbeat! So, he'd learned a lesson that would last him throughout his career: a player must set his price and stick to it! He would always remember to be like Will, ready to pick up his hat and walk away.[5]

For now, he had his second chance. He was going to play for the new Federal League.

THE OUTLAW LEAGUE

The start of 1914 was a great time to find a job in baseball. A third major league was being formed, and many cities needed to fill their rosters for the coming season. The newspapers were filled with daily announcements about this new major league. The "Feds" were offering long-term lucrative contracts and a guaranteed increase of five percent each year. Salaries would be paid during spring training. Uniforms would be new and cleaned regularly. Transportation to the spring training camp would be paid for by the teams. Players would even be given a copy of their contract—an unheard-of practice.

The American and National League owners dubbed the new league the "Outlaw League." Like in the old west, a new gang of "gunslingers" had ridden into their cozy, law-abiding towns and were threatening to steal some of their prize "horse flesh." They were quickly immersed in lawsuits to try to stop the bleeding as contracts were tossed aside and baseball went headlong into a freefall. They turned to their "sheriff," the powerful president and founder of the American League, Bancroft Byron "Ban" Johnson. He would devote enormous amounts of time, energy, and influence over the next two years to rid baseball of this "evil influence." But the time he spent anguishing over the Federal League would be a drop in the bucket compared to his involvement in the scandal of the 1919 World Series.[6]

There was much speculation and a great deal of support for the new league. They had taken it slow and done it right. They made their first bid under the leadership of John T. Powers in 1913 as a "semipro" minor league. Then the heavy hitters of the business world decided to take a chance. They attracted strong financial backing from Charles Weeghman, a Chicago restaurateur; Otto Stifel, a St. Louis brewer; Phil Ball, a Missouri ice plant magnate; and the Ward Bakery family of Brooklyn. They chose strong leadership in 1914 with President James A. Gilmore, a Chicago stationer with a glib tongue and a persuasive personality. Each of the eight clubs posted $25,000 as a guarantee to meet its obligations. They even established a minor league called "the Colonial" to feed the top circuit.

When the 1914 season began, the Feds fielded eight teams: Indianapolis, Brooklyn, St. Louis, Chicago, Baltimore, Kansas City, Pittsburgh, and Buffalo. They played in new stadiums and wore new Feds uniforms. They played on the same days as their AL and NL competitors to cut into their gate (a strategy used in 1901 by the American League teams). It was said that there would be more home runs in FL stadiums because some of the outfield fences were shorter than the required 325 feet, and the ball made by the Victor Sporting Goods Company of Springfield, Massachusetts, seemed "livelier" than the major league deadball.[7]

The sportswriters enjoyed covering the Feds games because they had colorful umpires who frequently expelled players and coaches after dramatic shouting matches. This was particularly reprehensible to Ban Johnson, who he had worked hard to establish a cadre of "professional umpires" in the American League to manage the games. His umpires were carefully selected and screened by a detective agency in Cincinnati that was run by his old friend and the former Cincinnati Chief of Police, Cal Crim. Johnson would seek help from the Cal Crim Detective Bureau again during the scandal of 1919.

Although Gilmore and his gang—known as "the brewer, the baker, and the ice machine maker"—were unsuccessful in enlisting Ty Cobb, Tris Speaker, and Walter Johnson, these players enjoyed major increases in their salaries to stay with their home teams. Baseball historian Harold Seymour reported that the average payroll of the AL and the NL more than doubled from

$30,000 to $75,000 during 1914 and 1915.[8]

When the final tally came in, the Feds had taken eighty-one players from the AL and the NL. Many of these players were in the twilight of their careers. Of the league's 264 players, twenty-five were from the minor leagues. A few were untested young "colts" who would prove themselves with the Feds and go on to enjoy brilliant careers. One of those players was Edd Roush.

In February of 1914 it was official. Edd Roush, a true Indiana boy would play for the Indianapolis "Hoosiers" of the Federal League. Everyone in southern Indiana was elated. The morning after Edd signed the contract, Will and Fred jumped in the milk wagon and went throughout the county to spread the news—just ahead of the postman.

DEAD BALLS IN WICHITA FALLS

If Lincoln had seemed like the end of the world to Edd, Wichita Falls, Texas, was its sister city. When he got off the train after the thirty-five-hour ride, he was hit full in the face by a gust of cold wind that almost knocked him off his feet. He would soon learn that everything was bigger in Texas—including the March winds. Wichita Falls was a little ranching town about 150 miles northwest of Dallas. It was forty miles due south of Lawton, Oklahoma, right on the edge of the spring tornado belt. The winds that swirled around Edd on the day of his arrival were still blowing in April when the team headed back north for the regular season. Edd would laugh as he reminisced years later that the weather was so bad, "You'd throw your glove up against the grandstand, and the wind would pin it and hold it up there." He said, "We spent most of our time jackrabbit hunting."

On the occasional day when the winds subsided, Edd noticed a change in his batting. This new Federal League ball seemed to fly farther than the balls they used in Evansville.

Although the true "lively ball" would not appear until 1920, the ball introduced in 1911 was livelier than in the previous decade of the Deadball Era.[9] Many baseball historians cite this era as the way the game of baseball was intended to be played. With a slower ball, the home run was very rare, so players developed what became known as the "inside game."

Historian Bob Schaefer writes, "The Deadball Era is perhaps the richest, in terms of the sheer spectrum of baseball skills necessary to craft a winning team. The prevailing strategy centered on the skills of bunting, sacrificing to advance a base runner, hitting behind the runner, the hit and run, stealing bases, and smart, aggressive base running...rather than simply slugging the ball."[10] Edd would become a master of the inside game. His training would be enhanced under the tutelage of coach Bill Phillips.

The relaxed spring training was also part of Bill Phillips' coaching style. He started the team with one hour of practice a day, then slowly increased it to three. Phillips said, "I'm not training these boys for a prize fight here. I'm training them for six months of hard, grueling work...by starting them in easy." Phillips had seen too many sore athletes and pitchers with bum arms from full-day workouts on rough fields in spring training. He wanted his men in good shape for the season. He had nothing to prove in Texas.[11]

The community fathers of Wichita Falls were delighted to welcome this new team to their city. The local newspaper carried daily stories about the league and the team. On March 25 a writer described Edd Roush with phrases such as: "keen of eye with free, easy movement at bat," and "covers territory like a jackrabbit." Rabbits seemed to abound in Texas that year.

The player who drew the most press that summer was Edd's competitor for a berth in center field, Benny Kauff. Edd was the freshman and Benny the sophomore on the club. Benny was born in the little town of Pomeroy, Ohio, and had come up in the coal mine leagues of West Virginia. Like Edd, Benny was a "lefty" and had a brief stint in the major leagues with the New York Highlanders in 1912. He would be touted by the sportswriters as the "Ty Cobb of the Federal League." Kauff was a short, pugnacious 24-year-old with a tenacity that echoed the personality of Cobb. He stole bases with panache (75 in 1914), hit doubles consistently (44 in 1914), and was loathe to let any ball that dared enter the outfield fall into the grass before his glove intercepted it. Rumor had it that Kauff was also something of a "dandy." He wore diamond stickpins and bragged of wearing pure silk underwear. He was the opposite of Edd. Where Benny was outspoken and flamboyant, Edd was quiet and reticent. Playing for McGraw was Benny's lifelong dream. He would get his wish in 1916. But then, so would his freshman colleague.

Another Hoosier was assigned to be Edd's roommate that year—a catcher named Bill Rariden. The friendship forged by Edd and Bill in Texas that year would last throughout their lifetimes. Bill was not a rookie when he joined the Feds. He had played five seasons with the Boston Braves and was a respected veteran five years Edd's senior. Bill and Edd were both from little burgs in Indiana. Bill was from Bedford, and, like Edd, he would retire to his hometown at the end of his career. Like Edd, Bill was soft-spoken and rather shy. He didn't drink, gamble, or cuss. Edd would later call him "my friend, B'gosh Bill." He was an excellent catcher and a loyal friend. Bill and Edd would be teammates again on the 1919 Reds.

On the night of March 14, Bill and Edd joined their teammates as the guests of honor at a dinner dance sponsored by the Wichita Falls Chamber of Commerce at Lake Wichita Pavilion. The Texas barbecue dinner was provided by a wealthy rancher named Luke Wilson, and on that night that Edd came to know another player who would become a lifelong friend.

After dinner the dancing began. Edd and Bill stood against the wall watching the festivities. Neither had any interest in meeting the local women. Edd was in love with Essie and Bill was happily married to Ruby. Benny Kauff was another story. Benny had been drinking heavily all night and was beginning to make a spectacle of himself. He was drooling over Wilson's wife when he started to undo his trousers to prove to her that he was wearing his signature silk underwear.

At that moment, three teammates sped from different parts of the room to avert disaster. Bill McKechnie got there first with Edd and Bill Rariden close behind. While Edd and Bill gave Benny the "bum's rush" out to one of the team cars, McKechnie handled the ruffled feathers of their hostess. The three of them put Benny to bed that night, hoping he would be in shape for the next day's opening game of the season against Kansas City. After they had secured their teammate in his room, the trio went to a local diner and laughed and talked for several hours over coffee and stale doughnuts. They shared a common dislike for their arrogant colleague.

Edd took an instant liking to this Scottish fellow from Pennsylvania. He'd heard the guys call him "Mac" and seen them show him respect. Mac had a mature, almost fatherly air about him at age 27. He was serious, yet friendly and not boastful. Edd listened closely as Mac described his five years in the Big Show with Pittsburgh, Boston, and New York. He was a northeasterner, and there was a slight twinkle in his eyes as he enjoyed gently rubbing that in on the two Indiana rubes. Rariden tried to better him with his Boston experience, but the farmer in Bill poked through the facade. They both seemed to be performing for Edd who innocently laughed and enjoyed every minute of their banter.

Neither Mac nor Edd could know what history had in store for them. Would that a time machine could have whisked them ahead fifty years, uprooting them from that Texas diner and dropping them onto the platform in Cooperstown, New York, where, together, they would become immortal.

The bond between the three men grew in the following weeks as the catcher, the third baseman, and the outfielder learned to respect each other as athletes. Edd, Mac, and Bill became a common trio at the dinner table and sat together on the bench during the games. When Edd came up to bat he knew there were at least two guys rooting for him. Wichita Falls didn't seem so cold anymore.

THE FEDS PENNANT RACE

On the morning of April 23,[12] the season opener, the people of Indianapolis threw a huge parade for their new team. More than 15,000 fans came to the new Washington Street Park. Governor Ralston threw out the first pitch. The trainmen

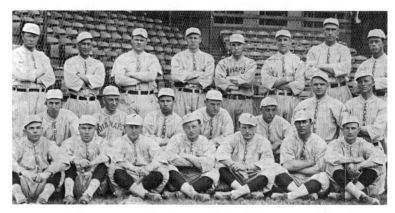

1914 INDIANAPOLIS FEDS
(ROUSH SECOND ROW, THIRD FROM RIGHT)

moved a freight car on the tracks behind the outfield fence and created temporary bleachers to watch the game for free. Although the Hoosiers lost 3-0 to St. Louis (3-0), the pitching duel between Hank Keupper and Cy Falkenburg (the Hoosier 20-game winner from Cleveland) was exciting. Kauff notched his first two hits of the season. In his book *The Federal League of 1914-1915*, Marc Okkonen called it an "auspicious debut."

As the season progressed the competition between the teams heated up. St. Louis maintained first place, but every month brought a new challenger. Both Pittsburgh and Chicago bore down hard, and Indy was right on their heels. Edd saw action in several games in May and June, spelling Charlie Carr at first base. Phillips tried to create opportunities to use Edd since he was assured a hit almost every time. Edd chuckled later, "I wasn't the greatest first baseman."

Indianapolis was just three games out of first place on July 28 when Austria-Hungary declared war on Serbia and World War I began. Baseball (and America) would not feel the repercussions immediately, but this action would contribute to the demise of the Federal League.

In early August, Baltimore took the lead over Chicago and the Hoosiers slipped into fourth place, just two games behind Brooklyn. The four horses ran neck-and-neck for the the next few weeks. Spikes flew all around the infield and veterans Frank LaPorte and Jimmy Esmond suffered serious injuries in late August. Captain Vin Campbell took a hard blow to the head on August 12—compliments of Baltimore pitcher Jack Quinn. According to baseball historian Dan O'Brien, the team was "pretty banged up physically at that time." Umpires seemed to look the other way and even encourage rough play.

In those days, baseball was a rough-and-tumble sport. Midwestern ballplayers looked less like rosy-cheeked, corn-fed kids with bulging muscles and more like lean, mean, hungry men who had somehow escaped from the coal mines and lumber fields. Ty Cobb once said of baseball, "It's like a War."[13]

Of course, the more players who got hurt, the more opportunities for Edd to get into the game. On August 10, George Holmes of the *Indianapolis Star* wrote:

> John McGraw once remarked that a ball club was only as strong as its secondary strength...it doesn't appear this Rousch [sic] has been getting all the credit due him....his .306 batting almost solely in pinches, stamps him a guy to be reckoned with.

Game after game, the newspapers listed four names as "game savers" with hits and sacrifices—Kauff, Roush, McKechnie, and Rariden. Finally, on August 12, Phillips retired Al Kaiser, and Edd won a permanent berth in left field for the remainder of the season.[14]

By mid-September two teams vied for the lead—the Chifeds and the Hoofeds. It was a bloody battle to the end and some of the most unruly baseball Edd would experience in his career. On October 4, Indianapolis drew the largest crowd ever to see a ball game in the local park. In front of 16,462 fans, the Hoosiers put Kansas City away.[15] Three days later James Gilmore declared the Hoosier Feds the champions of the Federal League by a one and one-half game margin over Chicago. Indianapolis had won the pennant!

Indianapolis celebrated its first (and only) major league pennant.[16] Hoosier pitcher Falkenburg came in second in the league in "total pitcher index." (*Total Baseball*, 2004). Mac McKechnie had the best season of his life, posting a .304 batting average. Benny Kauff won the batting title with .370, his lifetime best. The "Ty Cobb of the Federal League" was to be

JAMES GILMORE, FEDERAL LEAGUE PRESIDENT, AWARDS 1914 FL CHAMPIONSHIP MEDALS TO BILL MCKECHNIE, MANAGER IN NEWARK, NEW JERSEY. (ROUSH SECOND FROM RIGHT.)

1914 CHAMPIONSHIP MEDAL

a comet that flashed across the sky then sputtered a few more years on a downward spiral with the Giants then disappeared from sight.[17]

Although Edd didn't start in most of the games that year, he got 54 hits in 74 games for a respectable batting average of .333[18] and a slugging average of .440. In an *Indiana DailyTimes* article, general manager W.H. Watkins said, "I look for Rousch to become one of the greatest outfielders of all time."

EDD'S SECRET WEAPON

Nothing in game statistics or sportswriter's columns ever reveals the psychological aspects of an athlete's success. What is happening inside the *head* game of a star player is hidden from view and cannot be measured in numbers, percentages, and averages. Nonetheless, it is this invisible component that often spurs a player to his highest levels of achievement.

Edd enjoyed one of the best years of his life in 1914. It was a year of personal growth. He turned 21 on May 8. Answers to problems that had eluded him now crystallized. It all seemed so simple. He was left-handed, so he would bat and throw with his dominant, natural arm. His parents were good people and had tried to guide him to the best of their ability, but he had to take responsibility for his own life. He found a new confidence that wasn't there before.

Most importantly, he was in love with one woman and miserable without her, so he would marry her and live his life with her by his side. She was the one person in the world who *really* understood him. Essie Mae Swallow was, and would always be, Edd Roush's secret weapon.

One night in late March, when the ferocious Texas winds were lashing at the windows of his bedroom, Edd decided he could wait no longer. They had agreed to wait until he was 21, but two more months seemed like an eternity. The next day they agreed long distance to elope. She would come alone and meet him in Indianapolis the last week of April. He had sent her an envelope containing twenty-five dollars with instructions to pay for train fare and to buy a wedding dress. As she would do throughout their married life, she had saved ten of it for a "rainy day."

Edd sent a letter reminding her to keep the trip a secret from his mother. Although he had received willing permission to marry his sweetheart from "Pop" Swallow and her family, *his* mother was a different matter. Laura had never approved of Essie and openly expressed her feelings. Just before Edd left for spring training, Laura had told him, "You should play the field awhile like your brother. You and Essie are too serious. Why, she's two years older than you are."

So, on April 26, 1914, Essie Mae Swallow boarded the train to Indianapolis. She looked around to be sure she hadn't been seen. Luckily, she was the lone boarder that morning. She was grateful that her little brother, Arch, had brought her and her big satchel in his wagon. He handled her the bag with special care, knowing it contained her wedding dress

Essie spent the first night in Indianapolis at the home of her cousin, Eva, who was newly married to a rising junior executive with Standard Oil, Allen Hitch.[19] The next night Essie spent with Edd—as his wife.

Edd married Essie eleven days before his 21st birthday. Essie was 22. Luckily the old Justice of the Peace hadn't ask questions as Edd slipped onto her finger the simple gold wedding ring inscribed *Edd to Essie - April 27, 1914.*

Two days later, Essie wrote a letter to her little sister, Eva, on the stationary of the Grand Hotel in Indianapolis.

Dear Eva,

Just got a few minutes I can write to you. Have been so busy getting acquainted and also getting settled. The bunch is fine. All of the players are married now except 4 and we are mainly all here in the Grand. Edd and I go to our apartment tomorrow. We have a 3 room flat in the Belfour Apts. We also have the use of bathrooms.

Edd met me at the train and we were married at 9:30 yesterday. I gave the porter 50¢ to try to get me a lower berth. ...Well, Eva, we are happy as can be and I know I haven't made a mistake. ...I like it fine up here. Went to the game yesterday ...we have passes you know & our own especial boxes out at the park.

Edd is so nice. I'm crazier about him than ever. The fellows nearly had

a fit when Edd brought me into the hotel and introduced me as his wife. ...I'm as happy as a bird even if I am a Roush now instead [of a Swallow].
    With love, Mrs. Edd Rous

PLAYER'S WIVES IN BOX AT INDY BALL PARK
ESSIE ROUSH: TOP ROW MIDDLE, IN BLACK DRESS

Edd had told only two people on the club about his elopement—Bill and Mac. All three men held their breaths when their wives met for the first time. They were happy when the three women seemed to "bond" immediately. Ruby Rariden and Beryl McKechnie swept Essie under their wings, and the couples became close friends. Bill and Ruby lived around the corner from Edd and Essie and had the only car. On off-game Sundays, it was a common sight in downtown Indianapolis to see the Roushs, Raridens, and McKechnies sitting around on the steps of Monument Circle after church. Essie would later say, "When Edd finally became a regular on the team, we all celebrated together. We three couples stayed in touch with each other, even long after all of our baseball lives were over."

1 1913 was the first year that baseball cards were inserted in Crackerjack candy boxes.

2 Author's Note: Tinker may have remembered Roush's letter with chagrin when a year later, he offered Phillips a trade; Caruso Beck plus an "undisclosed" amount of cash for Roush.

3 On January 5, 1914, Ford Motor Company announced the 8-hour workday with a minimum wage of $5 a day.

4 Author's Note: Were it not for his jump to the "Feds," Edd Roush may have played alongside the infamous "Black Sox" in 1919 rather than on the opposing team.

5 It would not be until the late 1970's that athletes would break the stronghold of management in salary negotiations. By the end of the twentieth century, millionaire athletes would live luxurious lifestyles previously reserved for their bosses. But in the early years of baseball, only a few courageous souls fought for their worth. And, they did it alone, without sports agents representing them.

6 In 1876 William Hulbert of Chicago formed The National League of Professional Base Ball Clubs. This is the National League we know of today. In 1900 an "upstart" league took shape under the leadership of Ban Johnson called the American League. From 1900 to 1903, the new American League caused havoc by raiding the National League's prime players. In 1903 the NL and the AL agreed to respect each other's markets. Together they would be known as Major League Baseball (MLB) or "organized baseball."

7 According to SABR researcher Robert H. Schaefer, the Victor ball used in the Federal League contained a rubber core twice the size (two ounces) of the NL and AL issued balls. However, Schaefer quotes George Reach as saying in 1949, "The resiliency of the ball is governed by the way the wool yarn is wrapped around the core, rather than the texture of the core."

8 Harold Seymour. *Baseball: The Golden Age*. Oxford University Press, 1971.

9 Robert H. Schaefer, SABR historian. "The Dawn of the Dead Ball Era" Academic paper for SABR. "Although the ball was livelier in 1911 onward...the fundamental strategy of the game remained unaffected."

10 Ibid.

11 Note: Phillips's philosophy was the opposite of McGraw who forced players to compete for positions in spring training. If later managers would have held the same philosophy, Edd Roush may have attended more spring training events in his career.

12 The day before, April 22, in Baltimore, a young unknown pitcher named

Babe Ruth went 2 for 4 against Buffalo in the International League.

13 In the American League, Cobb suffers a broken rib from a pitch by Boston's Dutch Leonard. He stays in the game and on the next at-bat he drags a bunt down first base line and spikes Leonard.

14 Edd Roush was the youngest player on the team and the idol of one young Hoosier fan, Chuck Klein (age 10). Fourteen years later Klein would take his place in a major league outfield in Philadelphia.

15 Harry Roedersheimer. *Indianapolis Star Magazine*, 1978.

16 On October 14, the NL Boston Braves defeated the AL Philadelphia Athletics in a clean sweep, 4-0 to win the 1914 World Series. Gilmore offered $17,000 to Captain Johnny Evers to pit his "Miracle" Braves against the Hoosier Fed Champs in a post-season, post-world series contest. Evers said he wouldn't risk a "mediocre team" beating his Braves.

In 2001, a baseball statistician and member of SABR, Paul Wendt, explained a statistical assessment of the quality of play comparing the Federal League to the AL & NL, re: ERA+ & TPR. The results indicated that the two top FL teams (Hoofeds and Chifeds) were equivalent to average AL & NL teams that year.

17 Kauff would leave baseball in disgrace over involvement in an auto theft ring. Although he was not found guilty of car theft, he was found "guilty by association" by Commissioner Kenesaw Landis who banished him from baseball in 1920. Landis banished the eight 1919 "Black Sox" a year later.

18 Edd claimed he lost 2 points off his lifetime BA going into the National Baseball Hall of Fame. This was due to a recalculation of his statistics in 1962. The 1915 *Reach/Spalding Guide* listed Roush's 1914 batting average as .333. As late as 1961, the annual *Reds Yearbook* listed that average. When his statistics were recalculated, he was awarded one less hit (54) and two more times at bat (166) for 1914, bringing his 1914 BA to .325 and his lifetime average to .323.

19 Eva and Allen Hitch would be their neighbors in Bradenton, Florida, forty years later.

3

Top Dogs and Money Players

"I never ceased to try to get him [Edd Roush]
back from Cincinnati as letting him go was the biggest mistake
I ever made in my career."

– John McGraw, March of Dimes Benefit, St. Petersburg FL, 1934

JANUARY 1ST, 1915
TULSA, OKLAHOMA

Harry F. Sinclair was pleased with himself. At age 38, he was a millionaire several times over. On this New Year's Day he sat on his verandah overlooking the pool, nursing a bloody Mary. Thoughts that had been simmering for a while were popping into full boil in his mind. He was done with Tulsa; he'd outgrown it. Tulsa had been a great little city in which to make your *first* million. It was certainly a step up from his formative years in Independence, Kansas.[1] He remembered the thrill of that first oil well breaking black into the Kansas sky, and now he envisioned his oil wells all over the world. He'd heard that Russia was oil-rich and made a mental note to check into that.[2]

He saw the new name of his company take shape—*Sinclair Oil and Refining Corporation*. Since oil was a fossil fuel, he would use a new symbol for his company, a green dinosaur. He envisioned a national headquarters in Manhattan, a large office building with hundreds of smartly dressed employees going through huge bronze doors. Of course, he would have to live close to his offices, in a mansion in a prestigious neighborhood.[3]

Harry longed to live in New York. It was time to take his place there among the top dogs—Rockefeller, Vanderbilt, J.P. Morgan. He had the credentials and the money, but he needed more to gain acceptance with the elite. Suddenly the vision came clear. He should buy a baseball team. But which one? Ideally, it would be in New York. The Highlanders? The Giants? How much did a team cost? Well, if he ran out of money, there were always more oil fields to plunder.[4]

OAKLAND CITY, INDIANA

While Harry Sinclair was planning to buy a baseball team, Edd Roush was doing a little dealing of his own. As was to become his custom, he had held out for a larger salary through the winter. He had demanded $4,000, double his 1914 salary. His price seemed reasonable to friends and family because, during this period, his name continually appeared in the newspapers. The *Indianapolis News* and the *Indianapolis Star* kept the public informed on the cat-and-mouse games between management and players. Other teams were vying for his services. Chicago wanted him: *Manager Tinker...is said to have offered Beck and a cash consideration for Roush*. Pittsburg wanted him: *President Edward W. Gwynner, of the Pittsburgh Feds...announced that Outfielder Ed [sic] Roush of the Hoosiers likely would come to the Rebels in exchange for First Baseman Hugh Bradley*. And New York wanted him: *...John McGraw of the New York Giants tried to "steal" three Hoosiers, namely, McKechnie, Campbell and Rousch [sic]*.

The salary negotiations between Bill Phillips and Edd began in earnest in November, and they sparred throughout the holidays. The tone of Phillips' letters changed as the weeks passed with no signed contract from Roush.

My Dear Ed,   November 17, 1914

I have to say, I have at all times tried to help you in your profession. ...I have a position for you and if Demands is [sic] Reasonable I will Drop others...if not, must sign them and give preference.

My Dear Sir,   December 5, 1914

Seems you have ignored all my former letters in the past. ...the very BEST they would do for you the coming season is 3000. ...In my opinion I think you are treating the Indianapolis Club very Shabby and not becoming to a first class Ball Player.

P.S. Remember me to your Father and Mother.

Dear Sir,   December 10, 1914

...seems to me 3000 is pretty good salary for One who plays for love of the game. The Indianapolis Club...gave you 200 advance and more money than you ever received before and saved you from a Minor League....All I want to know is are you coming with us or not. I do not want to have a drove of oil fielders on my hands like last spring...

Finally, on January 15, the Hoosier fathers relented, and Edd signed his contract for $4,000. Edd was not the only Hoofed holdout that year. The other two—"Mac" McKechnie and team captain Vin Campbell—came in two weeks after Edd. And so the 1915 Hoosiers would remain intact for the next season. Edd had only one regret. He had signed his contract too soon. He would not have salary negotiations as an excuse to miss spring training.

SINCLAIR MAKES HIS MOVE

It was old home week when the Hoosier regulars gathered on a rainy March 8 in the little town of Valdosta in southern Georgia. The town was happy to have them. One sportswriter noted the German element within the team by citing the "Teutonic monikers" of several players; Rousch, Kaiserling, Scheer, Falkenburg, Huhn, Texter, Strands, Trautman, and a new addition, Herman "Germany" Schaefer.[5] He was both an experienced veteran and one of the best-known comedians in the business. Essie would remember how Germany and Harry Moran kept fans and team alike in stitches throughout the season.

CARTOON OF SCHAEFER, RARIDEN, AND ROUSH AS CIRCUS PERFORMERS

On January 2, Harry had met with his friend Pat Powers. As former president of the International League, Pat was his "ace in the hole." Pat suggested that Harry buy into the new Federal League. A month later Harry and Pat were sitting with league president Jim Gilmore at the Biltmore Hotel in New York. Sinclair pledged $200,000 to start. Gilmore was interested. Within days the deal was done. Sinclair had Gilmore's approval to raid the league in search of a team to call his own, and Sinclair made it clear that he intended to move his team to one of the boroughs of New York. On February 14 the *New York Times* quoted Sinclair: "The Federal League appealed to me as the league of the future." Since Indianapolis had won the 1914 pennant, Sinclair chose that team and moved it to Newark.[6] The Hoofeds would now be the "Newfeds."

The atmosphere in spring training was tense. By late March, the rumors were too plentiful to ignore. The newspapers ran headlines about the "Federal League War." Players were getting nervous. Maybe they shouldn't have jumped to this new league after all. Phillips announced that some oil man in Texas had bought the team.[7] But even he didn't know the extent of the politics transpiring on the level above him. The players noticed that their manager had become increasingly agitated and guessed that his job was in trouble. He'd left Valdosta, and no one knew where he'd gone or why.

It seemed to Edd and Bill that their friend Mac was more "in the know" than anyone else, so one night after dinner they asked him directly. When Mac told them that Sinclair was planning to replace Phillips, Edd felt a sharp pain in his stomach. Phillips had been Edd's mentor. In the early weeks in Indianapolis when Edd was not yet a regular, he had sat next to his manager throughout each game. He listened to his advice and soaked up his wisdom. When Edd decided to try a heavier bat, it was Phillips who said, "That bat will work for you because you have strong wrists and can swat it from the base." Edd would benefit from the lessons of Phillips for the rest of his career.[8]

Edd asked Mac, "So who's the new manager?"

"Don't know yet," Mac said. "Might be me." He forced a chuckle. "They asked George Stovall, but he's staying with Kansas. Sinclair really wanted McGraw. I heard he offered him a hundred thousand, but McGraw refused, has a five-year contract from 1912 for thirty thousand a year with the Giants. Big money up there."

"So where is Phillips now?" Edd was concerned.

"I reckon he's in New York with the rest of them. They're having some big meeting to get it all settled." Mac had another tidbit up his sleeve. "By the way, Sinclair is moving the team to Newark, New Jersey."

The next day Edd was up early. He made a beeline to the telegraph office.

WESTERN UNION

Mrs Edd J Roush   March 28, 1915
Oakland City Indiana

Team sold to Sinclair stop Moving to Newark New Jersey April stop Pack your bags Mrs. Roush stop Home next Saturday

stop Edd stop

By the end of the day everyone knew the story. The *New York Times* reported the meeting that Mac had described the night before. The article also confirmed that Bill Phillips would remain as manager.

NEWARK GREETS THE PEPPERS

The 1915 season opened with a whirlwind celebration. The festivities began on Thursday, April 15, when the City of Newark held a "Dollar Dinner" in Krueger Auditorium in honor of its new professional baseball team—the Newark Peppers. The next night the players and wives sat in special box seats at the Newark Theater for the performance of a new comedy titled *Potash and Perlmutter.* Saturday was the home opener of the season, pitting the Peppers against the Baltimore Terrapins (Newfeds versus Baltfeds).[9]

The Dollar Dinner was a lavish affair with 900 attendees including officials from throughout the state and the baseball world elite. When the diners were seated, Phillips trooped the team into the auditorium in single file as the audience jumped to their feet in thunderous applause. Mayor Raymond was enthusiastic when he declared, "We're going to have a city of play as well as of industry."[10] He was followed by "Herr

1915 NEWARK PEPPERS
EDD ROUSH: MIDDLE OF RIGHT SIDE ROW

Schaefer" who provided comic relief by mimicking Charlie Chaplin in a mock vaudevillian high wire act. He would repeat this performance many times to the delight of crowds in the Newark grandstands.

The highlight of the evening for Essie came as she walked through the receiving line. Beryl was in front of her and together they approached two gentlemen. They were both a bit overweight with full, fleshy faces. The taller one carried himself with a degree of authority and greeted Beryl warmly. He then turned to Essie, took her gloved hand, and with a smooth baritone voice said, "My dear Mrs. Roush. I am honored to make your acquaintance. My name is Harry Sinclair, and this is my colleague, Mr. Patrick Powers." Essie felt flustered and started to stammer a response when he said, "I've been watching your husband. I must say that I am favorably impressed with his talent. Is he a clean-living man, would you say?"

Essie was at a loss for words. Clean-living? What did that mean? The staunch British spine straightened as she looked at him pointedly and stated, "If you mean does he drink, gamble, and carouse, he does not. Do you?" Harry burst into laughter. For a brief moment he remembered the tenacity of her husband in demanding to double his salary that year. Birds of a feather, they were! From that point on, she became "Essie Mae" and she and Harry were fast friends. He would always stop and chat with her at the games. He'd tease her by asking if she and Eddie had been out "carousing" the night before and, as expected, she'd always have a quick retort for him. Harry made a mental note to include Edd Roush in his new enterprise—buying the New York Giants.

THE 1915 SEASON

The Peps started out with a bang. But, the people didn't come.

In late May, the team had a five-game lead, but the home games weren't close to sold out. As May stretched into June, attendance worsened. Some blamed it on the bad trolley service between Harrison and downtown and the difficulty in getting to the games. Essie described the situation in later years:

> The Harrison park was across the Passiac River from downtown. We had to walk across the bridge to get to the park. It was an ugly, smelly river because of the dye water from the silk mills north of Newark. You had to hold your nose as you went across.

The *Newark Evening News* reported, "The crowd simply jammed itself onto the narrow footpath of the Centre Street bridge....It took over a half hour to get from the grounds."

Sinclair lobbied the city to improve the public transportation and roads. He set up bike races to the park preceding the games and offered fifteen-cent tickets. Nothing worked. Exacerbating the situation, the Peps lost their lead to the Kansas City Packers and then Pittsburgh came on strong. Sportwriters called the Federal League contest "the closest race in the country just now." Sinclair responded by bringing in one of the new automatic pitching machines that propelled a ball every eight seconds.[11] Pitchers feared their jobs were in jeopardy.

On June 20, Sinclair fired Phillips and put Mac at the helm. Phillips would never again lead a major league team. Edd got the news in the hospital where he was suffering from pulled ligaments in his legs.[12] He felt a mix of sadness for the former manager who had treated him well and happiness for the success of his friend.

The team gelled under Mac. Falkenburg and Ed Reulbach pitched flawlessly. Rariden was consistent behind the plate. Al

Scheer and Vin Campbell murdered the league's pitchers. This was to be Campbell's final year in professional baseball, and he was going out with a bang. He was the top hitter on the team, finishing at .314, 12 percentage points above Edd. Both finished among the top ten hitters in the league.[13]

But Chicago would have the last laugh. When the season ended, the Whales were the 1915 Federal League champs, and Newark came in a poor fifth, one game behind Kansas City. "Prince" Hal Chase—soon to be linked with baseball gambling—led the Feds with 17 home runs.

"THE BEST YEAR OF OUR LIVES..."

Essie Mae Roush loved Newark. Although the grandstands were rarely filled, the fans who came adored the team and cheered wildly. The first full year of marriage for Edd and Essie seemed idyllic. They lived in a small Fleet Street apartment with another male tenant and a landlady with her two sons who adored the baseball player in their house. The landlady often invited the young couple to dinner, and, in return, Edd made sure she and her sons got passes to the weekend games. The Raridens lived around the corner and across the street was a Nickelodeon and tavern where they could enjoy a pitcher of beer and a picture show for five cents. Many of the players and their wives would meet Edd and Essie for a night of dancing at the Fleet Street Roof Gardens.

On special occasions they would go into Manhattan for dinner. Essie would later write in her memoirs: "I had the lead in our senior play about a wealthy heiress who disguised herself as a maid and went to Delmonico's in New York to eat chocolate sundaes. I never thought I'd ever see that big New York restaurant, but in 1915, I did."

More often they would go to Little Italy to have some of

that new pizza pie.

Gennaro Lombardi loved to see the baseball players and their wives come through the door of Lombardi's Grocery and Pizza Shop at 53 1/2 Spring Street. Essie loved this exotic new food with the tiny anchovy fish on top. In 1915 a Lombardi pizza pie replicated the colors of the Italian flag (red tomatoes, white mozzarella cheese and ample green basil) and cost a penny per slice.[14]

When they could get a babysitter, Beryl and Mac would come for dinner.

Essie's specialty that year was her prize mushroom soufflé. She was an excellent cook and cut new recipes from the newspapers, then glued them next to the articles about Edd and the Peps in her long, rectangular, cloth-bound, maroon scrapbook.[15]

Too soon the summer was over. There was a sadness in the final days of the Peps. They had slumped in late August and lost the championship. Edd felt badly, especially for Mac, who'd had a scant three months to prove himself as a manager. He'd shown great promise and a knack for working with pitchers. Edd respected Mac's approach to coaching. Although he carried the demeanor of a leader, he was also a "regular guy."[16]

The Peppers said goodbye on October 3. Their last game was all the more poignant because there was widespread doubt that they would be together again. With rumors of serious financial problems in the Federal League and out-and-out war with "Organized Baseball," the players left not knowing if they'd have a job next year.

DEMISE OF THE FEDERAL LEAGUE

Harry Sinclair would not give up without a fight. According to baseball historian Fred Lieb, Sinclair had been meeting the payrolls of Kansas City and Buffalo, in addition to his own team.

At the end of the 1915 season, Harry was still planning to move the Peppers to one of the boroughs of New York, possibly Queens,[17] when the bottom fell out.

Robert B. Ward, who owned the Brooklyn Tip Tops, died suddenly. Since Ward had been the second most important FL backer (next to Sinclair), his death threw the league into jeopardy. Other owners and angels of the Feds started to backpedal. They had poured money into a losing enterprise. They had fought "city hall" by filing an antitrust suit against Organized Baseball on which Judge Kenesaw Landis refused to act.

Although he did his best, Sinclair didn't have the muscles of Atlas to hold up the world alone. The Feds took their last breath on December 22, 1915. Organized Baseball would buy out the principals for approximately $650,000, of which Sinclair would receive $10,000 annually for ten years. Organized Baseball also took control of the Newark stadium. The Peppers would be only a footnote in baseball history.

Sinclair negotiated one more deal before the books were closed. Instead of releasing all the Feds players as "free agents," he served as the "league agent" with sole authorization to sell (for personal profit) the most valuable 84 players under contract with their teams for 1916.[18] Since he kept the most sought-after players as part of the buy-out, he realized a profit estimated at more than $120,000 for their sale.

The baseball world was indebted to Harry. Some called him the "savior of the game." John McGraw said, "The attitude of Mr. Sinclair throughout the negotiations has been commendable."

Harry landed on his feet. In an interview given to the *New York Times* on his way home to Tulsa on December 28, 1915, he said: "I'm out of baseball, but I went out the front door....I'm not out much. If I did lose anything, the fun was worth it."

In March, the *Washington Post* covered the "event of the

season"—the Jess Willard/Frank Moran fight at Madison Square Garden in New York City. The headline read: "Worlds of Finance and Politics, Society and Art at the Ringside." Famous names were listed including J.P. Morgan, W.K. and Reginald Vanderbilt, Jay Gould, Coleman du Pont, Ban Johnson, John Tener, and Harry F. Sinclair. In April, the *New York Times* announced a new corporate headquarters to be located in the city, an oil company capitalized at an estimated $50,000,000. Among its directors was Theodore Roosevelt, Jr. The name of the company was the Sinclair Oil and Refining Company.

Harry Sinclair never purchased the Giants. What he *did* purchase—via the machinations of his entry into the baseball world—was of much greater value to him. He bought membership into the elite and exclusive New York club. He had earned the respect of his colleagues and a national reputation as a Top Dog. He would soon meet another Top Dog. He would learn in 1919 that this dog had fangs. His name was Arthur Rothstein.

JANUARY, 1916: OAKLAND CITY, INDIANA

Edd, Essie, and Fred amused themselves in the 1916 winter by learning their lines for a play sponsored by the Presbyterian Church entitled *Jephthah and His Daughter*. But underlying their smiling faces was deep anxiety. Edd had no job.

Essie had loved her life in Newark so much. Would she ever see her dear friends Beryl and Ruby again?

Then in January the telephone on the wall rang three longs, their party-line signal. It was Bill Rariden calling from Bedford, Indiana. He was so excited he was "b'goshing" and "gee-whizzing" all over the phone. He said, "I'm going to the Giants. Did you hear me? The Giants!"

Edd turned to tell Essie as he offered his congratulations to his friend in the next breath. He knew that Bill had dreamed of playing for McGraw ever since his Boston days. Just as Edd was wishing he had similar news to share, Bill said, "They got Kauff and Fred Anderson, that big pitcher from Buffalo." As soon as he said it, Bill realized that the news about Kauff wouldn't sit well with Edd. "I'm gonna put in a good word for you, Edd, and for Mac. Sure hope you'll be going with me. It's not over, you know. They're just picking the players now. I'm sure you'll get picked. Don't worry."

But Edd was worried. He knew they'd picked Lee Magee, player/manager of the Brooklyn Feds first. And now Bill. Rightfully so. Bill was the best catcher in the league. But if they had Kauff in center, they might not want him too. Was he washed up at age 21? He wasn't going back to Lincoln and the minors, that was for sure.

What Edd didn't know was that there were many positive comments being made on his behalf behind closed doors. Sinclair had announced early that his three most valuable Newark players were Rariden, Campbell, and Roush. He would take care of Essie Mae and her husband if at all possible. And, he decided to keep Roush on his exclusive "list of 84." These were the "money players," the ones you could count on to deliver a solid performance in a pinch. Several of them, like Roush, were annual holdouts—money players who played *for* the money. In buying and selling Feds players as property, Sinclair and the owners were money players too.

Sinclair set the opening bid for Roush at $10,000. Reports estimated that he had already gotten $32,500 for Kauff, $25,000 for Magee and $10,000 apiece for Rariden and Anderson. The biggest bidders were Stoneham of New York and Herrmann of Cincinnati.

Throughout the month of January the announcements came in a steady stream.

The Reds had lost Rariden to the Giants, but they grabbed the number two Feds catcher, Emil "Hap" Huhn, Hal Chase, and a promising second bagger named Bill Louden. The Braves snapped up ace first baseman Ed Konetchy. The Yankees spent their bankroll on Magee and paid an additional $5,000 for Joe Gedeon. The Yanks decided to tap old Germany Schaefer while they were at it—for laughs, if nothing else. New Yorkers had to be entertained and loved Schaefer's antics. McGraw gave Schaefer a high compliment, "There is one of the most delightful and whimsical of personalities."[19]

Nothing about Roush. No mention of McKechnie either. Mac and Edd commiserated over the phone every other day. On January 20, The *New York Times* published a list of 123 Feds players who were "released as free agents" by Sinclair.

Sadly, Edd read the names of Newark teammates Brandon, Mullen, Texter, Trautman, and Whitehouse listed among the "unwanted."[20]

The paper reported that Captain Huston of the Yankees was interested in Edd and that both Charles Ebbets and Garry Herrmann had also expressed interest. George Stallings of the Braves had put in a strong bid. He was quoted as saying "Roush was the the best outfielder in the Federal League last year." But, Stallings wasn't willing to pay Sinclair's price of $10,000.

BEHIND THE SCENES

Three unrelated events interceded to secure a berth for Edd. Ironically, the first involved Benny Kauff. He refused to sign with McGraw. Although the Giants agreed to honor his $8,000 Feds contract, he insisted that he had been promised a $5,000 bonus on top of his salary. Further, he opened fire on Harry Sinclair, claiming he should have a share of the $30,000 that Harry put in his pocket from the sale of Kauff to the Giants.

The Top Dogs were furious—the gall of this little fancy man who arrived at spring training wearing silk, fur, and a diamond stickpin! Sinclair ignored him, but McGraw couldn't. If he had to spend the next season taming some prima donna in center field, it wasn't worth it. Maybe he should look at Roush. He could use him as competitive leverage on the bench against the arrogant Kauff.

To add to the pain of their task, both Sinclair and McGraw were sick with the "grippe" throughout the bidding wars of January. Neither was in the mood to wrangle with an outfielder whose nose was out of joint. (Kauff would finally settle for a slight salary increase.)

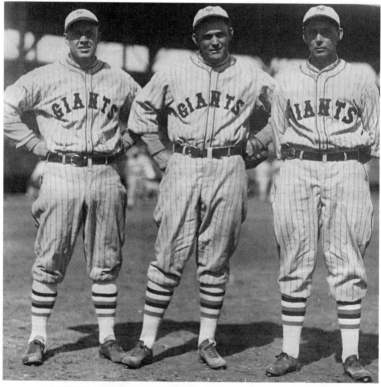

ROGERS HORNSBY, BURLEIGH GRIMES, AND EDD ROUSH
ON THE 1927 NEW YORK GIANTS

The second event involved Dave Robertson, the Giants' regular right fielder. In late January, McGraw learned that Robertson had a severe hip injury and would be out of the line-up until May or June. That left him one short of the six out-fielders he wanted to start the season. The press was all over it. Dan Daniel would recall prodding McGraw to "fill his void in his picket line by getting Edd Roush."

Finally, Edd's major league career was saved when he got a little help from his friends. First, it was Rogers Hornsby who, after a losing exhibition game with the Red Sox in Tampa, told sportswriter Fred Lieb:

> Our outfield stinks! They'd better get Roush in here quick, or those clowns out there will knock themselves out batting their heads together trying to get under fly balls. If the club doesn't hustle and get Roush, why it's simply crazy. McGraw hasn't asked for my opinion, but if he does, I'll tell him the same as I am telling you.

Next it was Edd's friend and former teammate, Germany Schaefer, who intervened on his behalf. Sportswriter Frank Graham described the scene in his 1944 "informal biography," *McGraw of the Giants*. In the midst of the bidding, John McGraw's trusted advisor, Schaefer, nudged him.

"Get Eddie Roush."

"What for?" McGraw demanded.

"He was the best outfielder in the league."

"How about Kauff?"

"He's a better ball player than Kauff," Germany insisted. "He's not as colorful as Kauff, but he can play rings around him. ...See what you can get Roush for," he urged. "I tell you he's the best buy in the lot and nobody knows it—not even Sinclair."

McGraw turned to Sinclair. "How much will you take for Roush?

"Ten thousand dollars."

"I'll give you $7,500." McGraw took a shot, hoping that Stoneham was willing to shell out a little more on top of the $60,000 he'd already committed.[21]

"He's yours." Harry wanted to take care of Edd and Essie. He also wanted to be done with all the haggling.

Retrospectively, Cullen Cain, publicity director for the National League, told the story a bit differently in a 1925 press release.

> When they had turned over all the players, goods and chattels of the ill-fated Federal League, one player was left and unaccounted for. Nobody wanted him. "But you have to take him," declared Sinclair. They dickered and haggled. Sinclair was sleepy and tired out. Finally...John McGraw offered to take Roush for the Waiver [sic] of $6,000...and an alarm clock, or a pair of clocked silk socks, or something. ..."Maybe I can trade him to the Minors," remarked McGraw wearily.

When Garry Herrmann heard the news, he was furious. He'd written a letter to Sinclair saying he wanted to bid on Roush for the Reds. The letter had arrived two days after Sinclair and McGraw finalized the sale. Herrmann had been cut out of the deal, and he wouldn't forget it.

In the final week of January, the call came through to Oakland City. John B. Foster, secretary of the Giants club, informed Edd that his contract had been bought by the Giants.

Original from *Baseball Magazine*

ROUSH & MCGRAW SIGNING
GIANTS CONTRACT[22]

"I'M LICKED!" CARTOON
WITH ROUSH &
MCGRAW

He was to report to the Texas training camp by March 5. Minutes after Edd hung up the phone, he and Essie were making another call—to Bill and Ruby in Bedford. They would be together again in New York.

On January 30, the *New York Times* broke the story, *Batsman Rousch [sic] To Play For Giants*. On February 10, a telegram arrived with reporting instructions for spring training. Then a contract came for Edd's signature. It offered the same salary he'd made in Newark, $4,000. Edd resealed the envelope and sent it back to New York. If they were paying Kauff $8,000, Edd wasn't going to play for half that amount. As Edd would later say, "Kauff talked a better game than he played."

Edd acquiesced to McGraw in the middle of March. By holding out, he had succeeded in increasing his contract by only $500, but he was pleased to have avoided at least three weeks of the dreaded spring training.

GIANTS INITIATE THE FEDS ROOKIE

He arrived, tough and ready, in Texas on Sunday, March 19. He was in great shape since he had hunted through December and then played basketball daily on the makeshift court in the Opera House in Oakland City. He was on the field Monday and McGraw immediately put him in the outfield with Kauff and his regular, George Burns. Edd knew this was his "audition" in front of the famous manager, and he wanted desperately to earn a regular berth.

Edd played that day like never before. He ran the entire outfield and stole every base in sight. In the fourth inning of the

ROUSH SLIDES HOME AT GIANTS SPRING TRAINING CAMP

intra-squad competition between the "Mattys" (Christy Mathewson) and the "McGraws", the rivalry between Edd and Benny Kauff became fierce, and they collided squarely in center field. McGraw had seen enough. These two rube outfielders had to learn to "yell" to each other. Edd later recalled, "[McGraw] had us out chasing flies for a couple hours and yelling like a pair of Comanches."

Christy "Matty" Mathewson was writing an occasional newspaper column in 1916, and he wrote glowing commentary on Edd. "None of our fine outfielders can afford to let down for one second. Eddie Roush is as eager as a fox terrier at a rat hole."

To earn a fulltime spot, Edd not only had "bashful Benny" to worry about; there was also George "Highpockets" Kelly and a quiet, reserved outfielder called "Silent George" Burns. George had a following of New York fans who sat in a section of the left-field bleachers that came to be known as "Burnsville."[23]

There was another outfielder with the Giants that year— Jim Thorpe, the Sac/Fox Indian of Olympic fame.[24] Edd and Jim became friends and enjoyed morning workouts by racing around the diamond. Although Edd was known for his speed, he was no match for the swift champion. He often regaled listeners by recalling, "I was taking three strides for every two of Thorpe's, just to stay even." As he loved to say, "I'd be running as fast as I could, and he'd just be trotting along beside me." Thorpe would attempt to make Edd feel better by telling him, "I never saw a runner I couldn't look back on."

Edd would never forget his first encounter with the New York pitchers. One day he was sitting on the bench between veterans Ferdie "Shoopie" Schupp and Jeff "Papa Tes" Tesreau. Edd heard them chuckling. He looked down and noticed that his shoes were wet with brown tobacco juice. The two pitchers were taking turns spitting on the "busher's" shoes.[25] When they saw that Edd was aware of what they were doing, they broke into full belly laughs.

Edd sat quietly for a few seconds. Since he didn't chew tobacco, he collected a big wad of saliva in his mouth and waited for the right moment. Tes turned to him in mid-laugh with his mouth wide open and Edd spit the wad directly into his mouth, hitting the target with perfect aim. The pitcher choked and spurted while Edd and Ferdie roared.

Edd told Thorpe what had happened, and Jim said two could play that game. Thorpe loved booze and hated pitchers—they made fun of him, mimicking the big Indian's drunken states. They also threw him those curveballs he couldn't hit to save his life. On the trip north, an inebriated Thorpe was careening down the corridor of the Pullman car and found Tesreau preparing to get into his bunk. With a great heave, he picked Tes up and threw him in the upper bunk, bruising his pitching arm. The next day McGraw fined Thorpe $500 and told his pitchers to lay off the teasing. This event and numerous other infractions caused McGraw to send Thorpe back to Milwaukee in the American Association for the 1916 season. But Edd would meet his big buddy, "the runningest son of a seacook," again in Cincinnati in 1917.

Throughout spring training Edd thought about McKechnie. The would-be manager had called both Edd and Bill with hearty congratulations when they were chosen, but he was one of the few remaining players still standing on the auction block.

As fate would have it, Hans Lobert, a 35-year-old veteran and McGraw's money player on third base, was injured in an exhibition game on Yale Field. Lobert slid into third base while running out a triple and cracked his knee. He was carried off the field. Edd and Bill started talking up Mac to players, coaches, anyone who would listen. The word finally reached McGraw, and he called Sinclair. He needed an emergency third baseman.

A few days later, Mac walked onto the field carrying his suitcase in one hand and, in the other, a small bag containing his glove and baseball shoes. Edd remembered how happy he and Bill were to see him. The friendly triumvirate was intact again. Beryl called Essie at home with the happy news. The old gang would spend another summer together in New York.

OPENING SEASON AT THE POLO GROUNDS, 1916

The Giants opened the season in Philadelphia and Edd got two base hits in four tries. Essie arrived in New York the next week and was there for the home opener, a second series with the

EDD IN GIANT'S UNIFORM, 1916

Phillies at the Polo Grounds. Beryl and Ruby hadn't arrived yet, so Essie took her place among strangers in the wives' box. Sitting around the wives were other famous New Yorkers such as George M. Cohan and Eddie Foy. In addition to the theater crowd, most of the Wall Street luminaries were in this section as well.

Edd would recall Essie's description of that eventful day. She had barely sat down when she was introduced to Mrs.

John McGraw and then to Mrs. Christy Mathew-son and Mrs. DeWolf Hopper. Essie was smitten. There she was, sitting behind the boss's wife, the wife of the famous pitcher, and one of the most famous names in New York—Hedda Hopper. Hedda would gain fame as a Holly-wood gossip columnist later, but in 1916 she was about to make her debut as an actress in *Battle of Hearts*. Essie would recognize her name because of her husband, the matinee idol DeWolf Hopper. He was immortalized in baseball circles for his 1888 rendition of *Casey at the Bat*. Hedda (born Elda Furry in Pennsylvania) was his fifth wife and twenty-seven years his junior.

Hedda turned to Mrs. McGraw and said in an affected manner, "Blanche, thank you so much for giving me the name of your furrier. He only charged me $3,000 to repair my coat. The mink is still good on it, even if it is five years old. It would have been $10,000 at any other place."

Essie blushed. Here she sat behind these three grande dames wearing used clothing—high-top, lace-edged shoes from a consignment shop in Ohio and a fake fur coat she'd bought for $9.95. "Until that moment, I thought I looked grand," she would tell Edd.[26] Essie felt like a backwoods rube that day. She quickly learned about the prestige associated with the Giants organization.

To add insult to injury, when Edd came up to pinch hit for Pol Perritt, the fans booed him. Essie wasn't used to this. Her husband had never received anything but adoration from home fans. She left the park in the fifth inning and never again sat in the wives' box with the Giants. When asked why, she would say, "I prefer to sit up with the fans where I can 'hoot and holler' all I want to."

Edd played regularly in left field for ten games. When asked about his new man,

McGraw said, "That Hoosier moves with the regal indifference of an alley cat."[27] Both Edd and Bill had a little problem adjusting to McGraw's rules. They weren't big city boys who liked to mix in the New York nightlife; they were farm boys and were raised to the tune of "early to bed, early to rise." They hated McGraw's habit of sending his assistant around from door to door in the hotels at 11:30 every night to be sure his players were in their rooms and in condition for the next day's game. Edd and Bill were consistently asleep by 9 p.m. and resented being awakened two hours later.

In the early weeks of the season, Bill had easily overtaken Red Dooin as catcher. As they had done many times in Indianapolis and Newark, he and Edd thrilled fans by connecting for several circus-style putouts down the third base line. The New York press loved writing about the two new "bushers" from the Federal League.

CARTOON OF ROUSH AND RARIDEN AS "BUSHERS" ON PEDESTALS—
WITH MCGRAW LICKING HIS LIPS

But the Giants floundered. They lost 13 of the first 15 games. McGraw raged. He swore, he stomped, he flailed his fists in the faces of players. During the games none of the players would sit next to him. By the time Edd got in from right field, there was often only one available seat—next to McGraw. The closest players would bear the brunt of his anger. He'd swear and sometimes punch players in the legs, seemingly unaware of what he was doing. The only person on the team he'd speak to with any degree of civility was his lifelong friend, Christy Mathewson. Edd saw the *real* McGraw and his antics for the first time. Soon these motivational tactics would be turned squarely on Edd.

John Joseph McGraw was a living breathing man walking around as a baseball legend. If there had been a *Time* magazine issue of "The 100 Most Influential People in America" in 1916, he would have been on the list. Harry Sinclair maybe, but McGraw definitely. He had managed the Giants since 1901 and made them the most powerful team in the sport. McGraw *was* baseball.

No one gets to that level without his supporters and detractors. McGraw had the baseball magnates in his pocket. Owner Hempstead (and Stoneham after him) gave McGraw free reign to spend his money and manage his team. Other owners could only salivate over this bankroll and remonstrate over McGraw's ability to steal their best players. The powerful Ban Johnson kept him at arm's length, disdainful of his power tactics and underworld connections[28] but respectful of his influence.

His management philosophy was "motivation by intimidation." When the team was losing, he flew into foul-mouthed tirades. He would often seek a scapegoat for the loss, and the unlucky player would be fined several hundred dollars. If pitchers and hitters failed to comply with his signals, they were fined. Umpires braced themselves against his blasphemies. It was a comical sight to see McGraw berate an umpire. The furious little manager would stand toe-to-toe against a six-foot umpire, yelling his heart out.[29] New Yorkers loved it.

Rogers Hornsby described McGraw's treatment of players to writer Daniel Scism in 1962: "He'd fine players for speaking to someone on the other team...or being caught with a cigarette. He'd walk up and down the dugout and yell, 'Wipe those damn smiles off your faces.'"

Players won his favor by meekly submitting to the great master. Several, including Edd Roush, refused to do so. Edd would remember the exact date—it was May 18, the second game of a four-game series in St. Louis. The Giants needed a hit. McGraw called Edd into the game. Edd grabbed his 48-ounce bat, the heaviest in baseball,[30] and lugged it to the plate. He popped out on the first pitch, straight into the glove of catcher Mike Gonzalez. On the way back to the dugout, he flung his bat down in disgust.

The bat had no sooner hit the ground than McGraw blasted out of his seat and rushed over to pick it up. He swung it at the air a couple times, then barked at Edd.

"Is this your bat, Roush?" He already knew the answer.

The whole bench held its breath. Infielder Hans Lobert nudged Edd to keep him quiet. McGraw didn't wait for a response. "Don't ever let me see you at the plate with that bat again. It's too heavy for you."

The marble statue melted. Edd saw red. "This is the first damn league I ever played in where the manager picked your bat for you." Lobert nudged harder.

"What league did *you* ever hit .300 in?'" McGraw growled.

"Why, I hit .300 in every league I was ever in, and I'm going to hit .300 in this league too...and with that bat you're holding." Edd was standing at the edge of the dugout now.

The two men stared into each other's faces. Both had

clenched fists. There was complete silence in the dugout. No one ever talked back to Muggsy. If you had a gripe, you took it to Christy. He'd intervene on your behalf. Everyone knew that. McGraw threw the bat down and walked away. Roush would pay.

As Hans Lobert told the story that Arthur Daley would later print:

> The other Giant players were aghast when Eddie Roush talked back to John McGraw, the autocratic manager of the Giants. None of them dared do that because the Little Napoleon ruled with a whim of iron. But Roush was new to the team and they had yet to learn that a ruggedly independent and hardheaded man was hidden behind that mild-manned facade.

On May 22, Edd saw his last chance melt away. Davis "Dave" Robertson, the "hoss doctah" from Virginia, returned to claim his outfield position. Dave had never been a star, just a steady, dependable gardener. But, with Edd breathing down his neck on the bench, he became a new man. By late June, Robertson was smashing home runs and hitting over .330 on his way to the best season of his career. McGraw put Edd in just enough to stir the competitive loins of Robertson. James Sinnott wrote:

> If Eddie Roush never does anything else, he has made Dave Robertson a great ballplayer. To his presence on the Giant club is directly traceable the Virginian's whirlwind play of this spring.

From that point on, Edd was riding the bench with Mac.[31]

Although the Giants came back with a 17-game winning streak in June, they slumped again in July. McGraw started unloading the losers. He sent veterans Fred Merkle to Brooklyn and Larry Doyle to Chicago. In return, he got Lew McCarty and Heinie Zimmerman. But he still had a problem at second base. He wanted Buck Herzog, player/manager from Cincinnati. He had to make a deal that would be attractive to Reds' owner Garry Herrmann.

McGraw knew that Herrmann was still steaming over Roush being jerked out from under him during the Sinclair auction. But the untested Roush alone wouldn't be perceived as equivalent in a straight-out trade for Herzog. McGraw would have to offer a bigger prize. He would have to trade his long-time compadre, Christy "Matty" Mathewson.

As the new manager of the Giants in 1902, McGraw inherited Matty. He and his wife, Jane, had been personal friends with John and Blanche McGraw for fourteen years. To his credit, McGraw developed the pitcher's natural talent, making him the greatest star in the Giants' sky and the toast of New York. It was generally accepted that the fans had dubbed him "Big Six" due to his height, but the name originated with sportwriter Sam Crane, who compared his speed to the Manhattan Big Six Fire Company.[32]

"Big Six" had enjoyed sixteen wonderful seasons with New York, but his pitching arm was done. Convincing Herrmann to take Mathewson would allow McGraw to put Christy out to pasture with proper respect, and Herrmann would have a big name for his new (though untried) manager. After several long and thoughtful dinner conversations, the decision was made. Matty agreed to go to Cincinnati as the manager of the Reds.

On July 20th, the big trade was announced on the cover page of every sports section of every newspaper. Buck Herzog would join the Giants, along with utility outfielder Wade "Red"

Killefer. In exchange, the Reds would get one of the most famous players of all time, Christy Mathewson. Then, the footnote...two additional players were "thrown in" to sweeten the deal for Herrmann—Edd Roush and Bill McKechnie. It would later be called the famous "Hall of Fame Trade."[33]

---

[1] Harry was the son of a pharmacist. He was a natural entrepreneur who found success by acquiring the necessary "partners" who could arrange oil leases in Kansas, Texas, and Oklahoma. The result was the Prairie Oil and Gas Company. From this company Harry would build the multi-national Sinclair Oil.

[2] In 1917, at the end of the Bolshevik Revolution, Sinclair would travel to Russian and attempt to purchase Siberia oil fields. Lenin would say "nyet" to the deal.

[3] The Sinclairs would live in Kings Point Village on Long Island with thirty servants and a theatrical producer, Edgar Selwyn, as his closest neighbor. Sinclair Oil would be located at 120 Broadway.

[4] Sinclair found himself in need of the cash to support his dreams in 1921 and convinced Albert Fall, the U.S. Secretary of Interior, to secretly lease him thousands of acres to drill for oil in the Wyoming Naval Reserve called the "Teapot Dome." Fall would resign in 1927 in disgrace over this famous scandal in the Harding administration. Sinclair would go to jail in 1929 for criminal contempt of court for hiring detectives to shadow the jury.

[5] Schaefer came from Washington and filled the weak first base slot for Phillips. Schaefer was at the end of his career, having debuted in 1900 with Kansas City.

[6] Sinclair attempted to buy the Kansas City Feds first, but his offer was rejected.

[7] Throughout his life, Edd referred to Sinclair as "that oil man."

[8] Edd would become known for carrying the heaviest bat in baseball, 48 ounces, authenticated by Hillerich & Bradsby.

[9] Newark would win the season opener, 7-5, in front of a sold-out crowd of 15,000. They sat in an unfinished stadium. The roof was not finished when the first pitch was thrown.

[10] In 1915 Newark was filled with cottage industries and small factories filled with talented immigrant craftsmen making everything from corsets and pillows to fine leather goods—including fine baseball gloves.

[11] The automatic pitching machine was developed by Alexander MacMillan at Princeton University in 1914.

12 Other than a brief foot injury in 1915, Edd Roush would not have another debilitating injury until 1928 with the NY Giants. That 14-year span puts him in the top five all-time players with the most time between walkoffs: Cal Ripken (16), Gabby Harnett (15), Andres Galarraga, Carl Yastremzski and Roush (14).

13 *New York Times* stats published in 1915. *Total Baseball* (2004) reported revised statistics at .310 for Campbell and .298 for Roush. Roush claimed "foul" on this number. He would insist throughout his life that he never hit under .300 until the last year of his professional career (1931) and he often said, "I lost 2 points off my average when I went into the Hall of Fame." In 1915 All-league stats, Roush was #4 Fielding Average (.977), #10 Triples, #8 in Total Bases, #2 in RBI's, and #6 in hits with 164 total and a slugging average of .390. Roush played in 145 games, the most games he would play in one season in his 18-year career.

14 Interview with granddaughter of original owner, Phyllis (Lombardi) Guerriero on Long Island. September, 2005.

15 This 90-year-old scrapbook has provided much original resource material for this book.

16 Bill McKechnie would get another shot at managing with Pittsburgh in 1922. He would enjoy a 24-year career as a manager in Pittsburgh, Boston, and Cincinnati that would eventually lead to the Hall of Fame.

17 Sinclair hired an architect to design a stadium to seat 45,000, exceeding the Polo Grounds by 12,000.

18 According to the January 1, 1916 issue of *Sporting Life* which defined the terms of the "peace treaty," this required all AL and NL clubs to waive all claims to former players who were under contract to FL, allowing the Feds to retain control of their players and realize some profit from their sale.

19 John J. McGraw. *My Thirty Years in Baseball*. University of Nebraska Press, 1923 [1995 reprint].

20 Author's Note: This was long before most athletes had agents, unions, and lawyers to speak on their behalf. Players were forced to "negotiate" with owners alone.

21 McGraw confirmed parts of both stories in his own biography, from *My Thirty Years in Baseball*. He acknowledged purchasing Roush from Sinclair for $6,000 and he said, "The only man who ever told me that Rousch [sic] was a better ball player than Kauff was 'Germany' Schaefer. A lot of them talk about it now [1923], but old 'Schaef' was the only one to hold that opinion in advance."

22 Photo depicts the famous signing of Roush's $70,000 3-year contract in 1927 when he was traded back to New York after eleven years with the Cincinnati Reds.

23 Richard Puff biography of Burns published in *Road Trips*: SABR, 2004.

24 Thorpe's 1912 Olympic gold medals (pentathlon and decathlon) in

Stockholm were stripped from him by the Amateur Athletic Union because he was under "professional" contract with the Giants. In 1983, long after his death, this decision was reversed, gold medals reissued, and honors officially recognized.

25 Author's Note: The term "busher" was made popular by writer Ring Lardner in a series of articles written in 1914 for the *Saturday Evening Post*. A busher was a derogatory term referring to an amateur ball player who played in rural sandlots and farm fields, also referred to as the bush leagues.

26 At the Hall of Fame induction ceremonies in 1962, the wives gathered on the terrace for mint juleps one afternoon. Mrs. Christy (Jane) Mathewson laughed as Essie told her the story of her initiation to the wives' box at the Polo Grounds in 1916.

27 Thomas Rogers. Roush Obituary. The *New York Times*. March 22, 1988.

28 McGraw's name surfaced in the 1921 Black Sox trial. It was reported that he was co-owner of a pool hall with the New York gambler being investigated for fixing the series, Arthur Rothstein. He also had interests in a racetrack and casino in Cuba. But, he had enough "top dog" credentials to emerge unscathed.

29 Some umpires actually found the courage to expel McGraw from games. Dan O'Brien, SABR researcher, reported that McGraw managed 4,801 games in 33 years with 131 confirmed ejections—giving him an ejection rate of once every 41 games.

30 On April 22, 1970, Jack Hillerich, President of Hillerich & Bradsby, confirmed in a letter to Peter Clark, HOF Curator, that according to company records, Edd Roush had "consistently used the heaviest bats in baseball (48 ounces)." Although not a large man (5'11",175 lbs), Roush claimed that his wrists and hands were strong from milking cows every morning as an Indiana farmboy.

31 William Phelon wrote negative comments in the July issue of *Baseball Magazine*...Rousch [sic], Kauff's former sidekick, has failed with the stick and been relegated to the bench.

32 Eddie Frierson is a well-known biographer of Mathewson who also wrote and starred in the one-man off-Broadway play, *Matty*. His Mathewson biography appears in the SABR publication *Deadball Stars of the National League*. Brassey's, 2004.

33 McGraw traded three future Hall of Famers to Cincinnati. He acknowledged that the trade of Roush in 1916 was the biggest mistake he ever made as a manager. McGraw's trade didn't help the 1916 Giants. Although they had a record 26-game winning streak after Herzog arrived, they finished the season in fourth place behind the winning Brooklyn.

4

Hudepohl Heaven

Last words of dying Umpire in Cincinnati:
"Boys, what were them things they hit me with?"
"Beer mugs."
"I thought they felt familiar. But boys..."
"What is it, Jim?"
"They wasn't loaded, was they?"
"No. It wouldn't be right to waste any of that stuff!"
"Bury me in Cincinnati."
– Boston Globe, 7/19/87 [1]

THURSDAY, JULY 20, 1916
NIGHT TRAIN TO CINCINNATI

Edd and Bill McKechnie sat on the outside deck of the observation car on the Cincinnati Special. In the rush from the Polo Grounds to Grand Central Station, they had nearly missed the train, throwing their bags on and jumping in after them. As the train headed to Ohio, McGraw's parting words rang in Edd's ears: "You can make a difference over there in Cincinnati. They need you."

It had all happened so fast. The team had been suiting up when Matty and Eddie Brannick, the club secretary, came in to get Bill. Minutes later, Matty returned and motioned for Edd to come with him to McGraw's empty office. As he walked in, Edd looked at Bill, trying to read his face. Matty handed him the phone, and he heard McGraw's voice. In seconds it was clear. McGraw, Harry Hempstead, and Garry Herrmann had made a deal. Edd, Bill, and Matty were being traded to Cincinnati for Buck Herzog and Wade Killifer. They were to report tomorrow at noon, details to follow.[2]

Of the three players, only Matty had been aware of the negotiations. However, even he got a surprise on the phone that day. Reluctantly, McGraw had to tell his friend that his transfer would be permanent. Herrmann had refused to agree to McGraw's stipulation that the Giants would have the option of recalling Matty after two years in Cincinnati. Herrmann wanted Mathewson as his new manager with no strings attached. McGraw knew it was the best move for Matty, so after a gallon of beer and a basket of Hermann's sausages, he acquiesced.

Back in the locker room Edd hurriedly packed his gear and took a cab to the apartment on the Jersey side to tell Essie. She was dumbstruck. He threw a few things in his satchel, gave her a quick kiss, and headed for the train station. All the unanswered questions were left hanging in the air. He'd call tomorrow from Cincinnati. They'd work it out. He'd be back

CHRISTY MATHEWSON AND EDD ROUSH AT REDLAND FIELD, 1917

in New York next Tuesday for the Reds-Giants series. In Essie's letter to her family she said, "I do NOT want to go to Cincinnati, Ohio!"

On the train, Edd and Mac were quiet. As Edd drew on his cigar, he turned to his friend and for the first time that day he expressed his feelings. "I don't know about Cincinnati, but I'll tell you I'm happy to get away from McGraw." Bill nodded. Edd had born the brunt of McGraw's anger on more than one occasion. Although Bill's experience had been less caustic, he understood his friend's feelings.

Bill had concerns of his own. More than anything, he wanted to be a manager. He had tasted management in Newark and wanted a bigger bite. Since it was clear that the trade would make Matty the new Reds' manager, he wouldn't have a shot. Although he knew he was a good third baseman, he also knew that the Reds' star Heinie Groh was firmly planted at third. So, what position would he play? Would he be a lowly utility infielder?

As the two men pondered their futures, a third man pulled up a chair behind them. It was their new boss, Christy Mathewson. Edd and Bill welcomed him, hoping he had more information to share. He did. Knowing Matty's usual reticence, Edd initiated the conversation.

"Bill and I are talking about how happy we are to get away from McGraw. Aren't you glad to get away from all that cussing and such?" Bill squirmed a bit, uncomfortable to be included in this statement. He had no personal beef with McGraw.

The comment was not totally inappropriate because Edd suspected that Matty might share his view. He remembered the day during the 17-game losing streak in June when McGraw stood in front of the team and blasphemed each player, one by one. When he got to Matty, he paused. He had never before said an ugly word to his friend in front of other players, but he lashed out with full venom. Matty remembered that day too. He also remembered McGraw's private apology to him afterward. Matty was kind and forgiving. He knew his friend's temperament better than anyone in the world, and he saw the good side too.

But now Matty had two players who deserved an answer sitting in front of him. He liked both Edd and Bill, and his response was heartfelt. "You guys have only been on the Giants a couple months. It's just another ball club to you. But I was with that team for sixteen years. To me, the Giants are home. Leaving for New York in the spring is like coming home to me." He paused for a moment. "Of course, I realize I'm done as a pitcher. Mac has done me a favor here, and I thanked him for it. He's giving me a chance to manage a ball club. It was Mac who arranged this deal so I could manage Cincinnati."

Edd shuffled around in his seat. The last thing he wanted to do was to insult Matty. He didn't know how to respond.

Matty did it for him. "I'll tell you another thing, Roush. The last thing Mac told me was to put you in center field. He said you'd make me a great ballplayer. So, starting tomorrow you're my center fielder."

The shocker came out of the blue. It must have been difficult for Edd to disguise the pleasure on his face. In one moment Matty erased the pain of the past months in New York. Edd's mind was reeling. He would have his dream position in Cincinnati—and all because of McGraw, the man he hated. He would later recall thinking, "Now I've heard everything!"

The next day's headlines focused on Matty, reporting his salary at $20,000 per annum. Most reminded readers of the great pitcher's 372-188 career win/loss record and 12 consecutive 20-win seasons with the Giants.[3] One writer called him "the McGraw of Porkopolis."

James Sinnott wrote an epitaph: "New York will miss Mathewson. He has been part of the very city itself, like the city hall and the Brooklyn bridge." Although it was true that the

Reds had been living just a floor above the cellar for the last three years, Sinnott postulated that this was an advantage for Matty: "...managers who have made big reputations have invariably done so through taking hold of what were considered hopeless propositions."

DEBUT WITH THE REDS

While Cincinnati was reading the news on Friday morning, Edd, Bill, and Matty prepared for a day's work at Redland Field. All players' eyes were on the new boss. Would he be a taskmaster like McGraw? Would he levy fines? Would he let Herrmann tell him what to do like other Reds managers, or would he be his own man? Would he lead them to that land where pennants wave?

The answers came quickly. Matty walked over to each man and shook his hand. Each one must have sensed he was meeting a leader. This new manager carried himself with a natural and easy grace. He appeared forthright, honest, and unassuming. He was a big man with blond tousled hair and kind blue eyes. When he met little Heinie Groh, he stooped over slightly in a gesture of deference. And no one in the room missed it when he loaded his gear into the empty locker on the end. He was actually going to dress with his players—unheard of in a Reds locker room.

In his first speech as a manager, he announced that Edd Roush would be starting in center field.

> Unless I am greatly mistaken, I have the counter-
> part of a Tris Speaker in Eddie Rousch [sic]. He
> is only a youngster yet and will improve steadily.
> He is a beautiful fielder now, can go back, come
> in, or to either side...he is chain-lightning on his
> feet and is possessed of a great arm...a crack-a-

jack runner. He will hit, never fear. With a fellow
of Rousch's [sic] glowing possibilities it should
not be difficult to construct a champion outfield.
–Christy Mathewson. July, 1916.

Edd would never forget his debut in Cincinnati on July 21,
1916. His performance was a preview of a brilliant career in
Redland. The game was the third in a series of five against
Philadelphia. The Phillies had won the first two. Groh led off,
and Edd hit in the number three slot. His first time up he hit a
single to right field. He popped out in the third inning but hit
another single in the seventh. Just to prove it wasn't beginner's
luck, he walloped the ball for a triple in the ninth and brought
in two runners to tie the game. The Cincinnati fans went crazy.
Yes, Roush would do.

Cincinnati officials awarded the keys to the city to their new
manager, and prominent merchants gave Matty keys to their
breweries, too. Although Edd Roush received no fanfare or gifts
that day, he made an impression on the baseball-loving people
of southern Ohio. Cincinnati papers lauded him. But most of
all, he had made Matty proud. Matty said nothing, but he put
his big hand on Edd's shoulder as they walked into the locker
room at the end of the game.[4] McGraw was right yet again.

The team left Sunday for New York, where they played a
series against the Giants. It was a poignant moment for Christy
Mathewson when he walked out onto the field of the Polo
Grounds in a Reds uniform. The entire grandstand rose and
stayed on their feet for what seemed to be an hour. Watching
their manager receive such an outpouring of respect inspired the
Reds to overwhelm their big city rivals that day for the first time
in a long time.

The next day's article in the New York Sun brought sweet
revenge to Edd. "The Reds have obtained a corking good ball

player in this man, who never had a chance, as a Giant, to display his real skill.

Essie was at the Polo Grounds to see Edd in a Reds uniform for the first time. Whatever misgivings she had about Cincinnati were washed away as she watched the Reds beat the Giants. The Reds went from New York to a series in Brooklyn the following week, and Edd and Essie spent the evenings packing for the move back to the Midwest. Essie would return to Oakland City as Edd finished the year with the Reds. If Edd was offered a contract for 1917, they would find an apartment in Cincinnati next year. After six years and so many cities, young Edd and Essie Roush accepted their fate. They would spend their lives as baseball gypsies.

NEW TEAMMATES, NEW FRIENDS

One Redleg was not happy about the trade, a big Scotsman and former college football star, outfielder Alfred Earle "Greasy" Neale. Matty had moved Neale to right field when he put Edd in center. Unbeknownst to Edd, Neale wanted his job and was willing to fight for it.

In those last two weeks of July, fans may have noticed strange behavior in the Reds outfield. Neale and Roush continually ran for the same fly balls and narrowly escaped collisions several times. According to Edd, "I thought the big football player was trying to run over me out there. Every time I'd go out for a fly, I'd holler three times, like I always did—'I got it, I got it, I got it!' I'd holler loud too." But Neale never responded with the correct protocol—"Take it!"—and he kept running toward the same fly.

Edd remembered his reaction, "I didn't have to watch the ball to know where it was going. If I thought I could catch it and get out of his way, I'd do it. If I couldn't, I'd cut behind him and let him try for it."

THE 1919 CINCINNATI REDS TOP ROW: DAUBERT, FISHER, RARIDEN
MIDDLE ROW: NEALE, ROUSH, GROH
BOTTOM ROW: RATH, KOPF, WINGO

For ten games the competition was fierce. In the final game of the series with Brooklyn, Neale sat down next to Edd on the bench and broke the silence between them. "I guess you know I've been trying to run you over ever since Matty put you in center. I wanted that job."

Edd said, "I figured you were trying to do something like that, but I'm pretty hard to run over out there."

Neale's response marked the full measure of the man: "I admit it. You're a better center fielder than I am. From now on I'll go along with you and I'll holler."

Edd looked into the pale eyes of his tall, West Virginia team-mate. He knew Greasy was a good man. Greasy would remind

Edd of McKechnie, but with a less saintly image. He was more sanguine, more robust, more a pure athlete. Edd would later say, "I knew right then Greasy and I were going to get along fine."

Years later in a little breakfast nook in Buckhannon, West Virginia, the two old Hall of Famers—Neale for football, Roush for baseball—would relive that day.[5] Like Rariden and McKechnie, Neale would become a lifelong friend.

Another player would be added to that list of friends in the summer of 1916: Edd's roommate, Heinie Groh. Heinie was the heart of the Reds. He was a little man with a big personality. He was the team's sparkplug—always the first to compliment the good work of a fellow teammate. He spoke with great enthusiasm, and when the Reds began to climb in the standings in coming years, Groh was their spokesman for the press. As Edd would say with a chuckle, "That Heinie sure loved to talk."

Above all things, Heinie loved the Reds and yearned for that elusive pennant. The minute he set eyes on Edd Roush, he knew they had a winner. He relished Edd's success that summer. When Edd got a triple, Matty would smile, but Heinie would jump up and down. He was like a kid, filled with enthusiasm and completely void of guile. Edd liked him immediately.

On long evenings in the hotels, the two roommates rehashed every play of the day's game. Heinie also informed Edd about their teammates. One of the first things he told Edd was, "Stay away from Chase." Edd didn't understand his meaning at the time.

Edd also admired Heinie's skill on the diamond. He was the ace third baseman.[6] Edd followed him at bat and could count on Heinie's well-placed bunt to set him up. With Chase following Edd and Heinie, the Reds began to click. But, the team still had a long way to go before that pennant would wave over Redland in 1919.

Ivey Brown Wingo was the catcher on the team and the

closest thing the Reds had to a "Georgia Peach." He had a southern drawl, albino blue eyes, and an innocent face that seemed to be permanently creased in a smile. He was a bit shy until he drank a few beers. Then he began singing. He loved to belt out the "doo dah, doo dah" in "Camptown Races."

Edd saw the playful side of Wingo first hand one August afternoon when Heinie invited him to "come along with the boys" after a home game. Heinie led the way as the small band of Reds exited the ballpark. As they stopped to chat with lingering fans,[7] Edd noticed that Hal Chase left the park walking in another direction. He wondered why Chase wasn't invited along.

They made their way six blocks down Freeman Street to the Foss-Schneider brewery. On the way in, Heinie warned Edd, "Last guy in has to pay for the beer. Then, we settle up later." The players were instantly recognized and escorted to a private room in the cellar. They sat on stools at a long bar made of smoothly sanded wood and savored the cold air of the dark basement room. After a long, hot game, this was heaven! The happy brewery host set three tall glasses of beer in front of each player. A few minutes later, he did it again.

The guys were all laughing and talking when suddenly Ivey's voice boomed out from the corner with a hearty "Take me out to the ball game..." Soon every man in the cellar joined him in song.[8] Together they sang the popular tunes of the day, capping off the night with a round of "Goodnight Ladies."

The Foss-Schneider brewery would become a Reds tradition that would last for a decades to come—even through Prohibition.[9] Visiting players from opposing teams would join in the camaraderie after games. In 1917, the brewery owners would create a "ladies room" upstairs where players could bring girlfriends and wives. Essie and Edd spent many wonderful hours there among friends: Ivey and Mattie Mae, Heinie and Ruby, Greasy and Genevieve, Bill and Beryl, and later, Bill and

POSTER FOR THE FOSS-SCHNEIDER BREWERY

Ruby Rariden, Rube and Helen Bressler, and Jake and Gertrude Daubert. The first place the Reds went to celebrate when they won the 1919 pennant was Foss-Schnieder.

MATTY TAKES CHARGE

When Matty first walked onto Redland Field he faced a team that had won 35 and lost 50. They finished in the cellar with a 60-93 record. Matty knew he would have his hands full even before coming to Cincinnati.

It was his goal to develop the Reds, particularly the young players. He had the valuable experience of watching McGraw build his team in New York, but Matty was not McGraw. Although his contract permitted him to "discipline by fine, suspension, or otherwise any player of the club,"[10] he was averse to such methods. He preferred to teach and mentor. His coaching style was more Socratic than Machiavellian. He was an educated man from Bucknell University and a more cerebral manager than McGraw. He would lead the horses to water, then allow them to determine when and how much to drink.

Heinie Groh said, "We called him 'Silent Sam,' in fun. He'd sit on the bench and wouldn't say a word."[11] Edd remembered asking his advice during a tight game and receiving the answer, "Suit yourself." To their credit, Herrmann and business manager Frank Bancroft didn't meddle as they had with the previous seven managers. Matty got respect.

Few people knew that Matty also did some personal coaching with young Edd Roush. When he noticed Edd's habit of pulling away from the first pitch, he encouraged him to overcome his fear by moving up in the box to meet the ball squarely. He arranged for Edd to work out for an hour daily with the battery of Fred Toney and Ivey Wingo. Edd took Matty's coaching to heart and spent hours in batting practice that season. This intensive practice would pay off in 1917.

During this time Edd developed his technique of constantly moving around in the batter's box. Future Hall of Fame pitcher Burleigh Grimes said, "I've been watching that fellow for years and I never found out yet whether he's going or coming, trying to slug or bunt...most disconcerting to pitchers."[12]

F. C. Lane described Edd's technique.[13]

> The pitcher eyes a pair of dusty spiked shoes sixty feet away. They do not kick the dust or fidget...they appear singularly at ease. The pitcher watches sharply for some premonitory sign of their owner's batting intentions. The moment that whirling sphere leaves his fingers, those

shoes are in motion. They step briskly in the
front of the batter's box....there is a crack of col-
liding wood and leather. ...Edd Roush is at bat.

Matty and Edd struck up a friendship that season. Since
their wives were not in Cincinnati, on off days Matty would pull
up in his car and take Edd for a drive. Edd would recall these
outings with great pride. The men found they had a lot in common. Both spent early years on farms (Matty grew up in
Factoryville, Pennsylvania) and both had practiced throwing
baseballs over a barn.[14] Both loved to fish and play cards.[15]

During these afternoon drives, the conversation would turn
to the Reds. Matty would ask Edd's opinion about other players on the team. Edd was cautious with his responses, but he did
share his concerns about Hal Chase making suspicious plays in
the field.[16] Long after Matty died and Edd retired from baseball,
Edd would say, "I told him about Chase in 1916. I played with
him in '13 in Chicago, and he was rotten then. Matty wouldn't
do anything about it. We lost the pennant in '18 because of
Chase and [Lee] Magee."

Edd ended the 1916 season with a .267 batting average.[17]
Although not attributable to Matty, the Reds did have one
bright spot in the 1916 season: Hal Chase won the National
League batting championship with a .339 average.

Despite his team's last-place finish, Matty enjoyed some
success in his first year. He began developing young players like
Edd Roush through skillful encouragement, and he shared his
vast knowledge with the existing pitching staff. Most importantly, his very presence gave the Reds respectability. With
respectability came confidence. Players would leave Redland
that season feeling better about their jobs and their team than
they had in years.

THE WINTER OF 1916-17

On Thanksgiving Day, after the noon meal, Edd and Will set off on their annual hunting excursion, this time in the upper peninsula of Michigan.[18] Edd left his unsigned contract for the 1917 season on the maple secretary in the parlor. The contract for 1917 was for $4,000, which was $500 less than he'd made last season. It was holdout time again in Oakland City.

The newspapers carried stories of financial difficulties in the major leagues due to the losses incurred over the Federal League debacle. Ban Johnson bemoaned the sad state of affairs: "As things are at present the players are getting so much money that the profits of the club owner are almost nil." Edd and Heinie had a good laugh over the vision of Garry Herrmann as a hobo searching through garbage for half-eaten sausages. It made Edd mad to think that the wealthy Top Dogs were barking over his measly $4,500.

In January, letters from the Reds began to arrive. On February 6th, Edd wrote his response. He enclosed the unsigned contract and, on a half sheet of plain white paper, he wrote two simple sentences stating his terms:

Cinn. Ball Club
Dear Sir:
    I received your letter yesterday also the contract a few weeks ago and will say I will not sign contract for that money. If you want to raise it two thousand dollars ($6,000) I will sign it, if not I won't.

Sincerely yours
Edd J. Roush

In mid-February, the phone rang and Essie handed it to Edd. It was Frank Bancroft, the Reds business manager. Edd knew that "Banny" was calling to do Herrmann's dirty work, as usual. The only thing Essie remembered was Edd saying, "I don't want to play. I'd rather buy a coal mine here in Oakland City. I'd be better off financially." She thought he'd been a bit curt with old Mr. Bancroft.

So, the Reds went to the training camp in Shreveport, Louisiana, without Edd.

Harry Stephens, club treasurer, wrote a long letter on March 8, offering $4,500. "Only three men in the National League are getting more than you. It is a great disappointment to Mr. Mathewson. Your loyalty to him should make you reconsider."

As the weeks wore on and Edd stood firm, Essie began to question the wisdom of these annual holdouts. She knew that Edd believed he would be rewarded with a higher salary and could avoid the dreaded March training camp. It was a great deal—for Edd.

But what about all the time Matty had spent with him last year? What about his friends on the team? Was he cutting off his nose to spite his face this time? When she asked these questions, Edd just brushed them off. The lesson his father taught him in Indianapolis was deeply ingrained. The stubborn German in him took over at contract time.

In Shreveport Matty decided he could not meet his goals for the coming season without Edd. The telegram arrived in Oakland City at noon on March 12.

Herrmann and his "gang of thieves" were one thing, but Edd would have real problems saying "no" to Matty. The following Saturday Edd was in Herrmann's office signing his two-year contract. Matty told an interesting story about that day in his newspaper column.

> When Roush signed his contract this year, he made a stipulation. 'I want you to agree to one

thing," he announced when he was ready to put his name on the dotted line.

"What is it?" I asked, figuring maybe he was going to demand some hard condition.

"I want you to put in there that you won't trade me from Cincinnati. I don't want to be moving around."

"That's a novel request," said Mr. Herrmann, who was present, "but I guess we won't hold you up on account of it. I don't know that it was ever made to us before."

Matty ended his story by saying, "That's what I like to see in a ball player—enthusiasm for his club." Perhaps Matty was also sending a message to Edd's teammates who had endured spring training for lower salaries. "Okay, so Roush didn't sweat through Shreveport in March like you did, but at least you see he is loyal to our team."

When Edd joined the team he noticed a slight change in Matty's attitude toward him. Instead of the friendly colleague of the summer automobile rides, the man who stood across from him wore the mantle of management. It had been important to Matty to have his full team at spring training. The one player to whom he had devoted personal time and energy the season before had let him down. He must have felt betrayed.

Edd's stubbornness had backfired this time. His relationship with Matty was never the same. He had lost an important friend and ostensibly damaged his team in return for just $500. The sad part was that he would do it again and again in years to come.[19]

But in March of 1917, Edd Roush was on top of the world.

He was about to begin one of the best seasons of his life and, most importantly, Essie had just told him he was soon to be a father.

BUILDING A CHAMPIONSHIP TEAM, 1917

Matty made major changes. He was constructing the 1919 pennant-winning team. As Edd would often say, "It was Matty who put that team together." He experimented with the lineup, trying several players in the leadoff position—Neale, Griffith, Smith, Kopf, even McKechnie. He found a winning combination in slots two, three, and four—Groh, Roush, and Chase. He purchased a solid outfielder from Boston named Sherry Magee. But he focused his energy in the area he knew best—pitching. He convinced Herrmann that, with the exception of Fred Toney and Pete Schneider, a major overhaul was required. He put his considerable feelers throughout the leagues for young, underdeveloped talent. The word was out, Matty was pitcher-shopping.

Four new pitchers walked onto Redland Field that year. Matty's judgment proved solid, and all four would make major contributions in the coming pennant races. He plucked a promising rookie from the Chicago Cubs, a southpaw named Walter "Dutch" Ruether, age 24. The other three were big gambles, but Matty had good scouting reports on them. Horace Owen "Hod" Eller, age 23, was drafted from Moline and was to become the Reds' "shine-ball" artist. The Philadelphia Athletics were happy to let Cincinnati take bench rider Raymond "Rube" Bressler, age 24, off their hands. Dutch, Hod, and Rube were all southpaws.

The fourth was Jimmy Ring, age 22, a handsome fellow who caused the women to swoon when he came to bat. He'd had a cup of coffee with the Yankees. They had tucked him away in Buffalo, and were surprised when Matty called him up for Cincinnati.[20] Jimmy was a fast-baller with a fast tongue to go with it. He was a big guy and a New Yorker by birth, the only Red with an eastern accent. It was humorous to listen to Wingo, the southerner, with Ring in the battery. Edd laughed remembering Ivey's perplexed looks as he tried to understand Jimmy's rapid speech. It took Jimmy awhile to learn that when Ivey said "y'all," he meant Jimmy.

In established Red's tradition, Heinie, Edd, and the boys initiated the new teammates at the Foss-Schneider brewery after the season opener. Edd and Hod hit it off from the beginning since both were Hoosiers. (Hod was from Muncie, Indiana.) However, Edd's pick of the new crop was Rube Bressler, age 23. Rube was intelligent, easy-going and, like Edd, a devoted hunter. Rube was popular among his teammates, and he would eventually become the proprietor of Bressler's Tavern on the Little Miami River, a favorite watering hole for the Reds after Prohibition.[21]

Of the four, Hod would see some action that season, but Fred Toney and Pete Schneider dominated the mound.[22] All the work that Matty had done with Schneider in '16 paid off in 1917 as Pete finished with a 1.98 ERA in 342 innings. Sadly, he also destroyed his pitching arm. Schneider would pitch his last major league game at age 23.

Matty tapped "Mac" McKechnie as manager for exhibition games. However, as Mac had surmised when he was traded, this was not his year.[23] In fact, both Edd and Mac were injured early in the season. On April 22 in a home game with the Cubs, Edd slid into second in the sixth inning and caught his left foot under the bag. Dr. Harry Hines, the club physician, said he has torn two ligaments and would be out for two or three weeks.[24] As he was carried off the field to the clubhouse, a fan in the grandstand reportedly said, "They just carried the Cincinnati ball club off the field."

Edd had started the season red hot. His average was .451 on

April 19, three days before the injury. Because of the injury Matty called Jim Thorpe over from New York.[25] Jim became a regular at Foss-Schneider, where his antics amused the players.

EUROPE'S WAR

On April 6th, 1917, the United States entered World War I. Baseball players registered in their local communities.[26] The Reds registered at city hall. Edd had the marriage exemption (Level 4) and no compulsion to fight in "Europe's war." However, like his married teammates, he showed his patriotism by writing "do not claim head of family exemption[27] on his form. Others wrote creative responses under the "disabilities" section of the form. Greasy claimed he was "a little baldhead-ed;" Ivey Wingo had a "bad finger; "Emil Huhn wrote "can't hear out of one ear;" and Larry Kopf had "bad eyes."

The biggest surprise was that two players had been lying about their ages. Pete Schneider, at 21, was four years younger than he had claimed, and Jim Thorpe confessed to being four years older and beyond the age to fight. There were two other Reds who were too old—Matty (36) and Hal Chase (34).

As war raged in Europe, Edd fought his own battle at home. He was a serious contender for the National League batting championship of 1917. In early August, Edd and St. Louis out-fielder Walton Cruise were jostling for the lead. When Cruise dropped back, up came George Burns of the Giants and for a few games they were neck-and-neck with .347 averages. When Burns broke stride, a young colt named Rogers Hornsby came roaring along the inside rail. At age 21 Hornsby wouldn't wear the roses this year, but would go on to win seven batting titles in the 1920s.[28]

Throughout September Edd suffered from severe charley horses and played sparingly in the last seven games of the season, but Hornsby had slumped to six points behind, so the injury had a negligible impact on the race in the end. When the final stats were published, it was young Edd Roush in the winner's circle.

There was great delight in Cincinnati since their Reds had won the National League batting championship two years in a row—Chase in 1916 and now Roush. Although the Reds finished fourth, the fans were happy. Their team was on the upswing. They tied for first in hitting with the Giants, and two of the league's six .300 hitters were Reds. Heinie Groh hit .304.

A special honor was forthcoming when F.C. Lane placed Edd on the *Baseball Magazine* 1917 All-Star Team. In Lane's article he said that Edd's win had "caused a mild furor in baseball circles" because he was in his first year as an "established regular" and had been cast off the prior year by McGraw. "This achievement is unique in baseball annals."

Heinie Groh had been chosen for the All-Star Team in 1915, and his name would be listed again in 1918 and 1919. As one SABR historian put it, "Roush paired with Groh were the Reds' two superstars. They were the Reds' 'heart and soul.'"[29]

HIGHLIGHTS OF 1917 SEASON

Edd would recall three events that bookmarked the 1917 season in his memory. The first was at the beginning of the season when he would meet his boyhood idol for the first time. By 1917, Ty Cobb was far and away the most famous baseball player in America. He had already won the American League batting championship nine times and would win it three more times before the lively ball was introduced in 1920. Edd would say later in dozens of interviews, "Cobb was the best of them all. Hands down."

Cobb happened to be in Cincinnati for a couple days before the season opened.[30] Matty invited him to Redland Field to give his young team some pointers. Those two days on the field with Cobb were like gold to Edd. He hung on every word. His eyes followed every movement—the grip of his hands on the bat, the total focus of his body on the ball flying toward him. Cobb didn't pull back; he had no fear. Edd listened as Cobb explained how to steal bases, one of his specialties. Edd would always remember, and often repeat, Cobb's ominous threat: "Infielders better get out of my way. When I'm on the run that baseline is mine." It should also be noted that Cobb was a highly publicized holdout at salary time, another pattern that Edd would continue to emulate.

Cobb seemed to "latch on to young Edd Roush"[31] and it was noted years later that Roush's batting average in 1916 was .267 and jumped to .341 in 1917. Indeed, two days of lessons with batting coach Cobb may have helped Edd.

The second highlight might seem small, but to Edd it was an important milestone. He jokingly said, "I had to win the National League batting championship and become a member of the All-Star Team for the writers to spell my name right." In the winter of 1917, the press finally acknowledged the proper spelling and of his name. The *Cincinnati Post* ran the article.

VERY WELL, EDD, WE ACCEPT IT

His name is not Edward Rousch, as so many of them spell it, nor Eddie Rousche, nor even Ed. Roush. It's some quaint and curious title. The real name of the Reds' center fielder is Edd Roush–no period after the Edd, either. Just "Edd," as it might be John, Anthony, or Gahookenstopp. An odd and unusual name, but it's his just the same, and it is blazoned all over sundry barns, fences and country stores on the broad baronial estates of the Roushes up in Indiana.

The third event etched in Edd's memory was a personal affair—one that would involve Edd in the sordid events surrounding the 1919 World Series. It happened in the middle of the September batting race. Edd was a new father longing to be with his family. Mary Evelyn Roush was born in August and, given the fragility of childbirth in those days, Essie had spent the entire season in Oakland City. Edd had not even seen his baby daughter yet because Essie insisted he stay in Cincinnati and remain focused on the batting race. Essie was always practical, even in affairs of the heart.

Edd decided that he wanted to do something special for Essie. He thought about the plain gold wedding band he had placed on her finger in front of the Justice of the Peace in Indianapolis three years prior. For Essie, it was enough. But now he was 24 years old and making a good salary. He decided to buy her a diamond wedding ring.

Edd had no idea how to shop for a ring in Cincinnati, so he asked his teammates in the locker room one day. Hal Chase suggested a local fellow named Jimmy Widmeyer. Heinie reminded Edd that Jimmy was one of the guys who hung around the ballpark a lot. He said Widmeyer claimed to be a part owner in the team.[32]

Edd remembered having talked with him a few times, but had never caught his name. There were many guys who came to the park during practice sessions or before games. They would stand around the field and engage players in conversation, then brag about it in their local bar later that night. Most players would attempt to be polite, knowing the importance of a solid fan base to the team.

Edd met Jimmy sometime in midseason and Edd remembered taking an instant liking to the man. He had a bulbous nose, pink complexion, round German face, and wide forthright eyes. He dressed plainly, unlike some of the "dandies" who strode around the field with their diamond rings and silk ties. He was not a pushy salesman or a showoff. In fact, he was self-effacing and more interested in learning about the other guy than in talking about himself. He seemed to genuinely like people and have a quick wit. Jimmy had played some amateur baseball, so the conversation between him and Edd flowed easily. Although Edd liked Jimmy, he knew little about him.

Edd found it interesting that so many of his teammates knew the guy. Chase told Edd that Jimmy could get him anything he wanted, from those rare foreign cigars to the finest Bourbon whiskey (Essie's drink of choice). Larry Kopf called him the "million dollar newsboy."[33] He said it was rumored that he had a million bucks stashed away. Edd thought this was just talk. How could a guy make a million dollars selling newspapers for buffalo nickels? Jimmy appeared to be just an affable fellow with a newsstand and a love for baseball, but this was no ordinary newsboy, as Edd would learn.

The Reds were leaving for a three-week road trip and Edd wanted that ring. He saw Jimmy on the field and walked over. Jimmy spoke amicably but said he couldn't get a ring, though he did have some "special" contacts for fresh cut diamonds. Wouldn't Edd's wife prefer to have a setting made to her own liking? Edd hemmed and hawed, having no knowledge of such things and said, "Okay, but get me a good one, Jimmy."

"No problem, but it'll cost you a hundred or more," said Jimmy. Edd wasn't worried about prices. Although Essie kept the Roush purse strings pulled tight, he would receive some extra money from the "Ohio Championship" coming up when the Reds took on the Cleveland Indians in a special post-season series. The winning players would receive a bonus of $100 or more, depending on the gate.[34] Edd had planned to surprise Essie with the cash, but now she would have a diamond ring instead.

Three weeks later Jimmy caught Edd coming off the practice field. He invited him downtown that evening saying, with a wink, that he had something "special" for him. Edd was delighted. Jimmy said to meet him in the lobby bar of the Metropole Hotel.

Edd arrived at the appointed time and almost didn't recognize Jimmy in his expensive tailored suit. They drank a couple beers then Jimmy invited Edd to his suite in the hotel. Few people knew Jimmy lived in the hotel during the week and went home to his wife, Jean, in Kentucky on weekends. Family members later claimed that Jimmy liked living in a hotel because he wanted the "grand life." This dramatic flair was a side of Jimmy that few of his customers saw. He always used the back entrance of the hotel and made sure to dress as a working man during the day. He told his nephew, little Jimmy, that he didn't want his customers to think he had any money or was "putting on airs."[35]

Once in the room, Jimmy offered Edd one of the Cuban cigars he'd heard about, then handed him a small gray velvet pouch. Edd opened it and saw a flawless, multifaceted, three-carat diamond that would grace Essie's delicate fingers for the rest of her life.[36] Jimmy agreed to wait for his money until Edd got his bonus. The exchange was complete.

Edd left the hotel that night with an eerie feeling. It had seemed upfront and easy—maybe too easy. He had the feeling that he wasn't the first player who had done business with Jimmy. And now he was in debt to a man he barely knew.

Nonetheless, he had accomplished his goal and the next day he put the precious pouch in an envelope and addressed it simply *Mrs. Essie Roush - Oakland City, Indiana*. He sent it via the U.S. mail, no insurance, no special delivery, no problem in 1917. Days later, Essie gasped as she opened the envelope and withdrew a three-carat diamond. She would laugh when she told the story over and over for years to come.

When it came time for Edd to fulfill his part of the bargain, he asked Jimmy how he had come by such a beautiful gem. Jimmy skillfully sidestepped the question. Years later Essie would swear that the stone was "hot." Edd would just smile, but he never denied it.

Edd couldn't have known that every Friday at 2 p.m. in downtown Cincinnati a young employee from the well-respected Hershede's jewelry store started his daily run to the Union Savings Bank, founded by Jacob G. Schmidlapp, one of the early German immigrants to the city.[37] The appointed runner was expected to dash the four blocks from the store to the bank, because he was carrying precious cargo in his pants pocket. Arriving at the bank, the youth headed directly to the vault. Once there, he would empty his pockets of the diamonds entrusted to him in the transfer. In 1917 Cincinnati, the Hershede's "diamond runner" was the equivalent of the Brinks truck of today.[38]

Sometimes the runner would be a few minutes later than usual. When this happened it was most likely because he had stopped to chat with his friend, that nice fellow who sold newspapers at Fifth and Walnut. He told the boy to call him "Jimmy" and he often had an ice cream cone waiting for the Hershede's runner. Such a kind gentleman he was.

Jimmy would reenter Edd's life in years to come. That friendship would be hard for Edd to explain. He had never been in debt to anyone before in his life. And, of all people, why this man whom he hardly knew? Why had he listened to Hal Chase's advice? He'd been warned about Chase. Why hadn't Edd asked one of his trusted friends before he got mixed up with Widmeyer? There were men of integrity and high standards in Edd's life. Matty, Bill McKechnie, or Bill Rariden would have given him good advice, had he sought it. But, he didn't. He was a center fielder who was "off-center."

Somewhere along the way he had lost his compass. Since he

was sixteen, that compass had been Essie Mae. Without her by his side that year, he had probably been lonely and, yes, even vulnerable. Instead of his usual habit of turning in early (and sober), he had fallen into spending evenings with his single teammates at Foss-Schneider. And even in 1917 there were "baseball Annies" who hung around ball players. At 24, he was handsome, virile, and lonely.[39] After the cheering fans went home, life could be hard for a young ballplayer alone.

But all in all, it had been a great year for Edd. He was a German man in a German city that loved beer and baseball. He had won the National League batting championship and now, that city loved *him*. He had received a congratulatory phone call in Oakland City from the American League champ when the final statistics were announced, a man he now called "friend," Ty Cobb.[40] He had a contract for the next year and a secure place on a team that was headed for the pennant. He was eager to return to Cincinnati for the 1918 season.

He didn't know there were evil forces conspiring in the wings—forces that had recently brushed by him, ever so softly. The diamond ring incident made the events that were about to unfold all the more credible, for Jimmy would play a part in the underbelly of the baseball gambling scandal. It was just a minor role, or, if not, history has been kind.[41]

---

1   Compliments of Joanne Hurley, SABR historian. June, 2005.

2   Herrmann was the Grand Exalted Ruler of the Benevolent Protective Order of Elks of America and had summoned McGraw and Hempstead to the Elks convention in Baltimore to finalize negotiations.

3   Mathewson had a lifetime pitching ERA of 2.13 in 17 seasons. (*Total Baseball*, 8th Edition, 2004.) Some writers noted that Cincinnati was correcting the mistake it made in 1900 when Reds owner John T. Brush traded the young Mathewson to New York for Amos Rusie.

4   The Phillies had won the game, 4-2. But the Reds were infused with new energy and rallied in the remaining two games that weekend, losing the series 3-2. In three games, Edd got seven hits, of which four were triples.

5   Bob Dellinger, Edd's grandson-in-law, was present that day in West Virginia. Bob was a 22-year-old high school football coach with little knowledge of baseball. He thought it odd that the old baseball player with Edd kept asking him questions about his football team, but he answered politely and asked Neale if he'd ever heard of the T-formation defense. Neale politely answered that he'd used it "once or twice when I was coaching the Philadelphia Eagles." Bob would never forget the day he drank beer with the guy who twice led the Eagles to national championships, the guy who created the 54 Eagle defense.

6   Groh was in his fourth year in Cincinnati having spent his first two years with the Giants.

7   Autograph seekers were rare in 1916. That practice was born in the Babe Ruth era of the 1920s.

8   "Take Me Out to the Ball Game" became the signature song for the Reds. It was written by Jack Norworth in 1908 and gained popularity in the nickelodeons of America and during the 7th inning stretch at ball games. Tim Wiles. *Baseball as America*. National Baseball Hall of Fame and National Geographic Society, 2002.

9   According to SABR researcher Jan Finkel, in 1922, pitcher Eppa Rixey, was tailed to the Foss-Schneider brewery by a Prohibition enforcer, known only as "Operative #40." In all likelihood, Operative #40 was Ora Slater, a principal with the Cal Crim Detective Bureau. No charges were filed.

10   Philip Seib. *The Player*. Avalon Publishing Group, 2003.

11   Interview with Lawrence Ritter for book *The Glory of Their Times*. MacMillan Co., 1966.

12   F.C. Lane. "Batting." *Baseball Magazine*, 1925.

13   Ibid.

14   Philip Seib. *The Player*. Avalon, 2003.

15   Edd remembered that Hornsby would organize a game of poker in the men's room on train trips while Matty was McGraw's bridge partner playing against Hal Chase in the private car.

16   This situation that would worsen in 1917 and 1918 until, finally, Matty would be forced to use his authority and take action against Chase. His failure to do so earlier was a management mistake that seriously affected player morale.

17   Edd hit .188 with the Giants in 39 games, and .287 with the Reds. He was second in the league in triples with 15.

18   In future years there would be trips into the upper reaches of Canada for deer and moose. He would become part-owner in a cabin in Loch Haven, Pennsylvania. His hunting buddies would become his Reds teammates—notably Rube Bressler and Eppa Rixey.

19   Author's Note: Edd jeopardized the 1919 Reds by holding out until three days after he season began. His most publicized holdout was in 1922

when he refused to join his team until July. Some experts postulate the Reds may have won the pennant that year had he played the full season. He also has the questionable distinction of holding out the entire 1930 season, but his team, the Giants, were not pennant contenders that year. If there was any one thing that kept him out of the Baseball Hall of Fame for thirty years after he retired, it was these tenacious holdouts that so exasperated owners, managers, and teammates—not to mention fans—throughout his career.

20 Lee Allen. *The Cincinnati Reds*. Putnam, 1947.

21 Rube Bressler would marry Helen Kopf, little sister of teammate Larry Kopf (derivation of name from German "dummer kopf"), the Reds shortstop. Rube and Larry settled in Cincinnati and owned a real estate firm there. Rube and Eppa Rixey (pitcher for Reds in the twenties) later owned gasoline stations and the Sky Galley restaurant at the Cincinnati airport. Interview with Tom Bressler, son of Rube. 2005.

22 Greg Rhodes & John Snyder. *The Redleg Journal*. Road West Publishing, 2000.

23 McKechnie would play in only 48 games (primarily second base) for a .254 average. Sadly, Edd would say "goodbye" to his friend of four years at the end of the 1917 season.

24 Edd Roush would not have another debilitating injury until 1928 with the NY Giants.

25 One of the most historic events in baseball occurred in a game between the Reds and the Cubs in Chicago on May 2, 1917. Fred Toney and Hippo Vaughn pitched the only nine-inning double no-hitter in major league history. Roush was back in Cincinnati that day.

26 According to SABR historian Rod Nelson and the research of the SABR Veterans committee, 368 known baseball players fought in World War I in 1917 and 1918. (Report: March, 2005)

27 Author's Note: On August 18, Edd would have another exemption. Mary Evelyn was to be the sole offspring of Edd and Essie. She is this author's mother.

28 Edd must have felt the pressure from Hornsby because he did his best hitting in 1917 against St. Louis. Tom Swope reported Edd swatted a percentage of .511 in eleven games there. Edd also claimed there was a very "liberal scorekeeper" during Hornsby's years in St. Louis.

29 David Karickhoff. Unpublished paper. Marshall University, 2004.

30 The real reason that Cobb came to Cincinnati was because he had gotten into one of his famous fights at an exhibition game between the Tigers and the Giants. He had threatened to kill McGraw and badly beaten Buck Herzog. Mathewson was giving him a place to cool off until the transgression blew over. Al Stump. Cobb. Algonquin Books, 1996.

31 James Weisberg. www. rec.sport.baseball newsgroup.com , 1999.

32 Author's Note: Although Widmeyer claimed to be a part owner of the Reds, this was never substantiated. It is possible, however, since Garry Herrmann did over stock options to local businessmen to infuse cash into the team after World War I and the Federal League debacle.

33 Joe Nolan, *Cincinnati Enquirer* sports editor first dubbed Jimmy "The Million Dollar Newsboy."

34 The Reds won the post-season Ohio Championship that year and the winning share for each player was $157.

35 Interview with Jim Widmeyer (nephew). October, 2004, Alexander, Kentucky.

36 Harry Winston Jewelers in New York would nestle the gem in the classic platinum and sapphire setting chosen by Essie.

37 In 1919, the Union Savings Bank became the Fifth Third Bank of Cincinnati.

38 Author interview with Robert Manley, prominent Cincinnati attorney and son of a former Hershede's runner, John M. Manley Jr. In later years the Cal Crim Detective Agency and attorney John M. Manley worked together to prevent the emergence of union strongholds in Cincinnati. Cincinnatian Hotel, 2004.

39 Author's Note: This passage arose from an interview in which Edd talked about how lonely it was for players on the road. He said, "There was nothing to do unless you played cards or went to the speakeasies at night. We didn't have television in those days." He would swear to his dying day that Essie had been the only woman in his life. He and Essie were part of a culture that grew out of the Victorian period of the nineteenth century, and they were both religious people. Although temptation may have been there, I believe that Essie was the only woman whom Edd ever loved.

40 Cobb topped both major leagues with a .383 batting average.

41 Years later it would be reported that Jimmy Widmeyer was, indeed, Cincinnati's "million dollar newsboy." He parlayed a $5,000 savings from his newsstand into $1.8 million by investing in stock tips given to him by customers in the financial world who stopped by his newsstand every morning to buy a paper and chat. In 1929 he lost it all in the stock market crash and became a struggling newsboy in his open-air office again.

5

Battles Home and Abroad

Roush, in many ways, is one of the most interesting athletes
who ever wore the Redleg livery, and certainly one of the greatest.
The memory of Edd tearing across the outfield to snare hits
that were tagged as doubles or triples is one of the proudest
recollections of Cincinnati fans.

– Lee Allen, The Cincinnati Reds, *1948*

HAL CHASE

Essie remembered how she felt about Hal Chase in the
beginning. She had never seen a man play first base like
he did. He played so far from the base that she held her
breath each time for fear he wouldn't get back to tag the run-

1918 CINCINNATI REDS WITH CHRISTY MATHEWSON, MANAGER
ROUSH: TOP ROW, SECOND FROM RIGHT

ner. But he was pure lightning. He was all over the infield, even running close to third base on catches behind the pitcher. His movements were fluid and graceful, and he seemed to pick the ball out of the air as if it were a meaningless tap in a practice session. Essie knew her baseball, and this guy could play first base.

Not long after Edd joined the team Essie met Chase's wife, Anna. She learned that Anna was Hal's second wife and she was from the Bronx. Although 1917 had not been a great season for Hal, he had won the National League batting title in his debut year with the Reds, 1916.[1] That solidified him with the fans, and he and Anna made Cincinnati their home.

On May 15, 1918, Anna Chase organized the other wives as ushers for the Bat and Ball Fund Day on behalf of the war effort.[2] Essie was happy to help Anna in this endeavor, and 4,000 spectators watched the Reds beat the Giants 3-2. That evening, the husbands joined their wives at Haberstumpf's restaurant and dance hall in Price Hill, a western neighborhood of Cincinnati, for a night of fun. On this night Essie would see a different side of Hal Chase.

As the team sat at the long table in the middle of the beer hall, they were drinking and the mood was jovial. Local fans loved having the Reds in the restaurant and took turns coming to their table to chat. Essie was sitting next to Hal and Lee Magee, and Edd and Anna were on the other side of the table. Essie soon felt something strange. Under the table Hal's foot gently stroked her calf, two feet away from her husband and his wife. Essie jerked her leg away and looked at him in shock. He withdrew his foot and flashed her one of his big signature smiles. Not a word was said, but at that moment Essie saw the true Hal Chase. Any other man would have been embarrassed, but Chase was arrogant. A pang of sadness for Anna passed through her.

Essie ignored Chase the rest of the evening. She kept the incident a secret until years later when she knew that Edd wouldn't kill Chase. She would say, "Chase was a womanizer. He learned not to play 'footsie' with me." This was Essie's first clue to Chase's character. Other flaws would soon become apparent.

On May 17, the Reds were on an eight-game winning streak moving them close to the leading Cubs and Giants. During the streak, Chase sat on the bench nursing a shoulder injury. When he returned to the lineup on May 23, things went downhill for the Reds.[3]

Chase had no chance for the batting title that season, but "Tiny Heinie" Groh was leading the league with a whopping .362. In Groh, Cincinnati hoped to have its third National League batting champion in as many years.

In June and July the Reds began to struggle.[4] On June 10 in Boston, Chase bobbled a slow grounder, giving the batter a key hit. On June 18, he muffed an easy throw, and the Reds lost to the Giants, 7-1. After

Heinie Groh May Be Third Red To Lead National Hitters In As Many Years

Cincinnati Enquirer

CARTOON OF CHASE, ROUSH AND GROH AS NL BATTING CHAMPS FOR 1916, 1917 AND 1918

nine consecutive losses, they beat the Cardinals 9-7 in a hard-fought game in which Chase made an error. A pattern was beginning to emerge.

By this time Heinie was angry. He later told Edd that he, Ivey, and Greasy had agreed to watch Chase closely in the coming games. Although Chase was hitting well, he made repeated blunders in the field at strategic moments. Edd later said, "He'd be just a couple seconds too late to the base, or the ball would deflect off his mitt at the last second, or the sun would get in his eyes on a pop-up." He'd made six errors in the last fourteen games—at least that's how many were attributed to him.[5] Often he was skillful enough to make his near miss look like it was Heinie's throw from third that was bad. Heinie would said, "Hey, Chase, who you betting on today? I just want to know how many errors I'm going to get."

One day Edd decided to try it. As he would later recall, "I just wondered if I was capable of losing on purpose or not. I chose a day when we were playing a meaningless game in the standings. Sure enough, late in the game we had a slim lead, and they had the bases loaded. I decided if a long hit came my way I'd let it drop." Edd got his wish. A batter slammed a long fly to deep center. "I said to myself, 'I'll let it go.' But while I was saying it, I began to chase the damn ball. As I got close to it, I kept thinking I'd just miss it, making it look good like Chase did. But then, something within me had more control than I did. While my mind said 'No,' my body leaped up and caught the ball. I just couldn't do it to save my life."

When asked about Chase in later years, Edd would say, "I couldn't see what he was doing from center field, but I knew something was wrong." But Essie remembered when Edd came home from a road trip and said to her, "I want you to stay away from Chase and his wife from now on. There's something going on out there, and if he's throwing games, we're not going to be part of it." Essie would remember the emotion on Edd's face that day.

Essie filed another claim against him. She recalled that Chase and his friends stole for fun. Although the Reds' groundskeeper, Matty Schwab, would lock up when the players went onto the field each day, things would be missing when they returned. Then, a few days later, an anonymous "gift" would turn up in someone's locker—a new hunting jacket, a silver pocketknife.

The problem was magnified when teammates began to realize that Chase had a partner in crime. His name was Lee Magee.[6] He had joined the Reds from St. Louis in April. Like Edd, Magee had played in three leagues; the National (St. Louis), the American (New York and St. Louis), and the Federal League (Brooklyn). In 1915, Magee had been highly touted with the Feds when he hit .323. In 1916, he was in the top ten for stolen bases (29). In 1918 the team would discover that, like Chase, Magee stole more than just bases.

Like Chase, Magee, was older, at 29, than most of the boys on the team. Chase and Magee struck up an instant friendship centered on gambling and carousing rather than playing baseball. Magee was positioned at second base, within spitting distance of his partner in crime.

Most importantly, as a native Cincinnatian, Magee knew the right people if you were looking for ill-gotten gain.

On July 19, Magee showed his true colors in a home game. He gave Boston four runs in the third by failing to touch second base and by making wild throws. The Reds lost 8-3. It was obvious, there was something rotten in the Reds infield.

The situation came to a head in late July when the Reds went on the road for a two-week eastern swing. Chase and Magee were more cautious at home and more blatantly treasonous on the road. On July 25 they had a doubleheader in Boston. Magee played like a vaudeville comedian. With a man on first in the bottom of the ninth, an easy bouncer came his way. Instead of tagging the runner or even throwing to Chase at first, Magee threw wild to third, and Greasy caught the stray ball out in left field.

The game continued into the thirteenth inning, when Magee hit an easy grounder to Johnny Rawlings, the shortstop, and it took a funny bounce and hit him in the face.

Rawlings went out with a broken nose. With Magee on second, Edd smashed a long drive to left-center and started running. Edd recalled that as he rounded second "Magee was just trotting along" barely ten feet in front of him. Edd yelled loud enough for the fans to hear him, "Run, you son-of-a-bitch!" Edd's hit was an inside-the-park home run and the Reds won 4-2. If Magee and Chase had bet against their team, Edd had foiled their plans at the last minute. Now Edd was convinced that Heinie and Greasy were right. Chase and Magee were dirty, but how to prove it?

Greasy didn't wait for proof. He'd seen enough. The Reds went from Boston to Brooklyn for their next series. On August 5, the team was working out in pre-game practice when Magee threw a ball over Greasy's head. Greasy ran at Magee with all the fury of a fullback carrying the ball for the winning touchdown. As Heinie told Edd later, "You should have seen it! Greasy knocked the hell out of Magee!"[7] The official report said that Neale hit Magee twice before their teammates separated them.[8]

Cincinnati would rid itself of one of these two poltroons a few days later. The final stop on the eastern tour was New York. In the ninth inning of the opening game an easy grounder came to Chase but instead of grabbing it, he kicked it away. As he ran to retrieve it, two Giants runners came in and the Reds lost. During that game he made two bad throws to the pitcher who was covering first on grounders. The pitcher was big Jimmy Ring, and he didn't like looking bad in front of his hometown crowd. When the game was over, Ring exploded in the locker room. As Edd would remember, Ring tore his uniform into shreds and yelled, "I swear I'll never pitch another game for Cincinnati as long as Chase is on this club."

After Greasy had taken on Magee and Ring fingered Chase, Matty must have sensed that his team was ready to mutiny.

Being a wise old pitcher, he couldn't have missed Chase's mis-
plays to Ring. In all likelihood he had a long talk with McGraw
that night. He knew what he had to do, and he knew he had
McGraw's support as a witness against Chase in New York.
The next day Matty walked onto the field and handed Chase
his suspension papers.[9] Chase went back to the clubhouse without a word. Grateful nods passed among the players on the
field. Chase was done. Sherry Magee was quickly moved to
first and Rube Bressler to left field, and the rejuvenated Reds
beat the Giants in a doubleheader that day.

One down, one to go. The players felt vindicated with
Chase's suspension. Jack Ryder's *Enquirer* column on August
10 said the Reds "have been wise to Chase's methods for some
time and they are tickled to death that he is through with the
club." Several players calculated that Chase had cost the Reds
as many as 27 games that season.[10] Edd would say many times,
"Chase cost us the pennant in 1918." Matty corroborated this
with Ryder, saying that the Reds would have finished in second
place with an outside chance for the pennant if not for Chase.[11]

When Chase left, Magee had lost his buddy and became an
outcast on the team. Edd would remember the last time he saw
Lee Magee in a Reds uniform. It was August 29 in Chicago, the
second game of a disappointing series with the Cubs. Edd was
walking out of the clubhouse onto the field when Magee
approached him going in the opposite direction. Edd noticed
he looked upset and asked, "Where you going, Lee?" Magee
didn't look at Edd and just mumbled something about the clubhouse. Edd said, "He packed his clothes and went back to
Cincinnati and I never did see him again."[12]

In the spring of 1919 another piece of the Chase-Magee
puzzle would fall into place. As Edd would later tell the story,
he and Bill Rariden were standing outside the Ansonia Hotel in
New York after a game at the Polo Grounds. A stranger came

up to them who looked like one of those "gambler types."

"Is your name Roush?" he asked. "I know Rariden, here."

Edd nodded.

"Do you know where Lee Magee is?"

Edd said that Magee had left the team last fall, and they hadn't seen him since.

"I'm looking for him cause he owes me five hundred dollars." Edd and Bill shared a knowing look. "You know that ballgame you won over there in Boston last year?" the man continued. "Well, Magee and Chase both bet five hundred dollars on Boston. Chase paid his part, but Magee never paid his. If I can get ahold of that son of a bitch I'm going to take it out of his hide."

Before he left, the man turned back and said, "You know, Roush, you gummed up the works when you hit that home run."[13]

ANALYZING CHASE

Questions continue to linger surrounding the imprint left by Hal Chase on baseball.

1. Why didn't Matty handle the "Chase problem" earlier?
2. Why did John Heydler, President of the National League, exonerate Chase at his hearing in 1919?
3. With full knowledge of his guilt, why did McGraw hire him in New York in 1919?
4. Why didn't baseball commissioner Kenesaw Landis expel Chase from baseball along with the eight "Black Sox" players?

Since it is clear that most of the Reds knew about Chase's despicable acts of sabotage against their own team, it is reasonable to ask why Matty did nothing about it for two years. Ed recalled, "Matty and McGraw were friends of Chase. They all used to play bridge together and who knows what else. I reckon Matty figured he could put up with him because he was the best first baseman in the league. But in 1918 it became terrible. He couldn't just ignore it anymore.

Sportswriter Tom Swope supported this theory.[14] According to Swope, Mathewson and sportswriter Jack Ryder played bridge in a regular foursome against Chase and Mike Regan, a relief pitcher. Chase and Regan were losing badly so Chase devised a "system of signals" using his ever-present cigar to alert Regan to the contents of his hand. Their secret codes would have remained secret except that before Regan left for the Army in August, his guilt overtook him and he confessed to Matty. Swope postulated that it was only when Matty became furious over Chase's cheating him at cards that he did "what other Reds had been asking him to do for weeks."

To Matty's credit, when he finally did take action against Chase, he did it correctly. He and Reds' owner Garry Herrmann filed a formal complaint with John Heydler, President of the National League. Although several players testified against Chase,[15] Heydler let him off because of "insufficient evidence." The real reasons may have been to avoid bad publicity for the game of baseball[16] and to prevent a lawsuit. (Chase was famous for filing lawsuits and winning them.) Ironically, after Heydler refused to punish Chase, McGraw took him with the Giants (traded for Bill Rariden in 1919). But, it wasn't long before the Top Dogs got their comeuppance and Chase was blacklisted by all teams. Although he was never formally "expelled," his major league baseball career was over. It was rumored that during he 1919 World Series scandal investigation, Heydler said that his only regret in his career was "not giving credence to Christy Mathewson in the Hal Chase case." Had he done so, the scandal may never have occurred.

Sportswriter Lee Allen believed that Chase suffered from "problems of personality."[17] Many writers have offered clues to his personality. Most accuse him of being "amoral" due to a lack of remorse for his actions. Fred Lieb said Chase had a "corkscrew brain."[18] Harold Seymour chose the words "a malignant genius," the "archetype of all crooked ball players."[19] In the rhetoric of psychology, today he might be diagnosed as a brilliant sociopath.

When asked about Chase, Edd would say, "He was always a loner. There was hardly anybody who ever wanted to room with him."

He was (and is to this day) an enigma. It appears that Chase had highly developed interpersonal insight. His primary weapon was his pleasant personality. This was likely a well-polished facade since anyone who risks thousands of dollars on games of chance must have strong competitive fires burning within. He wisely ingratiated himself to others by lavishing compliments on teammates and opponents in the press.[20]

When asked what Chase would do when teammates accused him of throwing games, Edd said, "He'd just ignore you, or sometimes laugh it off like it was all a big joke." So, Chase used two effective defense strategies: avoidance and laughing it off. These strategies result in confusion, obfuscation, and lack of closure, much like the continuing enigma of the 1919 World Series.[21]

The name Hal Chase would surface again in connection with the Black Sox Scandal. When his vocation ended, he turned to his longtime avocation of gambling. This time he would be instrumental in the corruption of some of his former teammates on the White Sox.[22] His involvement with other gamblers in the 1919 "fix" would also tarnish the name of the 1919 Reds. Their championship would forever be tainted.

By August of 1918 there was more for Edd to worry about than crooked teammates. The beginning of the 1918 Pandemic Influenza was taking hold in the Midwest. In the next two months this deadly scourge would sweep the planet and kill more than twenty million people. The Black Death and World War II claimed fewer lives than the 1918 flu.[23] Edd and Essie worried about their one-year-old daughter and listened closely for any cough or sneeze. Essie stopped taking Mary to the ballpark in August. She and Ruby Groh fretted over their husbands' road trips and their exposure to people in close quarters on trains and in hotels. Working in the sun and fresh air of the ball fields may have spared them, for no Reds died of the disease that year.

This was not the case with the other scourge of 1918—World War I. The summer saw players and owners alike wracked with uncertainty about whether or not they would be able to complete their schedule for the season. The pressure on organized baseball began on May 17, when Provost Marshal General Crowder issued the "Work or Fight" order. By July 1 all able-bodied men must be in the armed forces or involved in essential work. Sports were considered "nonessential work." This dictum sent waves of anxiety throughout the baseball community.

Cincinnati newspapers recorded the early responses from the Reds. Matty might become the athletic director for the local Y.M.C.A. Heinie, Ivey, and Edd would return to essential work on their farms in New York, Georgia, and Indiana.[24] Tommy Griffith was offered a job in a munitions plant that also had a baseball team. Jimmy Ring would be a linotype operator at home in Brooklyn. Neale, Eller, and Schneider were undecided. Ruether, Bressler, and Kopf joined the armed forces.

Essie held her breath waiting for the results of the Gibson County, Indiana, draft. She would rather have Edd take his chances with the influenza epidemic than see him go off to fight in Europe. Edd was lucky. His number was 1,012 and the county was given a quota of only 170 men.

The baseball owners worked behind the scenes to influence the administration of President Woodrow Wilson on their behalf. Club owners installed the five-cent war tax on tickets at the gates of their parks. All members of the baseball community were heavily "encouraged" to buy Liberty War Bonds.[25] At every ballgame in every city, servicemen were admitted free and local bands played patriotic songs. Police brigades and players were now required to march onto the field in solemn single file in honor of America's soldiers.

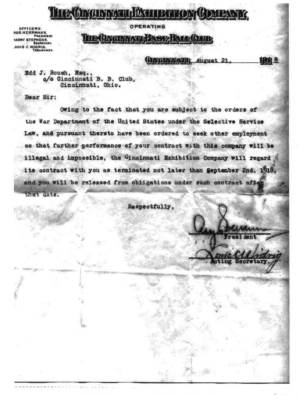

REDS RELEASE LETTER FROM HERRMANN TO ROUSH (WWI)

At this time the practice of throwing baseballs that landed in the stands back onto the field was changed. Ushers were instructed to pass any stray ball to a serviceman in uniform as a gesture of respect. After World War I was over, the fans rebelled against returning the balls to the ushers, wanting to keep the balls for themselves.[26]

Finally, in August the work of the baseball magnates with their government leaders paid off. The "Work or Fight" order was suspended until September 1 for baseball players, allowing teams to finish their seasons. Owners of all teams issued official compliance letters to players.

Within days, the government relented even further and agreed to allow the World Series to be played after Labor Day.[27] The Cubs and the Red Sox would represent their respective leagues in the annual contest.[28]

THE REDS LOSE A GREAT MANAGER

Even though he was too old to be drafted, Christy Mathewson chose to enlist. He was patriotic, and in his syndicated "Big League Gossip" column he admonished those who were able and yet unwilling to fight for their country. On August 27, the Reds were still battling for third place when Matty left for Washington, D.C., to ship out for France. His received a commission as a captain in the Chemical Warfare Service. He would join several baseball colleagues in the same unit in France: Branch Rickey, George Sisler, Grover Cleveland Alexander, and Ty Cobb."[29]

Matty would never return to Cincinnati.

Cobb later described in detail the event that eventually took Matty's life.[30] It happened near Chaumont, France. Cobb and Matty missed the warning signal that preceded the release of mustard gas. This signal allowed time for the eighty soldiers in their command to snap their gas masks into place and escape the building. Instead, the entire group was trapped inside and subjected to the gas without protection. Cobb said, "Men screamed when they breathed a smell of death. They piled up to escape...a hopeless tangle of bodies. Eight men died within hours of lung damage." Cobb himself described being weak and experiencing a colorless discharge draining from his chest for weeks afterward. He eventually returned to health. "I fell outside...I was damned lucky," he said. Matty was not so lucky.

Matty came home to coach the Giants with McGraw and became president of the Boston Braves in 1923. But, he developed tuberculosis in both lungs and died at a sanatorium in Saranac, New York, on October 7, 1925. He was 45. When they heard the news, Edd and Essie mourned his passing. He had been a loyal supporter of Edd since those afternoon drives in 1916. Not long before he died, Matty picked a "1924 All-Star Team" for *Collier's Magazine*. True to the end, he placed Edd Roush in center field.[31]

THE 1918 BATTING CHAMPIONSHIP

1918 was a great year for Heinie Groh. When Matty went to war, Herrmann chose Heinie to lead the team in the final two weeks of the season.[32] Although it was to be his only time in management, Heinie motivated his teammates to excellent results. The Reds won seven of the ten final games and ended the season with a six-game winning streak.

In the early months of the season, Heinie was a serious candidate for a third batting championship for Cincinnati. He was whacking balls in every direction with his short fat bottle bat. He was neck-and-neck with Red Smith of Boston, Fred Merkle of Chicago, and Jake Daubert of Brooklyn in early July. On July 10 he was listed as the number one hitter in the National

League with a .350 average. Edd sat in tenth place on that day, but he was Heinie's biggest cheerleader.

In early August Heinie went into a serious slump.[33] It looked like the Reds wouldn't have the batting honors this year. Edd later recalled a conversation with his friend that would give Edd the green light to go for the title. They were sitting on the bench in their usual spots. Heinie said, "I'm not going to make it this year, but you have a chance. If you can catch [Zack] Wheat

HEINIE GROH WITH HIS FAMOUS "BOTTLE BAT"

in the next few weeks, you can win it. I'm behind you a hundred percent." Edd said, "Okay, I think I'll try." Edd made a furious dash for the title, hitting .427 (53-for-124) over the last 32 games of the season.[34]

When Edd started his rally he was trailing Zack Wheat by 41 points. Throughout the month of August the sportswriters watched the race. Two weeks later, Edd had narrowed the margin to 18 points. W.A. Phelon wrote, "Pull for Edd Roush, ye Redland fans! Batting furiously, he has a chance....only one man stands between Roush and the summit–Zack Wheat of Brooklyn. Wheat is hitting .340 to Roush's .322–a formidable margin, with the season so near its end." A week later Wheat's 18-point lead was reduced to 14. On August 24, the Reds had 12 games (five doubleheaders) to go, and Edd was only 8 points behind Wheat. Then disaster struck the Roush family.

On Friday morning, August 30, Edd and "Manager Groh"

had just gotten out of bed in their hotel room in Chicago. They had two more games against the league-leading Cubs, and then they would head back to Redland Field to meet the Cardinals for the final four games of the season. Edd was determined to beat Wheat for the title. He couldn't wait to wrap his hands around the wood that day.

At 8 a.m. there was a knock on the door. A bellboy handed Edd a telegram. The message was curt.

Will in coma (stop) Fell off telephone poll (stop)
Come home (stop) Mother

Edd handed the telegram to Heinie without saying a word, but his eyes were pleading, "Help me." Heinie read the words and didn't hesitate in his response: "You have to go now." Edd knew he was right, but he also knew the price he was about to pay. He grasped for a ray of light in the darkness.

"I'll be back in time for the Cards games on Sunday," he said. Heinie agreed, but both men knew it was not to be. While Edd hurriedly packed, Heinie arranged for a taxi and a ticket on the first train to Oakland City. Ten minutes later Edd was standing at the door ready to go. Neither said a word as Heinie reached up and awkwardly patted his friend on the back. It was a heartfelt gesture.

Edd flew through the train station headed for the ramp. Only then did he remember that Essie was in Cincinnati with Mary. Did she know? He didn't have time to call her. He'd wait until he got there. When he was finally settled on the train, he noticed the headlines on the sports page of the man sitting across from him.

RED STAR AND DODGER VETERAN IN HOT RACE
ROUSH 3 POINTS BEHIND

When Edd walked into the little farmhouse that night, the situation was grim. Dr. John McGowan greeted him and quietly shook his head to indicate the gravity of Will's condition. Essie and Mary were already there. Edd gasped to see his father's head wrapped in layers of white gauze. His neck and upper body were purple as the blood raged below the surface of the skin. One arm was grotesquely crooked and badly broken. Edd knew then that he would never make it back to Cincinnati before the end of the season.

For the next few days family members took turns at Will's bedside, alternating between the patient's room and hushed conversations in the parlor with concerned friends. Edd learned that his father had been working on some faulty lines and had fallen from the top of a telephone pole.[35] He had been wearing his climber belt, but the belt had suddenly broken. The local papers reported Will's condition on a daily basis.

> ### INJURIES MAY PROVE FATAL
> Will Roush, local manager of the Independent Telephone Company, is lying unconscious at his home near the east end of town. There is little hope for his recovery. Ed [sic] Roush, his son, a member of the Cincinnati national league team, is home at the bedside of his father.
> – *Oakland City Journal*, 9/3/18

During those long and painful hours Edd didn't ask about the scores of the Reds games that he was missing.[36] He was lost in memories of this man whose love had always been there for him. Images of the hunting trips, the early morning milkings, the time his dad threw Aunt Fannie out of the house because she wouldn't let little Edd ride her horse to the store for milk. He thought of the day in 1914 in the office of Bill Phillips when his dad had taught him how to negotiate a fair salary. He remembered the countless times Will had fought with Laura so that Edd could play the game he loved. Tears came when he thought of the pride Will had taken in his success. Will was his mentor, his defender, his beloved father.

Will Roush lived a week in a deep coma. He died on Thursday, September 5, around afternoon milking time.[37] Will Roush was born in West Virginia in 1868. He was only 50 years old. There should have been so many more years; years to enjoy his grandchildren, years for Edd to tell him the things in his heart.

SEASON END

It would be several weeks before the final statistics for the 1918 season were published. By then, it was anticlimactic. The Reds finished third, and Edd received his player stipend of $175 from the World Series receipts. The standings in the National League batting race revealed that Zack Wheat had beaten Edd by 2 percentage points.[38]

Years later, baseball scholars would bemoan the loss of Roush in the elite company of players who won three batting titles in a row; Wade Boggs, Ty Cobb, Rod Carew, Tony Gwynn, Rogers Hornsby, Stan Musial, and Honus Wagner.[39]

In 1986, baseball researcher Joseph Wayman analyzed the 1918 batting race and concluded that Roush should have protested his title loss on grounds separate from the lost games due to the death of his father. Wayman argued that Edd was unfairly treated on the basis of a rule technicality.[40] A rule in 1918 said that if a team protested a game and won, all individual fielding, batting, and pitching records from that game were thrown out. It was as if the game had never been played.

In 1918 there were two protested games. Both would determine the batting title. Both games involved the St. Louis

Cardinals. The first protested game occurred on April 29 between the Reds and the Cardinals. Edd made a "wonderful catch of a difficult fly," Wayman wrote. In the eighth inning, Walt Cruise hit a beauty over the head of the shortstop and Edd "tore in for the short, fast-dropping fly." He caught it, but stumbled to his knees and the ball popped out of his glove. He then made a second great catch to grab it before it hit the ground. Umpire Hank O'Day called the runner on third out because he had left his base headed for home. The Cardinal manager, Jack Hendricks,[41] protested the play, claiming that Edd "momentarily held the ball." Hendricks convinced NL President Heydler to throw out the game. Edd lost his two hits and his "wonderful catch" cost him the 1918 title.

Wayman argued further that the second protested game favored Wheat. On June 3, the Cardinals topped the Dodgers 15-12. Wheat went hitless in five times at bat. This time, the Dodgers protested. The game, and Wheat's lackluster perform-ance, were thrown out.

Ironically, this rule was deemed unfair to players and was changed in 1920. Had the rule not existed in 1918, the final averages would have been .336 for Roush and .335 for Wheat.

One year prior to Edd's death in 1987, baseball scholar Stanley McClure wrote a long letter of protest to the commis-sioner, Peter Ueberroth. McClure concurred with Wayman's hypothesis concerning the April game between the Reds and the Cardinals. Further, he presented newly calculated statistics that gave Edd the win with a .3364[42] average compared to final numbers for Wheat of .3349. McClure wrote: "It is evident that the ruling of President John Heydler was incorrect....Edd Roush of Cincinnati would have been the champion batter of the National League for 1918."

Of course, by this time both Wheat and Roush were enshrined in the Hall of Fame. Wheat was inducted in 1959—

three years prior to Edd. Ironically, as many sportswriters remember, Edd constantly urged them to consider older players when they voted on the annual inductions. The two names that he most often mentioned for consideration were Max Carey and Zack Wheat.

---

1 Chase hit .339 in 1916 to lead the NL. He hit .277 dropping 62 points into 22nd place in 1917 and ended up with .301 in 1918.

2 Martin Kohout. *Hal Chase.* McFarland & Co. 2001.

3 Author's Note: Chase's cheating would pay him back in injuries. He had a bad shoulder and missed a number of games over several years because of ankle injuries. One could surmise that if a player's objective was to miss a ball instead of catch it, there would be times when he would have to suddenly twist his feet and upper body out of natural position (leaning in for the catch) in order to miss it. This sudden unnatural jerk may have resulted in the injuries that he sustained.

4 Ibid.

5 Chase holds the AL record for most errors at first base in eleven seasons–279. Thomas Gilbert. *Deadball.* Grolier Publishing, 1996.

6 There were two Magees on the Reds in 1918, Lee and Sherwood. They were not related.

7 Author's note: Edd didn't witness Neale's attack on Magee. He was in the clubhouse at the time.

8 Martin Kohout. *Hal Chase.* McFarland & Co., 2001.

9 Chase was suspended for "indifferent play and insubordination."

10 Martin Kohout. *Hal Chase.* McFarland & Co., 2001.

11 *Cincinnati Enquirer.* August 11, 1918.

12 Magee was traded to Brooklyn by the Reds for Larry Kopf. He began the 1919 season with Brooklyn, then was passed like a hot potato to the Chicago Cubs. His career ended there. He never again wore a Reds uniform.

13 Author's Note: It is likely that the stranger was a gambler named James Costello, who owned a pool hall in Boston. In the 1920 Costello-Magee trial that was a precursor to the 1919 World Series investigation, Costello testified that both Magee and Chase have given him blank checks for $500 to bet against their team. Chase told him that they had the pitcher in their pocket, Pete Schneider. When Schneider was replaced by Hod Eller and Roush hit the winning home run, the bet went sour. Magee's check bounced, and Costello sued him for the debt in June, 1919, in Boston.

[14] Source identified by Martin Kohout as Tom Swope to Lee Allen. June 23, 1960.

[15] Reds players Jimmy Ring, Mike Regan, Greasy Neale, and Pol Perritt and John McGraw of the Giants testified against Chase.

[16] Heydler admitted privately to Fred Lieb that he believed Chase to be guilty. Correspondence between Herrmann and Heydler strongly suggested a COVER-UP to prevent a "severe black eye for the game if the details became fully known." August 29, 1918. HOF BSS/AL files.

[17] Lee Allen. *The Cincinnati Reds*. Putnam, 1947.

[18] Fred Lieb. *Baseball as I have known It*. Grosset and Dunlap, 1977.

[19] Harold Seymour. *Baseball: The Golden Age*. Oxford University Press, 1971.

[20] Martin Kohout. *Hal Chase*. McFarland & Sons, 2001.

[21] Author's Conclusion: Hal Chase was the living embodiment of the Black Sox Scandal.

[22] Chase's teammates on the 1913-14 Sox who also played in 1919 were Cicotte and Weaver.

[23] John M. Barry. *The Great Influenza*. Penquin U.S.A., 2004.

[24] According to historian Lee Allen, 15 percent of major league players were farmers. *The Cincinnati Reds*. G.P. Putnam's Sons, 1948.

[25] Ban Johnson, AL President, claimed the baseball community (including stockholders) contributed 8 million dollars to the war effort via Liberty Bonds and Red Cross charities. Seymour. *The Golden Age*. Oxford University Press, 1971.

[26] Marc Okkonen. SABR Veterans Committee Report, January, 2002.

[27] Author's Note: U.S. government's decision may have been influenced by England. Soccer fans there had persuaded the British government to certify soccer as "essential."

[28] Arrangements were even made for the doughboys to follow the games in France via trans-Atlantic cable.

[29] Cobb said he joined the chemical unit because "Branch and Christy were my friends." Al Stump. *Cobb*. Algonquin Books, 1996.

[30] Ibid.

[31] Mathewson's 1924 All-Star Team lineup: Bassler (c), Vance (p), Fournier (1b), Hornsby (2b), Frisch (3b), Bancroft (ss), Ruth (rf), Roush (cf), Falk (lf), McGraw (mgr). Seven of these ten are in the Hall of Fame.

[32] Herrmann asked Edd if he was "interested in management" that year. Edd responded with a resounding "No." He always claimed he had no interest in managing a ball club. Author's Note: It is probable that Edd's stead-

fast refusal to join management delayed his entrance into the Baseball Hall of Fame for thirty years.

[33] Groh would end the season with a career high of .320.

[34] *The Baseball Page*, 2002.

[35] Will had only worked for the new phone company for a few days. He had taken the job to bring in a little extra money for Laura.

[36] Boston would win the 1918 World Series. They would not win again for 86 years (2004).

[37] He was buried in the Roush plot at Montgomery Cemetery in Oakland City. Services were performed by the pastor of the Presbyterian church. His death certificate listed "Trama [sic] Injury to Brain" as cause of death. Bill and Ruby Rariden and Heinie and Ruby Groh attended the funeral.

[38] The Wheat/Roush race for the 1918 batting title is one of the Top Twelve closest races in baseball history. The final statistics were: Wheat= .334963; Roush=.333333.

[39] Roush would win both the 1917 and the 1919 NL title. Wheat's only title was in 1918.

[40] Joseph M. Wayman. Grandstand Baseball Annual. 1986.

[41] Author's Note: Edd claimed that Jack Hendricks was one of the most unpopular managers in either league. He pushed his religion and favored the Catholic players. He became the manager of the Reds in 1924 over strong protests from the team who wanted captain Jake Daubert instead.

[42] Edd had impressive statistics again in 1918 landing in the top ten in several categories. Slugging % = .455 (1), OPS = .823 (1), On-base % = .368 (7), Hits = 145 (3), Triples = 10 (7), Stolen bases = 24 (6), Home Runs = 5 (4), Total Bases = 198 (2), RBI = 62 (6) Note: Roush was again listed in center field in *Baseball Magazine*'s "1918 All-Star Team." Wheat was chosen as an NL All-Star, but didn't make the all-league team.

PART II

THE CROOKED SERIES

6

Pennant Pride in Porkopolis[1]

The first of October, 1919, a Fourth of July all over again in Cincinnati....Everybody who was anybody would be at the game that afternoon. They were setting up direct-wire connection, follow it play-by-play on the scoreboard, getcher official line-up here, getcher autograph picture of Eddie Roush!

– John Lardner, **Saturday Evening Post, 4/30/38**

SEPTEMBER 28, 1919
WURLITZER SHOWROOMS
CINCINNATI, OHIO

The 1919 National Leage batting champion, Edd Roush, had just stepped out of the taxi when his teammates Heinie Groh, Greasy Neale, Bill Rariden, and Larry Kopf tumbled out behind him. They were laughing and poking each other like schoolboys, belying the fact that they were five of the most revered men in the city of Cincinnati on this day. No sooner had they reached the curb when another taxi pulled up and disgorged more young men. A mere hour before entering the taxis, these members of the Cincinnati Reds had been dressed in their white wool uniforms on Redland Field playing the final game of he season against the Chicago Cubs.[2] Now clad in tailored suits, they all looked like junior executives as

CINCINNATI "REDS" PENNANT WINNERS · 1919 · NATIONAL LEAGUE

1919 REDS IN WURLITZER SHOWROOM[3]

they scurried into the Wurlitzer showroom at 117-119 East 4th Street for their five o'clock photo session.

The guys calmed down when they saw their manager, Pat Moran, standing in the doorway. He had that act-your-age-boys look on his face. Jake Daubert was standing next to Moran. At age 35, Jake was the oldest player on the team.[4] He had a Marlboro Man look about him—rugged and square-jawed with clear blue eyes. Far from ready to retire, he had established himself as a wise elder and assisted Moran in leading this young team to a pennant. Edd had great respect for Jake. At first base, he was second only to Hal Chase. Unlike Chase, he was a man of integrity. He wasn't a cheerleader like team captain Heinie Groh. Daubert was more of a fatherly type—someone a young fellow could go to if he had a problem. He was a man of few words who made each one count.[5] Moran and Daubert had become friends during the season, and Pat often delegated management tasks to Jake. Jake reminded Edd of his first professional manager, Bill Phillips, in 1914 with Indianapolis in Federal League.

As wise a leader as Daubert was, he was no equal to the

squat Irishman with curly blond hair who stood next to him that day. Patrick Joseph Moran was chosen to manage the Reds in January 1919 when Garry Herrmann was unable to reach Christy Mathewson in France during the war. Although many credited "Matty" with the success of the '19 Reds, he had merely created the roux into which Moran would mix his magic ingredients. Moran's recipe was one part discipline, two parts training, and a dollop of inside advice from his friend, John McGraw.[6] (McGraw agreed to release Moran, his ace pitching coach, to the Reds, and when Mathewson returned from the war, he would join the Giants.)

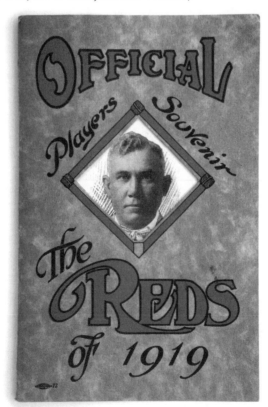

PAT MORAN ON 1919 OFFICIAL REDS SOUVENIR BOOKLET

When the Reds returned for spring training in '19, they were thoroughly prepared to dislike this new manager named Moran. They were "Matty's boys," after all. They were in for a surprise. As a former catcher, Moran had two indelible strengths. Deep in his gut, he *knew* both sides of the battery. He had been with the Chicago Cubs in the 1907 and 1908 World Series. Through the years he studied his position and developed an almost psychic ability to "read" the signals of opposing catchers—a huge bonus for Reds hitters. He devoted himself to understanding all manner of pitching from the various methods used in the deadball era (spit, shine, and emery balls) to the personalities who threw them. He is often credited with the development of Grover Cleveland Alexander who he coached in Philadelphia. Moran managed the Phillies to their pennant in 1915. Now he had led the Reds to their pennant, and the city called him "The Miracle Man."

For seventy years, when asked to identify the best manager of his career, Edd Roush would answer, "Pat Moran." He would explain, "Moran had strong principles. He didn't put up with any foolishness. He made you respect him, and you wanted to play good ball for him." Unlike McGraw, Moran didn't attempt to intimidate his players by throwing fits and swearing at them. A silent frown was all it took. Edd would later say, "It was like the guy had eyes in the back of his head. He always knew what was going on with the team even though he never went to the breweries with us players."[7] Like any good manager, Moran knew people. He knew his boys were brimming with rowdiness that day as they walked into the music store.

Greasy, Heinie, Bill, and Edd walked into the plush Wurlitzer showroom and were amazed. The room was filled with shiny musical instruments and grand pianos with mirror finishes. Reds teammates were scattered throughout the room enjoying the feast. The noise was deafening. Ivey Wingo banged on one of the grands. Rube Bressler strummed a big bass. Nick Allen and Jimmy Ring played the new Tonophone coin-operated piano, and a cluster of players surrounded the new player piano energetically belting out "Take Me Out to the Ballgame"—the song they had sung so many times at the Foss-Schneider brewery after games. A dozen anxious salesmen in bow ties and pressed white shirts stood nearby, too timid to stop the onslaught and looking totally baffled.

Edd stood at the doorway taking in the scene. For a few minutes he allowed himself to pause amid the flurry of the activities and take a breath. So much had happened in the last few weeks.

1919 SEASON RECAP

The world had known that the Reds were the National League champions on September 16 when Moran's prodigy, Dutch Ruether, beat Fred Toney and New York, 4-3. They were nine games ahead of their closest rival, McGraw's Giants, with only eight games left in the season.

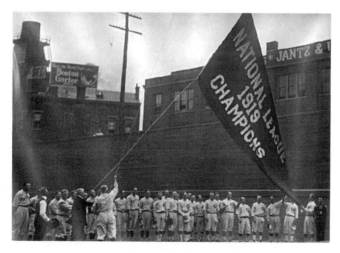

1919 NL PENNANT WAVES OVER REDLAND FIELD

CINCINNATI WINS NL PENNANT AFTER 50 YEARS

Cincinnati had gone mad that day. It had been over thirty years since Reds fans had a pennant-winning baseball team.[8] Most importantly, the Queen City had given her unbridled support to the fifty Reds teams that had represented their city from 1869 to 1919. With each new season, they had loyally marched to Redland Field to cheer. Year after year their cheers had turned to whispers as they saw one team after another go down in defeat. Until 1919.

The Reds started the season with a bang, winning their first seven games. On June 1, the Reds were in second place—five games behind the mighty Giants. The fans held their breaths.

By July 15, the Reds were only a half-game behind the Giants. The fans began to believe. On August 1, the Giants came to Redland for the last trip of the season. They found a new voice in the grandstands, the deep, low-pitched roar of a city that demanded blood. When Heinie Groh started a fight with Benny Kauff, teammates Morrie Rath and Larry Kopf started to jump in. The umpire, Bill Klem, threatened to clear out the Reds' dugout. Fans were delirious in the second game when Reds newcomer Slim Sallee pitched a 6-0 shutout. The Giants went home in second place.

But it wasn't over. Two weeks later the Reds would enter

the Polo Grounds for the final challenge—three days of back-to-back doubleheaders. Animosity between the cities ran so high that the Reds took their own bottled drinking water to New York for fear of being poisoned by local fans.[9] Moran used six different pitchers in that series and demonstrated beyond doubt the depth of the Reds pitching strength. He had nurtured each pitcher with his magical recipe throughout the season. Now he sat back and watched the yeast rise. The Reds walked away with four of the six games. Sportswriter Dan Daniel attributed much of New York's poor performance to Hal Chase, who fell down chasing balls several times.[10] (As Edd later claimed, it was bungled plays by Chase that prevented the Reds from winning the pennant in 1918.) Scurrilous cheating and game fixing by this same player may have also cost the Giants the 1919 NL pennant. Was there no loyalty among thieves, or did Chase have a *bigger* reason to assure a pennant win for Cincinnati in 1919?

A short article appeared in the sports section of the *Chicago Daily Tribune* on August 25 titled, "Now They Are Speading Yarns Belittling the Reds." I.E. Sanborn reported a rumor that a "Braves outfielder" said he was approached by a gambler to throw a game to the Reds. Were the gamblers lining up to assure the Reds played the Sox in the Series?

Billy Evans, American League umpire and columnist, described it best.

> What could possibly be a greater test of a team's greatness than to be forced to play three double-headers in as many days, with its strongest contender on the foreign field, before a hostile crowd of 75,000 people?[11] What the Cincinnati Reds did in this series is now a matter of history.

[They] took much of the fight out of McGraw's players.

From that point on—from New York to Brooklyn, Boston, Philly, Pittsburgh, Chicago, and St. Louis—it was all gravy for Cincinnati.

For Edd Roush, beating the Giants was also a personal victory. Because of his brief foray into the nest of the Polo Grounds in 1916, he had developed a true hatred for the arrogance of McGraw and his team. When New York traded him to Cincinnati he found a team and a town that were right for him. He left with a bitter aftertaste from that New York cup of coffee. There was no team on the schedule he wanted to beat more.

The Reds ended the season with a 96-44 record and a .686 winning percentage—the highest in the history of the franchise. Other stats were impressive too. They led the league with fewest errors (151), a fielding average of .974, and triples (84). But the teamwork was the real story. They got the hits when they needed them. Teamwork falls under the category of "hidden team assets" for which the Reds received a blockbusting +12.8 in 1919.[12]

On the last day of the short season, September 28, Edd Roush and Rogers Hornsby were still vying for the National League batting title. They both got two hits that day, giving Edd the final edge with a .321 average against Hornsby's .318. In addition to becoming the 1919 NL Batting Champion, Edd finished in the top ten in other categories: Slugging percentage .431 (#4); OPS .811 (#3); On-base percentage .380 (#5); Hits 162 (#3); Total Bases 217 (#4); Triples 12 (#3); Runs 73 (#5); RBIs 71 (#2). Edd Roush would be the third man in the history of baseball to both win the batting crown and play in the World Series in the same year.[13]

As Edd stood in the Wurlitzer showroom watching his teammates sing and play together, his heart must have swelled with pride. After six months, more than 1,300 innings, forty-eight long train rides, and seventy-six nights in hotels together, they had done the impossible. This ragtag group of Midwestern farmers had won the pennant. He loved every man in that room and trusted every man to play his best every minute. No Hal Chase or Lee Magee to siphon off their will to win. Every man focused on one goal—get the runner home. There were no stars. No one cared who was on third. If he wore the Reds insignia, just get him home.

Edd remembered his joy when Chase was traded to the Giants and his friend Bill Rariden joined him in Cincinnati. He remembered Bill's astonishment when he saw the Reds all going to dances and picnics together. After years of roaming the fields of Oakland City, Evansville, Indianapolis, Newark, Chicago, and New York, Edd knew that, at last, he was part of a real team. His pride in his teammates knew no bounds.

PENNANT-WINNING REDS ON SEPT. 28, 1919[14]

None of the pitchers had the raw ability of a Grover Cleveland Alexander, but Moran had massaged the natural talent in each one. Each had returned the favor by winning games when they were most needed. As an extra bonus, Moran had brought in old Chief Bender, a full-blooded Chippewa Indian pitcher, now the retired star of the Philadelphia Athletics.[15] Whatever Moran didn't know about the fine points of pitcher development, coach Bender did.

Hod Eller (19-9) and Jimmy Ring (10-9) had returned from the 1918 season. Although Jimmy often blew up on the mound, Hod was slow and steady, and his shine ball was perfected in 1919.[16] He had practiced and practiced, and he had the "hop" down pat now. By rubbing the ball hard against his pant leg he made it "shine" on one side. Then with his tremendous speed behind it, it would hop up and break to one side at the exact moment it reached the plate—right in front of the startled batter's eyes. Hod insisted there was no paraffin or dirt on the ball. His practice would pay off for the Reds on October 9 when he would pitch the deciding game of the 1919 World Series.

Adolfo Luque (10-3) also returned to the Reds from his 1918 rookie year and provided strong relief in the pinches. "Dolf" was one of the first Cuban players in the major leagues. Edd took a special liking to Dolf, perhaps because he felt a certain affinity with the "Pride of Havana." Hurtful rumors had circulated in 1919 that Edd was part Indian.[17] Dolf would later say that he relied on Edd to show him how to pitch to the batters. If Edd was veering a bit short to right, he'd say to himself, "Eddie thinks I should throw this bird a low inside curve," and he'd do it.[18]

Southpaw Walter "Dutch" Ruether had been a cast-off by the minors before being drafted for a short stint with the Chicago Cubs in 1917. He had only won three games in the majors in his career.[19] But in the spring of 1919, Pat Moran saw gold buried beneath his quiet German exterior. Of all the pitchers, Ruether benefited most from Moran's training. Ruether posted the team's best ERA (1.82) and a 19-6 record. Moran's investment was to pay off again in the first game of the World Series.

The new additions to the pitching staff were Ray Fisher from the Yankees and Harry "Slim" Sallee from the Giants. At 33 and 34 respectively, they were in the older group on the team. Michigander Ray was at the end of his decade-long career but had given his best during the season (14-5). It was Slim who had surprised all the experts that season. When Moran worked a deal with McGraw to trade Slim, the experts thought he was crazy. Portsider Sallee was considered washed up. Moran didn't think so. The lanky 6'3" Ohioian who looked and acted like a country bumpkin, proved Moran right. Slim had "retired" midway through the 1918 season with the Giants. He was willing to come back for the Reds because he owned a tobacco farm in Higginsport, Ohio, a short drive from Redland Field.[20] With newfound confidence instilled by his manager, Slim compiled the team's second best ERA of the season at 2.06 and a 21-7 record.

Slim also made a personal contribution to the 1919 team. He befriended the 25-year-old Dutch Ruether. Dutch would later say that Slim had been a mentor to him. Slim knew the ropes after a dozen years in the National League. He'd started with St. Louis and was traded to New York, where he learned from McGraw. Like Edd, he'd seen games thrown by Chase and seen gamblers hovering around ballparks. When the team headed for the local brewery after the games, Slim drove two hours home to his farm in Higginsport. It wasn't that Slim didn't drink. His drink of choice was Jack Daniels—no German beer belly for him.[21]

Although they saw little action during the season, Roy Mitchell, Ed Gerner, and Raymond "Rube" Bressler were relief pitchers. Bressler was a team favorite. He was a big, burly guy with a kind heart and a quick wit. Edd and Essie always included Rube and his new wife, Helen, in social activities. Rube was the first player Edd introduced to Bill Rariden when he joined the club in April, and Edd would remember when he and Greasy Neale convinced Pat Moran to take Rube off the bench and put him into the outfield.

It was when the regular left fielder, Sherry Magee, was sidelined in May. Moran was desperate for a third outfielder. He tried a young rookie named Billy Zitzmann. Moran told Billy to watch Edd and do what he did. Billy would later say, "In the short while I was with the club, I discovered Eddy [sic] Roush to be one of the finest fellows I have ever met in baseball. He really tried to help me."[22] Although Billy didn't work out in 1919, he would return to the Reds in 1925 for five seasons.

When Zitzmann proved unworthy, Edd told Moran, "Rube's a good hitter and a fair bet for left field. Neale and I can carry the load and I'll move Bressler around and tell him where to play." Edd found Rube to be an apt pupil, but said, "Rube did what every other pitcher does until he got the hang of it. He'd keep backing up on a long drive until he fell down." Years later, Edd would chuckle as he remembered the day Rube came back to the bench and said to his mentor, "I know we're doing it right out there. We're right in front of every line drive. The thing I can't understand is why we have to move around so much."

Rube would later remember Edd's tutelage with fondness. "What a beautiful and graceful outfielder that man was. He taught me how to play hitters, how to judge line drives, how to yell for the ball, how to shift on different hitters and even on the same hitter." When Rube first joined the outfield, Edd said, "If I can help you in any way, I'll be tickled to death." Rube later told Larry Ritter, "Hah! The understatement of the century. The greatest center fielder in the game saying to me 'if I can help you.' Terrific!"[23] Edd and Rube became fast friends and went deer hunting every November for thirty years after their baseball careers ended.

With renewed pitching strength and Wingo and Rariden at the catcher's post (big Nick Allen in relief), the Reds battery was second to none. The outfield combo of Roush and Neale was finally complete when Moran picked Pat Duncan out of obscurity in August. Duncan was playing in the minors in Birmingham. He had a reputation as a fiery competitor who had once been banned from baseball because he socked an umpire. Moran liked this fellow Irishman and pulled him up to replace Bressler in left field. Duncan would play for the Reds for five seasons and would have the distinction of hitting the first home run over Redland's left field fence in June, 1921.[24] He would also do his part in the coming Fall Classic. The outfield relief consisted of Hank Schreiber, Jimmy Smith, and Charlie See.

Moran was less confident in his infield. Although the book-ends were firmly secured with Heinie Groh at third and Jake Daubert at first, the middle was weak. During spring training in rainy Waxahachie, Texas, Moran scoured the league for a strong second baseman and a shortstop. No managers had a man to spare. So, he took a chance with Morrie Rath (33) and Larry Kopf (29). Both were lackluster veterans who had bounced around the leagues for several years. Morrie[25] had quit the Reds after the 1917 season in frustration about Matthewson's indecisiveness but was happy to return under Moran. Kopf was joining the team after military service and a trade for Lee Magee with the Dodgers. Edd would later say, "Rath and Kopf were never great players, but they both played their best season in 1919." Rath became the lead-off hitter and turned in a .267 average for the season. Bill Rariden and Ivey Wingo spent hours working with both men to perfect double plays. This extra effort between catchers and infielders would pay dividends in October.

The Reds were unquestionably a strong defensive team, but what of the offense? One oddity was exactly half the team (11 players) were left-handed batters. Of the starting lineup, six were lefties; Daubert, Roush, Neale, Rath, Kopf, and Wingo. Of the pitchers only Ruether and Bressler batted left.

There were two star hitters—Roush (.321) and Groh (.310). Unlike some stars on other teams, both men refused to *act* like stars. Edd and Heinie were team players, willing to reject the long drive for a well-placed bunt. For this reason,

Edd was often identified by competitors as "hard to dope."

> I don't know how Eddie Roush will fare against
> the White Sox pitchers in the big series....He
> must have a weakness. But if this baby has one,
> I, for one, am free to admit that I don't know
> what it is. I know he hits about everything I
> throw at him. – Fred Toney, New York

> Roush is the hardest batter to figure. He hits 'em
> anytime and anywhere. He can walk up on a
> slow one, time a fast one and hook a wide curve
> into the opposite field....The pitcher doesn't live
> who can catch him flatfooted. On the hit-and-
> run play he is the most dangerous batter in the
> world. – Dave Bancroft, Boston

Reminiscent of Cincinnati's "Big Red Machine" of the 1970's, the 1919 Reds were in the game from start to finish. They simply refused to give up, and Groh and Roush were the heart and soul of the team.[26] As Greasy Neale, Edd's outfield partner, would later say, "Never would he [Edd] hit the cripple, that juicy three-and-nothing pitch, unless it meant the ball game. But he wouldn't do it just for himself or his batting average."[27]

The day after the Wurlitzer visit, Jack Ryder's article in the *Enquirer* would tell Cincinnati fans about their "musical" heroes.

> So, the noble Reds of Cincinnati, Baseball
> Champions of the National League and con-
> tenders for the World's highest honor in their
> profession, have been cheered and inspired on
> their forward march to Glory by their devo-
> tion to Music. In fact, they all own a Wurlitzer

Musical Instrument now.

Heinie and Ivey ordered a player piano and Edd walked out with a bugle. Although he would have preferred a piano, Essie held the purse strings in the family and any large purchase required her approval first. The bugle would be put to good use in the future as little Mary would play taps on it at many summer camps for Girl Scouts in years to come.

Edd walked home that day since he and Essie spent the summer season in the Gilbert Avenue apartment—just blocks from the Wurlitzer showrooms downtown.

SEPTEMBER 28, 1919   CINCINNATI

Essie Mae Roush was in a tizzy over her wardrobe for the coming week. She wondered, *What does one wear to a World Series?* She had never been to one. Worse yet, what does the wife of a star player wear to his first World Series? She knew Ruby Groh would wear a fine new outfit or two from Giddings department store, but when Essie shopped downtown, she preferred Mabley and Carew. She thought Giddings was overpriced and didn't want to "put on the dog" like Ruby did. But she had to look nice for Edd and for the photographers. She chuckled at the thought of Edd looking up at her from the outfield and thinking to himself, "Oh dear, my wife is wearing the red hat instead of the nicer beige one." Ha! Edd would be completely oblivious to her appearance, as usual.

The past few days had been a whirlwind of congratulatory letters and phone calls. Half of Oakland City had called them, it seemed. Even Bill and Beryl McKechnie had called from Pennsylvania. Edd's brother, Fred, and mother, Laura, were coming for the opening games in Cincinnati. Although Essie never relished a visit from her mother-in-law, even Laura could not quell her happiness now.

The Business Man's Club of Cincinnati had a lovely dinner party the previous weekend in honor of the Reds winning the pennant. A lumberman named Fred Mowbray was listed as the organizer of the event. Each player received a beautiful vase from the local Rookwood Pottery. The best part of the dinner was the speaker—Ring Lardner. He told the audience he'd been invited to speak because someone had to tell the players "what to do with those vases." He told lots of funny stories and really connected with the crowd. Lardner said he was a sports-writer, and he was having trouble predicting the outcome of the "World Serious." They'd have to "Luque and see" what happened. Everyone laughed when he said the hardest part was predicting what the umpires would do. He poked fun at indi-vidual players on both teams, calling White Sox manager Kid Gleason an "effeminate guy who owned a handkerchief facto-ry in Philly." Bill Rariden roared when Lardner said, "Catcher Rariden won't be dazzled by the big crowds since he was born in Bedford, Indiana." He added, "When I need to think, I have Hugh Fullerton push me in a go-cart."[28]

The Reds Boosters and the Cincinnati Chamber of Commerce staged gala events on Saturday, September 27. The ticker tape parade downtown started promptly at 12:30 at 4th and Broadway and ended at 9th and Plum. The parade included over 2,000 uniformed baseball players from amateur adult teams and every school team in the surrounding area. There were more than twenty bands, and two-year-old Mary Roush squealed with joy in Essie's arms when she heard the music. Then they rushed to the ballpark where Mary watched her daddy get a hit in the seventh inning to win the game against the Cubs, 7-4. Finally, they rushed home to Gilbert Avenue to prepare for the banquet that night at the distinguished and ornate Gibson Hotel.

Essie remembered her pride when Mr. Moran chose Edd to

stand in the receiving line to greet the guests at the banquet. Even Governor James Cox and his wife were there. And the boss, Mr. Herrmann, had been in such a jovial mood that night. When around the players' wives, he was usually terse and rather formal. But at the dinner he was charming and witty. Sporting a cigar, he worked the room with uncanny skill.

After the Cincinnati Glee Club performed and the evening was over, Herrmann invited everyone to the hotel bar, saying the drinks were on him. Edd graciously refused the offer, saying he had to prepare for the final game of the season the next day. As they said their goodbyes, Essie thought she saw a couple of the pitchers heading toward the bar with some slick-looking fellows from out of town. She thought nothing of it at the time.

Outside the hotel, throngs of people still lined the streets and celebrated. Although many people were inebriated, the happy crowd was relaxed and polite, with no appetite for foul play. The newspapers said there would be no hotel rooms available in the city once the Series began, and people might have to sleep in the parks. The newspaper also announced that because of an "expected shortage in rooming accommodations" General Passenger Agent D.M. Bowman offered parked Pullman cars for guest lodging.[29] The Chamber of Commerce announced that more than a thousand guests had taken rooms in private residences. Cincinnati was sold out!

Essie had seriously considered taking in a family of visiting fans, but Edd wouldn't hear of it—particularly now that they had little Mary and his family was coming. Of course, Edd was not as naïve as Essie. He had seen the gambler-types hanging around Redland Field for weeks. He had seen them clustered in the "gambler section" of the stands opposite third base. (This was the gambler section in several ballparks.) Prior to the building of Redland Field in 1912, the third base line was known as "Rooters Row." The rowdiest fans gathered there at the field level behind a wire barrier. They bought beer (twelve for a dollar) and threw insults and sometimes bottles at opposing teams.[30]

Heinie kept tabs on this section from his spot at third. He'd sometimes tell Edd, "Those slick Jews were up there at it again today. They must be making a lot of money on us!" In August, fans complained about "loud and obstreperous" professional gamblers making bets in that section.[31] Edd and Heinie wondered why Garry Herrmann did nothing about it. Edd laughed as he told Heinie, "They buy tickets, don't they?"

Essie was innocent of such things. She could not have imagined the inner workings of a Peeble's Corner pool hall—just a few blocks away from the safety of her little nest. Essie lived in the sunshine. She didn't know there were shadows gathering around her and the city she loved.

---

[1] Author's Note: The author is deeply indebted to Gene Carney, SABR researcher and co-creator of the 1919 Yahoo.com Internet site, for valuable information and insight into this chapter.

[2] Only known photo of entire 1919 Reds team in "citizen clothes."

[3] The Reds lost this game to the Cubs, 2-0.

[4] Sherry Magee, Slim Sallee and Roy Mitchell were each 34.

[5] Jake Daubert is one of the unsung heroes of the deadball era. In a 15-year career he hit .303 and won NL batting championships in 1913 and 1914. He was traded by Brooklyn to the Reds in 1919 for Tommy Griffith. He was an active player for the Reds when he died suddenly in 1924. Roush and Reds teammates were pallbearers at his funeral. Many experts feel he has long deserved a plaque in Cooperstown.

[6] "McGraw loved Moran like a brother." *New York Times* obituary. March 7, 1924.

[7] One of the saddest days in the history of the Reds was when Moran died at age 48 on March 7, 1924 at the Reds training camp in Orlando, Florida. He died of Bright's Disease, a failure of the liver and kidneys attributed to the consumption of alcohol prepared under Prohibition standards. When Moran died, Roush and the core Reds supported Jake Daubert for manager, but Moran was replaced by Jack Hendricks who caused dissension within the team because he favored Catholic players. Roush believed that had Moran lived, the Reds would have won the 1924 pennant.

[8] Reds last won a pennant in 1882 with the American Association.

[9] Lee Allen. *The Cincinnati Reds*. G. P. Putnam's Sons, 1948.

10 Martin Kohout. *Hal Chase*. McFarland & Co., 2001

11 Ibid. Kohout cites a crowd of 40,000 on August 13,1919, as the largest in Polo Grounds history.

12 Linear Weights is a sophisticated computer analysis devised by SABR (Society of American Baseball Research).

13 Honus Wagner (1903 & 1909) and Ty Cobb (1907-9) were the first two. Stan Grosshandler. *Baseball Research Journal #24*, 1993.

14 Note: See back row. Adolfo Luque (relief pitcher) is holding up a bat behind Heinie Groh and pointing with pride to Edd Roush, newly minted NL batting champion.

15 Charles Albert "Chief" Bender was inducted into the Hall of Fame in 1953.

16 When the National Commission changed the rules in 1920, they outlawed "freak" pitching. Eller's career was basically over. He pitched his last season in 1921.

17 Author's Note: Edd's Aunt Fannie had started this "rumor" by tipping off a sportswriter in southern Indiana. The Roush family tried to stifle it, but, in truth, Edd's grandmother Harrington had a husband who was of Native American heritage. Though Americans take pride in this heritage today, mixed blood was considered an embarrassment in 1919.

18 Luque interview with Ken Smith, Director Baseball Hall of Fame, 1955.

19 William A. Cook. *The 1919 World Series*. McFarland & Co., 2001.

20 Interview with Eric Sallee, cousin of Slim Sallee and SABR historian.

21 Ibid. Eric Sallee interview. Slim owned a tavern in Higginsport, Ohio, after he retired from baseball.

22 *Appleton Times-Signal*. December 21, 1924.

23 Larry Ritter. *The Glory of Their Times*. MacMillan Co., 1966.

24 Author's Note: Duncan's home run was the first National League home run at Redland Field (June 2, 1921.) The very first home run was made by Negro Leaguer John Beckwith on May 22, 1921. Greg Rhodes and John Snyder. *Redleg Journal*. Road West Publishing, 2000.

25 Morrie Rath shot himself, committing suicide after a long illness at age 58 in 1945.

26 Author's Note: The sheer heart and hustle of the 1919 Reds is comparable to the 1970's Big Red Machine. "Charley Hustle" himself, Pete Rose, met Edd Roush in 1969 for the Reds Centennial celebration in Cincinnati. Rose was a gentleman as he shook Edd's hand, and they chatted for some time. Throughout the conversation Rose kneeled on the floor in front of Edd showing respect for the old-timer who once wore the same uniform.

27 Arthur Daley interview with Neale. "Sports of *The Times*." *New York Times*. February, 18, 1960.

28 For the speech Lardner received $500, which he immediately bet on the White Sox. The *Washington Post*, October 4, 1925.

29 *New York Times*. September 28, 1919.

30 R.J. Lesch. *Deadball Digest*. August 18, 2005.

31 Harold Seymour. *Baseball: The Golden Age*. Oxford University Press, 1971.

7

SHADOWS GATHERING

It was a makeshift job; compounded in equal parts of bluff and welsh and cold gall, no [one] knowing what the man next to him was up to....the biggest, sloppiest, crudest fix of a sporting event that ever was known to man.

– *John Lardner,* **Saturday Evening Post,** *4/30/38*

SEPTEMBER 28, 1919 CHARLEY'S SALOON
PEEBLE'S CORNER, CINCINNATI[1]

Jimmy Widmeyer stood on the fringes of a handful of men who hovered at the bar. Although to the casual observer he looked nonchalant, every fiber of his body was focused on the conversation in front of him. He had to be careful not to be too obvious. After all, he was just recently admitted into this exclusive fraternity and didn't want to appear eager.

Jimmy had gained admission to this private club through his long association with local businessmen and, in particular, with the Reds Boosters Club, to which many of these Cincinnati businessmen belonged.[2]

They were well-heeled gentlemen gamblers. They worked in honest professions and merely dabbled in a few well-placed bets for sport. The hardcore men who made their living at the tracks, the wrestling matches, and the baseball fields referred to these men as "piker gentry." Such businessmen were often the targets of professional gamblers who sidled up to them with a "hot tip" and walked away with their money.

In 1919, Jimmy was 38 years old and had sold "sheets" (newspapers) since he was eight. He grew up in Newport, Kentucky, the seamy community called "Sin City" just across the bridge from Cincinnati. Newport housed a number of gambling casinos, and it was rumored that they were controlled by the Cleveland mob. It was the "layoff" center for national gamblers. They would layoff their excess action in Kentucky in preparation for the next big gig. Jimmy's relatives ran the kitchen at the Victory Club. His brother Jack would later own one of the first floating restaurants on the south side of the river. Jimmy had two brothers, Jack and Harry. Harry's wife gave birth to fifteen children on the old claw foot table in the living room but thirteen died. Survival was at a premium in the early 1900's across the river from Cincinnati.[3]

Everyone in southern Ohio knew about Newport. They called the state "Cain Tuck" and local philanderers considered

Cincinnati Enquirer

JIMMY WIDMEYER AT NEWSSTAND ON 5TH AND WALNUT, CINCINNATI

Newport a safe haven where nobody knows your name. A decade before Edd met Jimmy, the Cincinnati police made a deal with the political bosses to ensure that Cincinnati remained clean of the vermin who crashed in Newport. The police chief at the time was Calvin Crim. He created a "hotel squad" assigned to make frequent visits to the front desk personnel at downtown hotels, such as the Metropole, Sinton, and Gibson. If any "gangster types" registered, they would receive a four a.m. visit from Crim's men. The police squad was trained to burst into the room, grab the unsuspecting visitor, and dangle him by his ankles out his hotel room window. They would tell him that if he was still registered the next day, he would have another visit from them the next night, and this time he would have an unfortunate fall from his window. Jimmy called Cincinnati "the gay white way" whereas all the "filth" was relegated to Newport.

Not wanting the life of poverty he saw around him, Jimmy sought ways to escape. At age nine he began selling newspapers at the busiest corner in town—Walnut and Fifth Street. He was taking home fifty cents a day to support his invalid aunt and four little brothers. He was determined to "own" this corner where the trolleys stopped and employees scurried to their downtown office buildings. When older boys attempted to take it away from him, he learned to use his fists to defend his turf. As a result, Jimmy had picked up a little cash in the boxing ring in his teens and once had a promising career as a professional boxer, fighting seventy bouts. He became a promoter and was looking to manage a boxer in 1905.[4]

It was during this time that Jimmy hooked up with a local boxing promoter and (later) racing commissioner, an Irishman named Jimmy Shevlin.[5] For years Widmeyer's second office was Shevlin's Oyster and Chop House around the corner on 6th Street. Other members of the boxing circuit gathered there such as Billy Ryan, Jim Corbett, Abe Attell, and Remy Dorr. These boxing connections would prove to be noteworthy as the sordid events of the World Series unfolded.

The Widmeyer newsstand was now a fixture in Cincinnati. Much of Jimmy's success was based on his contacts. Jimmy seemed to know everyone, and everyone knew Jimmy. Players, sportswriters, businessmen, and politicians all stopped to buy their morning newspaper from Jimmy. All had a friendly greeting for him and a handshake. Jimmy called his customers by their first names and remembered the names of wives and children.

He not only knew everyone in town, he knew everything about everyone in town. When he heard that the city manager, C.O. Sherrill, intended to prevent him from selling both major Cincinnati newspapers—the *Times-Star* and the *Post*—he was infuriated. He walked into Sherrill's office, went behind his desk, and hit him so hard he knocked him off his chair.[6] Jimmy continued to sell his sheets. Such stories abounded about Jimmy Widmeyer.

It was reported that one of the most powerful men in town, Republican Party leader George B. "Boss" Cox, used to drive up to the newsstand when it was closing in the late afternoon and take Jimmy for a ride to pick his brain. When Cox died on May 20, 1916, his friend Jimmy was quoted as saying he never knew a man like Cox who could say so much with so few words.[7] Underhanded dealings were nothing new to Jimmy. He grew up in a Cincinnati where the gambling houses on 6th Street were wide open and Cox's office was right above the infamous Mecca Café on Walnut Street. He would later say, "Cincinnati used to be like Mardi Gras every night."

It was a private meeting on Sunday afternoon when the pool hall on the corner of Gilbert and McMillan, known as Peeble's Corner, was closed.[8] The owner, Charley Marqua, had told everyone to come through the back entrance so as not to arouse suspicion among the locals across the street at Graeter's Ice Cream store. It was the usual group: the tavern owners Marqua, Keller, and Watter; the lumber company magnates Fred Mowbray (Robinson-Mowbray Lumber Co.) and Dan Moul (Moul Lumber Co.); and the race track guy Dick Williams of the Williams Brothers. To the outside world it would appear that these upright businessmen were merely enjoying an afternoon of camaraderie after the successful banquet at the Gibson the night before. In truth, their purpose was much more serious.

The man with the most clout in the group was Dick Williams. His family had been associated with race horses since old Colonel R.D. Williams had helped form the National Fox Hunters' Association in Lexington, Kentucky, before the turn of the century.[9] Dick had been in the sporting world all his life and had reserved tickets in the best section of Madison Square Garden in New York where he mingled with the Vanderbilts, Moores, and Tafts. He had a lot on his mind that day since his colleague, J.W. McClelland, was kicking up a fit over the poor conditions of the turf at the Kentucky tracks.[10] Dick had more to worry about than this little meeting in Marqua's back room. He doubted this "fix" thing would pan out anyway.

Charley Marqua, at 62, was the senior member of the group. Hi owned a successful café at 613 College Street in addition to the Peeble's Corner saloon. He also was a chicken breeder and promoted cock fights in various locations throughout southern Ohio and northern Kentucky.[11] Charley was heavily involved in local politics as Democratic leader of the 16th Ward. His friends, Charlie Watter and Keller, were co-owners of a little tavern on 5th Street.

The lumber executives, Mowbray and Moul, were leaders in the Reds Boosters Club and active in the same Elks club as Marqua. They were also active members of the Cincinnati Club and the Queen City Lodge of Masons.[12] Like Dick Williams,

Fred Mowbray was well known in town and owned lumber yards throughout Ohio and Kentucky.

Fred Mowbray, age 49, was the brain of the group and the unofficial leader. The Mowbray family was descended from Thomas de Mowbray, first Duke of Norfolk in 1366. Fred was one of eight children of Ebenezer Mowbray of Peru, Indiana, and he became a lawyer by reading his father's law books after school. Described as a math genius,[13] he got an accounting degree from the University of Chicago. In 1910 he moved to Ohio with his younger brother, Albert, and went to work for Karl Krippendorf, member of a founding family in Cincinnati, at the Crane Lumber Company. But Fred Mowbray would not work for someone else for long.

Fred foresaw the future of the lumber industry. To cash in, he needed land. He found a bank in Louisville that agreed to a $1,000,000 loan. He purchased 15,000 acres of prime woodlands in the Quicksand, Kentucky, area. The motto of his company was "Oak floors have no equal." Fred partnered with an expert lumberman and sawmill owner named E. O. Robinson. Over the next few years, Fred Mowbray developed numerous contracts with the U.S. government for the expanding railroad system. When America entered World War I, the Mowbray-Robinson Lumber Company sold lumber for ships. Fred negotiated the first contract with Fisher Brothers Company in Detroit to create wood paneling for automobiles.

Whatever Fred touched turned to gold. Coal reserves were discovered on his land. Along the way, he purchased some stock in a new company called International Business Machines. In 1922, Fred and his partner would donate a large portion of their land (including $9,000,000 in mineral rights) to the University of Kentucky.[14]

In 1919 Fred was still handsome with a shock of pure white hair that had suddenly appeared when he turned 30. He was an affable fellow who "could get along with anyone, even the drunken Fisher Brothers executives." He had a great sense of humor and a love for thoroughbred racing. (He had a head for figuring the odds.) He split his time between his thirteen-acre estate on Linwood Road in the prestigious Cincinnati suburb of Mount Lookout, a winter home in Arizona, and the racetracks of Saratoga and New Orleans (the home of Louise, his beautiful wife with jet black hair).[15]

At Kentucky's Latonia track Fred met an intelligent, young boxing referee named Remy Dorr. Dorr listed his profession as a "real estate salesman," but everyone in the sports world knew he was a gambler. Remy spent his days at the tracks and his nights in the boxing ring. He was highly respected in boxing circles for his fair and impartial work as a referee. Sportswriter Hugh Fullerton lauded Dorr as an "eminent citizen (...with a high reputation) from the sunny south."[16] For some time Fred had both benefited from and underwritten the gambling activities of Remy Dorr.[17] Fred didn't know that Remy supported an aunt in New Jersey named Louisa Rothstein.

Dick Williams had been a little nervous about having Jimmy around in the beginning. After all, Widmeyer's relatives worked in the casinos of Newport and didn't have quite the right pedigree. But Charley spoke strongly on his behalf. It helped that Jimmy had become something of a local hero in the spring of 1919 when he brought the great Reds holdout, Edd Roush, back into the fold.

WIDMEYER/ROUSH HOLDOUT STORY

In February 1919, Reds' owner Garry Herrmann offered Edd a contract for $4,500, a cut of $500 from his 1918 salary. Always thought to be the "generous" owner (as compared to Charles Comiskey of the White Sox),[18] Herrmann's argument for the lowball offer was three-fold: (1) the club had suffered financial loses as a result of the Federal League fiasco and low attendance due to World War I,[19] (2) because of the 1918 losses, the new season had been shortened by three weeks, (3) Roush's batting average was 8 points lower (.333) in 1918 than it had been the prior year. These reasons had been clearly spelled out in Herrmann's letters to Edd from January through March. Each letter ended with an invitation for Edd to bring his wife to Cincinnati (at Herrmann's expense) to discuss his salary.

When Edd learned that his salary was being cut because his batting average had dropped, it struck him to the quick. Herrmann knew Edd had been forced to miss the last games of the 1918 season because his father was dying. Further, Edd had been the 1917 batting champion and only missed 1918 by two percentage points. It made him so mad that he decided to more than double Herrmann's offer and demand $10,000. In true Roush form, having set his price, he wouldn't waver.[20] Neither would Herrmann.

But, these were the days when baseball was a game of the people. With two weeks left of spring training and no Roush, the people of Cincinnati got involved. Letters poured into Herrmann's offices. Fans offered money to help pay their star. One fan letter (signed only C.E.B.) offered to start a "Roush Dollar Fund" in the city. He suggested there were five thousand fans who would each pay one dollar to "assist Cincinnati staying on the baseball map." On April 16, at the request of Herrmann, noted sportswriter Bill Phelon decided to try his hand at grabbing the credit for bringing in the stubborn holdout.

Roush wrote back saying a visit from Phelon would be "inconvenient."[21]

But there was one man to whom Edd couldn't say "no." Jimmy Widmeyer drove up and parked in front of the Roush family farm in Oakland City on April 18, six days before the season opener against St. Louis. Edd greeted his friend warmly. When Essie saw that Edd genuinely liked this fellow, she fluttered over him, making sure he had a home-cooked meal and a warm feather bed to sleep in. Of course, Essie also hoped that Jimmy would convince Edd to return to Cincinnati. She had long ago wearied of this holdout battle.

Oddly enough, it was Edd's obstinate mother who would make the final decision for him. When Edd and Jimmy went into the parlor to "talk business," Essie tactfully disappeared, but Laura planted herself in the old rocking chair within earshot of the men. Neither man had the courage to ask the large German woman with the dour face to leave the room.

Edd began by telling Jimmy about the raw deal Herrmann tried to pull on him. Edd called Herrmann a spoiled "playboy" who never had to work for a buck. He was a "politician" who was more concerned with looking good than doing the right thing. Old Bancroft ran the club but didn't know which end was up half the time. All they cared about was making money.[22]

Jimmy let Edd vent his feelings. He knew that some of what Edd said was true. Herrmann had been a political henchman for Boss Cox for years and had become an owner of the Reds through these same political connections. Sitting in the humble farmhouse where Edd had grown up, Jimmy identified with him. They were both poor boys who, by sheer determination, had achieved a higher station in life.

Edd's fury spent, the two men sat in silence.

Jimmy broke the silence and began telling Edd about the pain of the fans over his absence. He told Edd of young boys holding signs in front of Herrmann's office that read "We want Eddie" and "Herrmann is a Tightwad." He told Edd about how Reds' Director Julius Fleischmann had called him, Jimmy Widmeyer, up to his office to ask him to go to Oakland City and "bring Eddie back for the people of Cincinnati." He spoke of the excitement over the new manager, Pat Moran, and the glowing reports coming out of the training camp in Texas about this being the pennant-winning year for the Reds. He pulled at Edd's heartstrings when he spoke of a telephone conversation he'd had with Edd's closest friend on the team, Bill Rariden, and how all the boys in Texas said it wouldn't be the same team without Edd.

Finally he said, "They've authorized me to offer you a contract of eight thousand dollars. Will you accept it and drive back to Cincinnati with me tomorrow?" (Jimmy wanted to bring back his big fish personally.)

Edd calmly answered, "I asked for ten thousand, and I won't come for a penny less."

Then Jimmy pulled out the big gun. "Okay, Edd, I'll tell you something. I'm convinced they will pay your price IF you come back to Cincinnati with me tomorrow." He paused. "I give you my word on it."

"I give you my word." These words resonated in Edd's memory. He remembered the first time Jimmy had said this to him. And indeed, he had kept his word. Edd never got a chance to answer. From across the room a low-pitched, raspy voice said, "My son will accompany you to Cincinnati tomorrow, Mr. Widmeyer." At which point Laura Roush placed her walking stick in front of her and pulled her large body out of the chair. Before walking away she turned and said, "Edd, go pack your things now. You'll need to get an early start."

For a moment Edd felt like he was sixteen again. Then, he laughed, a deep hearty laugh that seemed to wash away all the tension of the last hour. It was sweet irony after all the years he and his father had pleaded with his mother to allow him to play baseball. He smiled and offered his hand to the bewildered Jimmy, "Well, looks like you've got a deal, pal."

Two days later the *Cincinnati Post* ran the headline.

JIM'S TALK OR THE LONG RIDE?
ROUSH HAS SIGNED!

Jimmy Widmeyer was an instant hero in his hometown.[23]

And now, three days before the opening game of the 1919
World Series. Jimmy Widmeyer strained to hear the conversation at Charley's tavern. Dick Williams and Fred Mowbray were
doing all the talking now. It seemed that Fred had the inside
track on the Series. He talked about a gambler friend from St.
Louis named Ben Levi. The Levis had been family friends when
Fred and Ben were growing up in Peru, Indiana, twenty years
ago. He claimed Levi ran a respectable shirt manufacturing business, and he had connections with fellows in the garment district in New York and New Jersey. He had given Fred solid
advice on casual sports gambling in the past. Levi was placing a
bet for $6,000 on the Reds and advised him to do the same.
When Fred asked him why, he just said, "Trust me."

Williams corroborated Fred's story by saying he had gotten the same tip just yesterday at the Latonia stables from New
Orleans trackman Remy Dorr. Dorr's advice to Williams had
been to put all his loose change on the Reds to win the Series,
but he warned him *not* to bet on individual games. Dorr told
Williams that the Sox were going to take a dive. He had it on
good authority from the Saratoga track.

Fred made a split-second decision not to mention his relationship with Remy. It was enough that Williams had shared
the information. No reason to light the candle from both ends.

Marqua suggested they confirm these tips with Phil Hahn,
betting commissioner at the Latonia track who had inside
information on the odds, but Mowbray and Williams thought
it best to keep it to themselves. If Hahn knew, he didn't get it

from them. They agreed the information from Levi and Dorr was solid. The White Sox were going to throw the World Series to the Reds. It was a sure bet.

Jimmy concluded that although his associates were not professional gamblers, these weekend pikers had connections to those who were. He left the saloon with the same question on his mind as the other men. How much money could he scrape together in the next twenty-four hours? They had to lay the bets now while the Sox were heavily favored, 4-1. If the word got out, the odds would change.

As he walked away, his mind was racing. Could a World Series be fixed? How many players would it take to pull it off? Two? Six? A whole team? Unthinkable. Who was in the best position to do it? The catcher or pitcher, of course. Why did the New Orleans gambler warn Williams not to bet on individual games? If you bet on individual games you could increase your bet each day by plowing your winnings back in. A fellow could clean up!

Then, an idea hit him. He lived in the Sinton Hotel, where the Sox would be staying during the Series. Maybe he could convince Harry O'Neal, the young hotel clerk he'd been schmoozing, to put some Chicago players in a room close to his. With any luck, he could eavesdrop on them and figure out which games to bet on. He chuckled at the brilliance of the idea.

SEPTEMBER 28, 1919
ZELCER CIGAR STORE AND POOL ROOM
DES MOINES, IOWA

Carl Zork, age 40, gathered his troops for one last meeting before departing for the opening game of the World Series in Cincinnati. Zork was a well-connected manufacturer of ladies shirts in east St. Louis. Surrounding him in the back room of the pool hall on 714 Locust Street were four men. Abe Zelcer was one of four Zelcer brothers born to Polish immigrants in California. Ben and Lou Levi were born in Indiana to a Russian father, Jacob, who listed "peddler" as his trade in the 1910 U.S. Census. Officially, Ben owned a "loan and mercantile shop" (pawn shop) at 600 Walnut Street in St. Louis. Unofficially, he supported his wife, Esther, and five children as a traveling gambler. Rounding out the clique was Ben Frankel of Omaha, "mule merchant." Regardless what professions were listed in the U.S. Census, in truth, all five men made their living as *gentlemen* gamblers.[24] They had one other thing in common—they were all Jewish.

There were two members missing. One was there in spirit, Henry "Kid" Becker, known as the "King of Gamblers" in the Midwest. The whole thing had been Becker's brainchild. He had started plotting in 1918 to throw a World Series, then, suddenly (and mysteriously) he was shot dead in April 1919.[25] His partner, Zork, went into hiding for a while but came out even more committed to his dead friend's plan. In July, he began to put the plan in action. He wanted to keep the group small with he and Ben Levi as the ruling brain trust. Ben persuaded Carl to bring in his brother Lou and Ben's brother-in-law, David Zelcer. David brought in his brother, Abe, and his associate, Ben Frankel. The Frankels were clothiers in Des Moines.[26] They closed ranks with a half dozen conspirators.

David Zelcer was not present in Des Moines that day because he had a much more important meeting to attend on the group's behalf. He was in New York at the Ansonia Hotel in a private meeting with four ballplayers: "Prince" Hal Chase of the New York Giants, "Sleepy" Bill Burns, former pitcher for Detroit, Cincinnati and Chicago, and two members of the 1919 Chicago White Sox pennant winners, Eddie "Knuckles" Cicotte and Arnold "Chick" Gandil. Two of the four were also known gamblers, Chase and Burns. With his usual caution, Zelcer used a pseudonym for the meeting. He introduced himself as "Curley Bennett" from Des Moines. He didn't relish the spotlight in these affairs. He much preferred to skirt the fringes.

One other man was present at the meeting in New York. He was Abe Attell, former featherweight boxing champion and known henchman of Arnold Rothstein. Every petty gambler from Jersey to Denver knew of Rothstein. Based in Manhattan, he was the true King of the Gentleman Gamblers in America. Attell had moved in the same gambling circles with Chase, Burns, and Zelcer for years, and he knew Zelcer was using a fake name, but he went along with the ruse in front of the naïve players, Gandil and Cicotte. Attell used his own name because Burns and Chase knew him anyway, and, unlike Zelcer, Attell *loved* the spotlight.

Zork's gang in Des Moines had spent weeks in preparation for this day. Since July, they had followed the top teams in each league from one city to the next. When Cincinnati began to overtake New York in August, they were chagrined. The Giants (with Chase) would have been easy pickings, but the Reds were different. The Levis were assigned to scout the Reds for players amenable to taking a bribe. Ben Levi had a friend in Cincinnati who could give him inside information about the team—Fred Mowbray.

At 51, Ben was the senior member of the group. He had been a friend of the Mowbray family for many years and had enjoyed parties at the Mowbray mansion. There was always plenty of booze, gaming tables, and even live entertainment in the 2,500-square-foot ballroom on the fifth floor under the huge thatched roof.[27] Levi laid it on thick about how Mowbray had made his millions in the lumber business just as the nation needed railroad ties to feed the tentacles of progress from one coast to the other. Levi figured that Mowbray would be an unsuspecting ally. If anyone could get him into the ballpark where he could mingle with the players, it was Mowbray, who, on occasion, also was known to make a wager.

Levi decided to give Mowbray the "inside tip" on the Reds without giving him all the details that might eventually get him into trouble. It never occurred to Levi that his tips were shared by Mowbray with other Cincinnatians.

During the first week of August, Levi visited the Mowbrays in Cincinnati during the Reds-Giants three-day series. Mowbray was delighted to introduce his friend from St. Louis to the players as they were warming up on the field. The players all knew Mowbray and his friend, Dan Moul, from the Reds Boosters group.

Levi expressed interest in meeting Edd Roush that day. Roush had a reputation for keeping to himself, and Mowbray didn't know him. But, as luck would have it, Mowbray spotted someone who did know Roush well. He saw Jimmy Widmeyer chatting with Heinie Groh and waved him over. Jimmy was all too happy to oblige and to acquire a Mowbray "chit" for his arsenal. Levi had the pleasure of shaking the hand of Eddie Roush that day while Fred and Jimmy stood beaming behind him.

The following day Levi was out on the field early to begin his work in earnest. His conversation would appear completely innocent, just an out-of-town fan wanting to meet a few ballplayers so he could go home with stories. He concentrated primarily on the battery, engaging Sallee, Ruether, Eller, and Rariden in questions about the team, their manager, and their chances for a pennant win. With every answer, he carefully looked into the player's eyes and took the measure of the man. He would make his approach to the subject of gambling in a subtle, chatty way. What did the player think about that wonderful horse that had won the first Triple Crown this summer, what was his name? If the player instantly said, "Sir Barton," maybe he was a gambling man.

Then the big question: would the player advise him to make a small wager on the game today? If the respondent was a gambler, there would be that tiny flash of greed in his eyes, like the elusive green streak from the sun as it dropped into the ocean at the end of the day. It would be quick, momentary. Every gambler had it, a genetic flaw in the breed. Levi had seen it many times before. He thought he caught a glimpse of it in the eyes of young Ruether, but he couldn't be sure. Probably just wishful thinking.

When Levi got back to St. Louis, his news was disappointing. The Reds were out. He doubted they could be persuaded to "play ball" with gamblers. They were a tight-knit group of fellows and unlikely to respond to the offer.

However, David Zelcer had good news. He had scouted the White Sox and thought there were real possibilities. It was a team divided, composed of cliques that resembled street gangs. There was the "in group" led by Captain Eddie Collins, Ray Schalk, Dickey Kerr, and Red Faber, who were closely aligned with the new manager, Kid Gleason. They were well paid,[28] better educated, and did the bidding of management.

Then there was the group of rebels led by Chick Gandil who openly expressed dislike for management and felt underpaid and underappreciated. Gandil's group hated the Collins cadre. Zelcer learned that Collins and Gandil, side-by-side in the infield, hadn't spoken to each other since 1917.[29] Half the team would stand apart from the other half, not wanting to mix, while they waited for their turn at batting practice each day.[30] The stars of the team—Joe Jackson and Eddie Cicotte—seemed like loners who could go either way. The Gandil contingent would be prime targets for a fix. It was already rumored that certain players had fixed games before.

They all agreed to go forward with their plan if the Sox

won the AL pennant, which looked promising. The final hurdle was the money. How much would it take? Fifty thousand? A hundred thousand? It was a World Series, after all, and the players on the winning team would get a bonus, so the offer would have to be considerably higher. Zelcer told the group that the winning Red Sox players of the 1918 Series had only received $1,108 apiece.[31] Zork reminded him of the low gates because of the war in 1918. This year would be different. People had flooded the ballparks after the war, and this Series should make big money because it was to be a nine-game affair. Player bonuses should be much higher.

Ben Levi piped up with a happy thought: Unless, of course, the Sox lay down and hand it to the Reds in five straight games! Everyone laughed. The perfect scenario...a World Series shutout.

It would take big money for sure, more money than Levi had on hand. They all looked at each other and the same idea struck them simultaneously—Arnold Rothstein. Zelcer had the best entrée to the big man, because he moved in racetrack circles and often met him at Aqueduct. Rothstein had always called him, "the cowboy." In truth, there was still a feel of the old west in Des Moines, more than in St. Louis. St. Louis had become sophisticated; it had hosted a World's Fair. Zork was the second choice because he was the former manager of Rothstein's henchman, boxer Abe Attell. They decided to go directly to Rothstein. Zelcer would go.

Zelcer came home a week later with a smile on his face. The deal was done. The plan that Kid Becker had hatched in St. Louis months ago would finally become a reality. The fix was on!

Unbeknownst to Ben Levi and the Cincinnati gamblers, there was another fellow scouting around Redland Field on the same days they were there. This man had a little notepad in his vest pocket and carefully made notes about who and what he saw that day. He knew the local men—Mowbray, Moul, and Rubin—but he'd never seen the out-of-town stranger they were escorting around to the players. He'd have to investigate. He had a hunch it might come in handy in the future.

This dapper-looking fellow was Calvin Crim, the former Chief of Detectives for the Cincinnati police. In 1919 he was the principal owner and primary investigator for the Cal Crim Detective Bureau. He was also an old friend of a powerful man in Chicago, the President of the American League—Ban Johnson.

SEPTEMBER 28, 1919
LINDY'S RESTAURANT, TIMES SQUARE
NEW YORK CITY[32]

ARNOLD ROTHSTEIN

When Arnold Rothstein walked into his favorite haunt, the waiters flipped a coin to see who would get to serve him. They knew he was the biggest tipper in Manhattan. They didn't know the source of the money, but Mr. Rothstein was a charming fellow to serve. He was always polite and respectful, a classy gentleman, not to mention wealthy. Lindy's was quickly becoming his office-away-from-his-office on West 57th Street.

Rothstein's new gambling house in Saratoga, the former Bonnie Brook Farm, was pulling in cash by the thousands every night. He'd spent a wonderful month in August there with Bobbie Winthrop[33] from the Ziegfeld Follies. Of course, there had been so many others before her, including his current wife, Carolyn. Arnold Rothstein was a multi-millionaire, and the big money of Prohibition rum-running hadn't even begun yet. Capone's Chicago was in its infancy. There was some good action in Boston and Cleveland in 1919, but every gambler knew the big game was in Manhattan. If you wanted to play with the big boys, you paid your respects to A.R.

Rothstein was feeling particularly sporting tonight. He'd had a great week and saw a better one to come. The World Series would begin in three days, and his patsies were already sitting neatly in the separate baskets of his brain. First, the magnates: he had gotten through to Harry Sinclair in his Long Island mansion on the first try. Harry always took Arnold's phone calls because Harry wanted to maintain his connections with the powerful men of New York. There was still a glimmer of the "Okie" in this Midwesterner that had never been quite erased even after he had become established in the northeast. When Arnold offered him a "sure bet" on the Chicago White Sox, Harry plunked down his pocket change of $90,000. Harry imagined that round figures like $100,000 appeared somehow low class.

Harry asked no questions because, after all, Arnold always had inside information so the bet must be good. At least that's what another magnate, Charley Stoneham, had whispered to him last year. Unfortunately for Harry, he didn't know all the inner workings and complicated relationships in Manhattan yet. He didn't know that it was Rothstein who had financed Stoneham's purchase of the Giants or that Rothstein was McGraw's partner in the popular Herald Square pool hall.

Rothstein was humming "remember me to Herald Square..." as he was escorted to his table. He loved George M. Cohan songs, maybe because he had also placed a bet for George on the doomed Sox. Money in the pocket.

Waiting for him was a short man smoking a big cigar. Abe Attell had been Arnold's bodyguard since losing the featherweight boxing championship in 1912. Whereas Arnold took great pains to dress in an expensive but understated fashion, Attell was flamboyant and looked like a crook. Arnold had taken care of his nose years ago, to take away that "Jewish look" that Attell still sported. Arnold prided himself on blending with the Waspish magnates and officials in the city. He went to great lengths to eschew the "Jewish thing."[34] Sinclair would have been shocked to see his friend Arnold with this character who looked unsavory and spoke the language of thugs. Arnold felt safe moving among the artsy theater crowd here at Lindy's. Everyone looked like they were "in costume" here. Of course, the table of Tammany thugs nearby made him feel safe too.

The conversation was brief. As his boss insisted, Abe went down his list, and Arnold nodded approval or frowned. A frown meant there was a problem. Abe hated the frowns. He used initials as codes just to be safe from eavesdroppers.[35]

H.C. informed and paid.	*(Nod.)*
B.B. at Ansonia today. Bought the bluff.	*(Nod.)*
D.Z. in and leaving New York tomorrow.	*(Nod.)*
C.Z. working Midwest arriving Sinton Tuesday.	*(Nod.)*
S.S. meeting C.G. tomorrow in Chicago.	*(Frown.)*

Abe froze. Then he realized why Rothstein had frowned. He quickly recovered.

S.S. and N.E. meeting C.G. tomorrow.	*(Nod.)*

The Little Champ pulled out his pocket watch: "Okay, I've got to hurry to catch my train now. Anything else?"

Rothstein spoke in his hushed, modulated voice for the first time. "Remember, the hook's already baited. You catch the fish." This time it was Abe who nodded and abruptly got up. He knew he had a job to do—the most important one of all. He had to "catch the fish." That meant he had to get the bets in. Rothstein had already "baited the hook." The fix was in. He also knew the fix itself was worthless unless they could get enough patsies to give them money on the Sox. Rothstein expected at least a half million profit as a return on his investment.

To a casual observer the coded names meant nothing. To Arnold Rothstein each was a cog in the wheel of his plan. Hal Chase (H.C.) had done his job well. He had been the inside player who made the "assist" in the Giants' lost pennant. This put Rothstein right on track. If it all blew, the heat would be on the Midwest, not on West 57th Street. His hands—and those of his law enforcement and government protectors—would be clean. He chuckled as he thought of the botched attempts to throw a World Series in the past. Everyone in the gambling world knew about 1914 and 1918.[36] But he wasn't involved in those efforts by lesser colleagues. This time it would be done right.

Arnold felt bad about McGraw. He'd make a mental note to tip him off. It was the least he could do. They were partners, along with Giants owner Stoneham, inside the casino underbelly of Havana, Cuba. And, of course, Stoneham was a silent partner in the Brook. Arnold enjoyed sitting in Stoneham's elite box for the Giants games. They wouldn't like what was going on under their noses and, doubtless, McGraw would figure out that Chase was involved. So be it. He shouldn't have brought Chase to the Giants in the first place. He put the cheater right in Arnold's lap, for God's sake. And then he wondered why he lost the pennant. Well, let McGraw get even with Chase.[37] It was all just business to Arnold.

A scary thought crossed Arnold's mind. What if McGraw tipped his friend Pat Moran? The whole thing might collapse. Moran might be a drunk, but he was honest. Better to wait a couple days to tip McGraw.

"Sleepy" Bill Burns (B.B.), Texas rancher, former White

Sox pitcher, and known gambler, with his sidekick, stupid Billy Maharg, a former boxer and ball player, were trying to get in on the deal. When they came to Rothstein to finance their enterprise, he turned them down, claiming it couldn't be done. He was bluffing. He'd already done it and they weren't in. He knew they'd continue to skirt the edges, and that was fine as long as Attell kept them in control and kept his name out of it. That was one good thing about Chase—he was as good at sidestepping bullets as he was at sidestepping baseballs.

David Zelcer (D.Z.) and Carl Zork (C.Z.) were the Midwest connections. Along with Ben and Louis Levi, they hatched the plan early and brought it to Arnold first. Arnold's pick of the lot was Zelcer. He liked his quiet, understated, and cautious manner. The "cowboy" and the New Yorker had something in common. All roads led to Rothstein. He was the only gambler with both the bankroll and the clout to fix a Series. And, in Arnold's mind, he was just the moneylender in the deal. Innocent Arnold.

Joseph "Sport" Sullivan (S.S.) was assigned the task of go-between with the players. The leader of the dirty Sox was first baseman Chick Gandil (C.G.). But it was Nat Evans (N.E.) whom Rothstein chose to handle the $80,000[38] payoff money. Nat had Arnold's confidence. They had built the Saratoga business from the ground up. Nat was the perfect bag man. He was instructed to give the ballplayers their money in increments, holding $70,000 out for bets.

According to Rothstein's plan, Sullivan would bring Nat (posing as Mr. Brown) to meet Gandil at the Warner Hotel on the south side of Chicago for the first payoff installment of $10,000 the following day. That installment was earmarked for the one man who refused to "cooperate" until he got his money—opening day pitcher Eddie Cicotte. The other Sox conspirators would get theirs if they held up their part of the bargain. Gandil would give Nat his word as collateral. Nat reportedly answered, "In my book, that's not much collateral for eighty grand."

And, of course, Rachel Brown would be in Cincinnati to make sure Arnold's interests were covered. Rachel had been Arnold's trusted bookkeeper for several years.[39] Arnold took pride in the fact that she was his one employee "outside the faith." Imagine, an Englishwoman handling the books for a Jewish financier? He loved the irony. She and Nat had a "thing" going on right now. Nat liked the idea of posing as "Mr. Brown" in Cincinnati so they could be together.

Arnold had even hatched a plan for sleeping arrangements in Cincinnati. Zelcer and Levi would check into the Sinton first thing on the morning of September 29. Levi checked into Room 512 and wrote down his residence as Chicago. Then, when the front desk personnel changed in the afternoon, Zelcer would re-register under an assumed name. He chose W.B. Cavender, perhaps in honor of the Chief of Police in his hometown of Des Moines.[40] Attell and the gang members would reside in the second room (660). David and the boys would simply switch rooms so that Nat and Rachel would have their own room (512) anonymously. If anyone asked, they were Mr. and Mrs. Brown—no loose ends creeping back to Rothstein.[41]

Of all Rothstein's people, Attell was the key man. The rest didn't matter as long as Abe got the bets in on the Sox. He was the moneyman.

Arnold had it on good authority from his National League friends, Stoneham and McGraw, that Moran had the better team in the Series. He counted himself lucky that the sportswriters in Chicago—who were reportedly on Comiskey's payroll—were singing a different song. Comiskey was a smart public relations man who always stocked the press room with a big spread of food and libations. In return, the writers called the Sox the "team of the century" and the ignorant public was buying it. The odds were lopsided, and it was a perfect situation for the dark horse to win. No trifecta this time, just a straight winning ticket would do it.

There was only one problem. Attell was a little man with a big ego. If he started shooting off his mouth, the road could curve back to 57th Street. Arnold knew he was taking a risk with Attell, but if Abe turned pigeon, he could be sacrificed too.

There was one other *small* problem. Too many people knew about it—a dozen gamblers and probably as many ballplayers by now. He'd have to stay put and lie low in New York next week. Arnold was worried. He could only handle the strings of so many marionettes at one time.

SEPTEMBER 28, 1919

SPORTS DESK   *NEW YORK TIMES*

NEW YORK

Sportwriters gathered around their typewriters hoping to make the right call. Christy Mathewson was chosen by the sports editor to be the point man writing on the Series. Enormous weight was placed on the fact that the '19 Sox were primarily the same pennant-winning team of 1917 and the Reds had been cellar dwellers for years. But some whispered the possibility that the Sox had reached their peak in 1917, and the Reds were just now peaking. But this was a quickly discarded theory.

The first comprehensive statistics, odds, and predictions were published on September 28, the day after the Reds and Sox were confirmed as the NL and AL pennant winners.

CATCHERS	Games	At-Bats	Runs	Hits	Batting Avg.	Fielding Avg.
Schalk, Sox	129	393	56	111	.282	.979
Wingo, Reds	75	241	30	65	.270	.971
Rariden, Reds	73	212	16	45	.212	.981

FIRST BASEMEN	Games	At-Bats	Runs	Hits	Batting Avg.	Fielding Avg.
Gandil, Sox	111	420	53	124	.295	.997
Daubert, Reds	136	521	75	142	.273	.992
SECOND BASEMEN						
E.Collins, Sox	136	508	85	162	.319	.978
Rath, Reds	134	520	75	138	.263	.977
SHORTSTOPS						
Kopf, Reds	132	493	51	133	.270	.946
Risberg, Sox	115	399	47	100	.251	.949
THIRD BASEMEN						
Groh, Reds	120	440	79	185	.307	.970
Weaver, Sox	136	558	88	165	.296	.972
LEFT FIELDERS						
Jackson, Sox	136	511	79	179	.350	.968
Duncan, Reds	27	75	7	19	.253	.1000
CENTER FIELDERS						
Roush, Reds	129	490	69	158	.322	.987
Felsch, Sox	134	404	64	138	.279	.973
RIGHT FIELDERS						
Leibold, Sox	119	427	81	128	.300	.936
Neale, Reds	136	489	57	120	.245	.953

For the back story, the *New York Times* led off with Frank Chance, leader of the Chicago Cubs in four World Series. The Cubs hated their Sox brothers across town. Chance set the tone.

There is more uproar over this series all over the

country, than I've seen in twenty years...It will be the biggest series ever played, and morale will win it one way or the other. ..and everybody, outside of Chicago, seems to want the Reds to win. It's impossible to pick a winner...[42]

In the same newspaper was a column by "neutral" Billy Evans, American League umpire and senior official-to-be in the 1919 World Series. Evans was a dignified graduate of Cornell University and had been one of Ban Johnson's respected "men in blue" since 1906. Evans gripped the rail and would not sway toward either team. The headline read: "Famous umpire sees no weakness in lineup of either World's Series contenders." However, Evans seemed to favor his league's star team in the body of his article:

> (The Sox) are a ball club prone to have one big inning. It is a ball club with such confidence in itself...the word quit is not listed in the vocabulary of the White Sox. While I am not as familiar with the ability of the Red hitters....I have always been a great admirer of Eddie Roush.[43]

Two days later (when the odds changed), Billy Evans seemed to change his mind. This time his column favored the Reds:

> If "Red Faber" of the Sox was pitching in 1917 form, I would say without any hesitation...White Sox. But...I am much in doubt as to Chicago's chances. It is my opinion that no National league club that has met the American league entry in the big series in the past ten years entered the classic with a better chance to win than the Reds.[44]

Christy Mathewson fashioned a positive review for his former team[45] entitled "Matty says Reds may Fool Experts." Mathewson wrote:

> In my opinion, the Cincinnati Reds of this season are one of the best hitting clubs that has been seen in the National League in some years. …It is my opinion that the White Sox will need all their defensive strength…to hold the Reds safely.[46]

Of course, Cincinnati sportswriters Ryder and Phelon predicted a Reds win. Fred Lieb[47] gave the Series to Chicago in six games.

Hugh Fullerton, a baseball statistician of some note, had also picked the boys of the Windy City as the winners. He was so sure his team would win that he offered to quit his job if the Sox lost. On the eve of Game One, the headlines declared, "Fullerton says Sox Dope to Win 5 out of 8 Games."[48] Fullerton is often credited as the first sports analyst to create the concept of "doping," predicting the outcome of a game or Series in advance by studying the past performance of the team and individual players. Fullerton's dope was highly respected and, if it didn't pan out, he was likely to lose his excellent reputation. Fullerton, a personal friend of Sox owner Comiskey, would play a major role as the events of October 1919 unfolded.

For weeks every major newspaper in the country had compared the rivals player-by-player and position-by-position. By general agreement of the majority of the sportswriters, the Sox doped out ahead by a close five games to four. The individual player dope was generally accepted.[49]

| Right Field: | **REDS** | Greasy Neale over Nemo Liebold/Shano Collins |
| Center Field: | **REDS** | Edd Roush over Happy Felsch |

Left Field:	SOX	Joe Jackson over Pat Duncan
1st Base:	SOX	Chick Gandil over Jake Daubert
2nd Base:	SOX	Eddie Collins over Morris Rath
Shortstop:	SOX	Swede Risberg over Larry Kopf
3rd Base:	REDS	Heinie Groh over Buck Weaver
Catcher:	SOX	Ray Schalk over Ivy Wingo/Bill Rariden
Management:	REDS	Pat Moran over Kid Gleason

One piece of information was missing. What about the pitching strength of each team? Both Evans and Mathewson wrote an epitaph for Eddie Cicotte, calling him an "old timer" and "well past the age when most pitchers are at their best."[50] Several writers mentioned Cicotte's poor performance in the final games of the season and suggested he had a "lame arm."

Even the managers of each team placed importance on pitching. In press conferences, they took their shots. "Kid" Gleason claimed, "...we have the greatest hitting team that ever played for the title. The Reds have some good pitchers, but they can't stop us." Pat Moran countered with a chilling prediction, "If we beat Cicotte in the first game we ought to win the Series." Although the Sox were 8-5 favorites for the Series, they were 2-1 underdogs for the two opening games in

GLEASON AND MORAN, OPPOSING MANAGERS
IN 1919 WORLD SERIES

Cincinnati.[51] Many agreed with Moran that Game One would tell the tale.

John McGraw went on record as predicting the pitching would be worth "at least 65 percent." He said since Cincinnati had the deeper pitching staff and the Series was the first best-of-nine contest, he "favored Cincinnati."[52] (We have to wonder if McGraw's prediction was based on a tip from his New York friend.)

The ace in the hole for the Reds was the depth of their pitching staff. With five solid starters and one good relief man (Luque), they would have fresh arms for six games, whereas the Sox were counting on two pitchers (Cicotte and Williams) now that Red Faber was injured. Dickie Kerr was a wild card. Another advantage was the low error rate for the Reds, a key element ignored by the writers. The divisive Sox made 176 errors in the 1919 season compared to only 151 by the Reds. Another statistic favored the Reds: they won 96 games compared to 88 season wins by their opponent. Were the writers too filled with Comiskey's elegant spread of wine and caviar or Herrmann's beer and sausage to examine the stats? Were the dopers doped?

But there was something else that couldn't be doped. It was called the "X" factor. This was that elusive quality known by various terms: team spirit, morale, heart, sheer desire to win. The X factor could sway the balance for the Reds. Whereas the Sox were riddled with internal conflicts and players with hungry egos, the Reds liked their manager, they liked each other, and they played as a team. It was this powerful component that could prove the dopers wrong.

On the final morning of Game One, the *New York Times* printed these words:

NERVES MAY DECIDE IT.
...nerves must be weighed in the balance as the

Chicago White Sox and the Cincinnati Reds parade to the post for the first game in Cincinnati this afternoon. Will either of the teams blow? And if such a thing happened, which team will it be? Those are the important questions that present themselves at the eleventh hour.

---

1 The description of this meeting is hypothetical and based on Detective Calvin Crim's investigative report on Cincinnati gamblers submitted to Ban Johnson on September 23-24, 1920. Baseball Hall of Fame BSS/AL ("Black Sox") files.

2 The Widmeyer family claimed that Jimmy owned part interest in the Gibson Hotel and the Cincinnati Reds. Interview with grand niece, Barbara Widmeyer Trout. Cincinnati, Ohio. July, 2002.

3 Author interview with Jim (Jimmy's nephew) and Betty Widmeyer, (Jim's wife.) October, 2004.

4 *Cincinnati Post.* October 7, 1905.

5 Shevlin's son, James C. Shevlin, played first base for the Reds, 1932-34. *Cincinnati Enquirer.* November 12, 1944.

6 *Cincinnati Enquirer.* May 14, 1950.

7 *Cincinnati Times-Star.* George Cox Obituary. May 20, 1916.

8 The author is indebted to SABR member Stanley Bard of Cincinnati for researching this information. Mr. Bard postulates that the Marqua Saloon may have been in the Mueller Building, built in 1910 and still standing.

9 *New York Times.* November 18, 1901.

10 *The Atlanta Constitution.* December 11, 1919.

11 *Cincinnati Post.* June 1, 1942.

12 Ibid. December 18, 1926.

13 Author interviews with Mowbray family members, Jack O'Mara and Loveren Sharp. June, 2005

14 Appalachian Archives #20. Hutchins Library, Berea College, Kentucky.

15 Jack O'Mara, grandson of Mowbray, interview.

16 "On Sports' Screen." *Washington Post.* May 18, 1921.

17 Frank Navin, owner of Detroit Baseball Club identifies Fred Mowbray as the "party in Cincinnati" who is furnishing the money for NL gambler Remy Dorr of New Orleans. Letter to Ban Johnson, September 9, 1920. HOF BSS/AL Files.

18 Author's Note: A central reason given by experts for the Sox player "fix" of the Series was the stinginess of their owner, Comiskey. Here we have proof of the Red's owner, Herrmann, attempting to cut his star player's meager salary on the eve of a world championship year.

[19] WWI armistice signed between Germany and Allies on November 11, 1918.

[20] Edd would hold out in succeeding years. In 1930 he would sit out the entire year. The first player to do this was Amos Rusie in 1896. Notes: Dorothy (Seymour) Mills, SABR historian.

[21] Edd had no love for the eccentric *Times-Star* sportswriter Bill Phelon, who wore a string tie and carried around a pet monkey as his companion. He was the butt of many player jokes.

[22] "Baseball owners essentially turned ballplayers into indentured servants..." Dan Nathan. *Saying It's So*. University of Illinois Press, 2003.

[23] Widmeyer would repeat this performance in 1922 when Roush held out until July.

[24] Description of Midwest gamblers based on research of Ralph Christian, SABR historian. "Beyond Eight Men Out: The Des Moines connection to the Black Sox Scandal." SABR 35, Denver. 2003.

[25] Becker's obituary said he was shot by a "highwayman." David Pietruzsa. *Rothstein*. Carroll & Graf, 2003

[26] Frankel used the name "Franklin" at this time. Philip Ball, owner of the St. Louis Browns, first identified him during the Black Sox trial of 1921. HOF BSS/AL files.

[27] Interview with Chris Trautman, Mowbray family friend and caretaker of Mowbray Gardens. June, 2005.

[28] Captain Eddie Collins was the highest paid player on the Sox (or the Reds) making $15,000 a year. Catcher Ray Schalk had a 3-year contract for $21,250. The salaries of the players who became the "Black Sox" were, as a group, lower. Joe Jackson made $6,000 in 1918 and Eddie Cicotte made $7,000. William Veeck, *Hustler's Handbook*. Berkeley Publishers, 1967.

[29] John Lardner (son of Ring). "Remember the Black Sox!" *Saturday Evening Post*. April 30, 1938.

[30] Description of Sox team conflict based on observations of Ray Schalk. *Chicago Tribune*. September 29, 1920.

[31] Ty Waterman & Mel Springer. *The Year the Red Sox won the Series*. Northeastern University Press, 1999.

[32] Descriptions of Rothstein and his life in New York based on *Rothstein*. David Pietrusza, Carroll & Graf, 2003.

[33] Winthrop would commit suicide in 1927, one year before Rothstein was shot to death.

[34] Ironically, when Rothstein was murdered in 1928, he became a sort of folk hero in the Jewish community with whom he had tried so hard to disassociate himself. David Pietrusza. *Rothstein*. Carroll & Graf, 2003.

[35] Author's Note: Conversation is hypothetical device through which to introduce the gamblers associated with Rothstein.

[36] Baseball and gambling had been aligned from the beginning. "Suspicion of 'fixes' began early in the 1860's, as the game grew in popularity." Dan

Ginsburg. *The Fix Is In*. McFarland & Sons, 1995.

[37] McGraw did get even with Chase by ensuring that he never played professional baseball again and that his name was on the indictment list for the 1920 Grand Jury hearing in Chicago, but Chase escaped again and never testified. Don Dewey and Nicholas Acocella. *The Black Prince of Baseball*. SportClassic Books, 2004.

[38] After Rothstein was murdered on November 4, 1928, "affidavits were found in his files testifying that he paid $80,000 for the World Series fix. Harold Seymour. *Baseball: The Golden Age*. Oxford University Press, 1971.

[39] Rachel Brown first identified in biography of Rothstein titled *The Big Bankroll*. Leo Katcher. Harper & Bros., 1958.

[40] Sinton Ledger, Sept. 29, 1919. HOF BSS/AL files.

[41] This plan worked well until Attell arrived at the Sinton and was told he had no reservation. He immediately took over Room 660 and, with arrogant stupidity, listed the names of Attell, Zelcer, and the Levi Brothers on the ledger. He also listed two unknown names—Sam Lauswick and J. Davis (Zork and Frankel?).

[42] *New York Times*. September 28, 1919.

[43] Ibid.

[44] *Evansville Courier* from *New York Times*. October 1, 1919.

[45] See 1916-17 Chapters for more on Mathewson as manager of the Reds.

[46] *New York Times*. September 28, 1919.

[47] Fred Lieb was writing for *New York Morning Sun* and also syndicated.

[48] *Chicago Herald and Examiner*. October 1, 1919.

[49] Victor Luhrs. *The Great Baseball Mystery*, A.S. Barnes & Co., 1966.

[50] *New York Times*. September 28, 1919.

[51] William A. Cook. *The 1919 World Series*. McFarland & Sons, 2001.

[52] Philip Seib. *The Player*. Thunder's Mouth Press, 2003.

8

The World Serious

Edd Roush, star fielder in the world series and a boy who has put Oakland City on the map in national sports, returned Sunday from Cincinnati, driving through in his touring car. ...The writer remarked that he had that day witnessed his first series contest. "The first world series game I ever saw," said Eddie, "was the first game of this series and I played in it."

– Oakland City Journal, *10/14/19*

SEPTEMBER 30, 1919   SINTON HOTEL
CINCINNATI, OHIO

Jimmy Widmeyer couldn't believe his luck. His mother had always said, "Jimmy is shot clean through with the luck of the Irish." That was one of the few memories he had of her before she died when he was six. He had been successful in talking Harry O'Neal, the Sinton desk clerk, into giving him a separate room in the "sold-out" hotel for the Series. He said it was for his out-of-town uncle from Cleveland. It only cost him two tickets for dinner and wine at the Victory Club in Newport, Kentucky. Harry and his girl were delighted. What Jimmy got in return was the cheapest guest room in the hotel, about the size of a big closet. It was kept for late-night-arriving businessmen who just needed a bed and a washbowl for one night. However, to Jimmy it was paradise since his little room (712) was right next door to Sox players Eddie Cicotte and Happy Felsch (710).[1]

The night before the opening game, Jimmy stood with a water glass pressed up against the dividing wall. He'd waited hours, not wanting to be seen coming or going from the room. He wasn't overly worried about being seen however, since none of the Sox players knew him and he looked like every other paunchy, middle-aged German man in southern Ohio.

Finally, he heard voices in the next room—multiple voices. He gripped the glass tightly. The words were garbled. He grumbled to himself. It must be the damned glass! The many facets of the fancy Sinton cut-glass must be distorting the sound. He made a mental note to get a smooth glass for tomorrow night.

Two names kept coming up—Rothstein and Kerr. He knew Kerr was a Sox pitcher but had never heard of Rothstein. He would ask Mowbray about Rothstein. His sleuthing was also impaired because he wasn't sure who was speaking at any given time. Although he recognized the players by sight, he didn't know their voices. He would watch through the transom tomorrow night to see who came into the room.

He did think he recognized a yelling, high-pitched, rapid-fire voice. It sounded like it belonged to the little man who had been standing on a chair in the Sinton lobby earlier that day, the one who was grabbing all the money on the Sox. It was pretty obvious that the gamblers knew about the fix, even if the public didn't. Whoever it was, Jimmy determined that the others were mad at this fellow about something. He heard "but that was the deal." Numbers were batted about—eighty thousand, twenty thousand. Then he heard the gambler voice yell, "after you lose tomorrow."

One thing he knew for sure, Cicotte and Felsch must be the leaders of the gang since everyone came to their room to plot the strategy. He also heard enough to know that the Reds would win the opening game. He'd been able to scrape

$10,000 together to bet at 3-1 odds, and now he knew his investment was secure. With the windfall advantage of his "spying post," he'd decided to take it one game at a time.

Tomorrow morning when it was silent next door, Jimmy planned to quickly dress and scoot out into the hall and through the servants' exit to his suite upstairs. He needed to get to the ballpark early to meet his cohorts. He knew he could gain early entry into Redland Field

SINTON HOTEL, CINCINNATI, OHIO, CIRCA 1919

through his friend Maxie at the west entrance. He would then find the Reds Boosters sitting around the band and tell Mowbray that their bets were good—at least for one game.

SEPTEMBER 30, 1919   TRAIN STATION CINCINNATI, OHIO

Hugh Fullerton, age 46, nationally known sports columnist for the *Chicago Herald and Examiner*, arrived by train early Tuesday morning, September 30.[2] He was looking forward to seeing his friend Christy Mathewson later that evening. They would be roommates at the Sinton Hotel during the Series.

"Matty" had been asked to write special columns on the Series for the *New York Times*. Along with Ring Lardner, their syndicated columns were the most widely read and oft-quoted in the business. Fullerton had over thirty years as a writer, and Matty had sixteen playing years and three of managing the Reds.[3] With the two combined lifetimes, they had spent in the sporting world, they knew just about every major league player over the past thirty years. Reporters rode on the trains with players from city to city and often played cards and got to know them.

Hugh had the usual excitement of a sportswriter covering the biggest sporting event of the year. Although he had doped the Sox to win, he was prepared for an interesting contest. He had no idea how interesting the week was about to become. In a succession of interactions, Hugh would become privy to a secret he would have preferred not to know, a secret that could destroy his career.

He first glimpsed what was to come through fellow scribes. Jim Crusinberry of the *Chicago Tribune* was standing outside the Sinton when Hugh's taxi drove up. He greeted Hugh and prepared him for what he would see inside the hotel lobby. "It's crazy in there, Hugh. Wait till you see it. Some little guy is standing on a chair waving thousand-dollar bills. He's yelling for everyone to give him money on Chicago. Says he'll cover any amount."

The little man standing on the chair was just doing his job. His orders were to "catch the fish." Unfortunately, his method of doing so was exceedingly more crass and blatant than his boss, Arnold Rothstein, would have preferred.

All day the rumors were flying. It seemed to Hugh that everyone he met was talking about "something wrong in Cincinnati," "mysterious changes in the odds," "Sox might try to throw the Series." That evening, Hugh and several sportswriters went to a Newport, Kentucky roadhouse for dinner. As they were coming in, "Sleepy" Bill Burns was coming out. Although he hadn't seen him for a while, Hugh knew Burns and they exchanged greetings. Bill Burns was a former pitcher for Chicago who had knocked around the major leagues in the first decade of the twentieth century. Hugh had always liked this "odd, interesting character."[4] As a young reporter in Chicago, Hugh had given Bill good reviews during his playing years. He'd also heard that Burns had a become a professional gambler in recent years. Hugh always had his ear to the ground.

When Bill saw Hugh, he hung back as if he wanted to talk. Hugh walked outside with him. Bill gave Hugh a strange look and said simply, "Get wise and get yourself some money, Hugh."

For the next few minutes Hugh and Bill stood outside the roadhouse talking. It was Bill who talked and Hugh listened intently. He told his old friend the whole story, what he knew of it anyway. The Series was a done deal, fixed for Cincinnati to win. Some St. Louis gamblers had gotten to Cicotte. He was going to lay down tomorrow. The word was out. That's why the odds were dropping.

Hugh asked for names. Only one was forthcoming—Abe Attell, former featherweight boxing champion. Hugh realized it must have been Abe in the Sinton earlier that day. Hugh had covered some Attell bouts years back but didn't recognize him. Hugh asked if other players were involved. Burns said he'd heard the first baseman, "Chick" Gandil, was in on it. But he was quick to say he wasn't sure. Gandil was known as a wild man, no one to fool around with. Hugh asked if Kid Gleason knew what was going on. Burns doubted it. He knew he'd already said too much.

When Hugh got back to the hotel, Matty was there in the room. He told him the strange events of the day. When he told him what Burns had said, Matty exploded. "Damn them. They have it coming. I caught two crooks and they whitewashed them." Hugh knew exactly what he meant. Matty had caught Hal Chase and Lee Magee throwing games when he managed them in Cincinnati. He had submitted affidavits against Hal Chase, but National League President John Heydler had let him off claiming the evidence was inconclusive. Matty was in the war in Europe and couldn't be there in person. He'd been furious about it ever since.

Hugh asked Matty if he thought it was possible for players to actually "fix" a World Series. Matty shook his head and gave reasons why this seemed impossible to him. A pitcher couldn't do it alone. He'd be yanked. Too many players would have to be involved or bribed and then the secret wouldn't be safe. Hugh asked if a manager could do it. Matty said no. He couldn't control the players. They'd hustle anyway. Matty then said, "No player would want to risk everything—his career, his future, his income—for a bundle of quick cash."[5] Hugh would remember Matty's prophetic words in the difficult months to come.

Their conversation was interrupted by a rap on the board. They looked at each other wondering who would be knocking at two in the morning. Their colleague Ring Lardner stood in the hallway. He said he was on his way to bed, but had a bedtime story for them that couldn't wait until tomorrow. Lardner had been dining at another Newport hot spot that evening and spotted a member of the Reds in a booth "drinking heavily with companions who bore earmarks of professional gambling." The player was Dutch Ruether, starting pitcher for the Reds the next day.[6] He said that when Moran found out who Dutch was with, he was hopping mad.

Matty and Hugh looked at each other with the same thought: "The Reds too?" What was going on here? First the Sox, and now the Reds. Were both teams planning to throw the Series? Now *that* would be interesting.

Hugh and Matty agreed to carefully analyze the play of

both teams the next day to see if anything fishy was going on. As a former pitcher, Matty would watch Cicotte and Ruether while Hugh would concentrate on the field. They were putting this plan into action when they were observed by one of the players' wives in the stands the next day.

OCTOBER 1, 1919
REDLAND FIELD CINCINNATI, OHIO

"The World Series had attained such a devoted, quasi-religious mass following that in the century's second decade it out-ranked all native sports classics—heavyweight title fights, the Indianapolis 500 auto race, the Kentucky Derby, any tennis event, and even the Olympic Games when the U.S. was heavily represented."[7]

At 9:15 a.m., Essie held her mother-in-law's hand so tightly that Laura Roush winced with pain as they pushed through the throngs of people waiting outside Redland Field for the gates to open at ten. The City of Cincinnati was a living, breathing creature of one mind on this day. Unlike the sprawling diversity of New York or Chicago, Cincinnati was a compact, German-Irish culture. The mass energy of the smaller city was focused on one place—Redland Field. Essie could feel the pulsating electricity that seemed to emanate from the earth beneath their feet. As they reached the press gate entrance off Findlay Street, Essie was out of breath. She presented her pass to Lou Wolfson[8] and motioned for Laura and Fred (Edd's twin brother) to follow her.

As she located their seats and got them settled, she thought about Edd's father, Will. What a shame he couldn't be here to see his son play in a World Series. How proud he was of Edd, whose baseball career he had fought for. Why did God have to take him so soon, just a year ago?

Essie waved goodbye to her in-laws and made her way to the wives' box. She would have much preferred a place in the stands where she could be just another anonymous fan and "hoot and holler" to her soul's delight. The desire had also grown out of her embarrassment on those occasions when her husband decided to throw one of his angry fits and everyone looked at her. She knew the signals. It would begin with him dragging his forty-eight-ounce bat behind him as he marched toward the pitcher's mound. That was Essie's cue to start screaming "No, Edd!" That was also the cue for the rest of the Reds to pour off the bench, fists clenched and ready to fight.

When Edd's face was within spitting distance of the pitcher, he'd begin his tirade: "You sonbitch! You keep throwing at me and I'll clean out your infield. My cleats are long and sharp!" It was usually the opposing team's manager or catcher who came running out to make peace. If they could convince Edd that the beaners would stop, he would return to the batter's box. If not, the shouting would continue until the Reds bench unloaded and all hell broke loose. Then, as the fans went wild, Essie wanted to dissolve into a small puddle under her chair.

Luckily, the Reds' wives had an unspoken agreement in such situations.

If someone's husband goofed up, everyone remained silent. As the fans cackled and booed around them, the women would be stoic. If Essie was sitting next to the embarrassed wife, she would keep her eyes on the field while subtly placing her hand over the woman's hand. That reassurance would calm her. They'd all been through the pain. They were a special sorority unto themselves.

Surely that wouldn't happen today, not in a World Series. Essie chuckled as she remembered Ring Lardner calling it the "World Serious." Surely they would all be gentlemen today. She smirked at the thought of her own naiveté. How many times had she heard Edd say, "On that ball field, all friendships cease." And this contest was worth several thousand dollars to each player. She knew the Reds wanted it badly; she could only assume that the White Sox felt the same. They all wanted to be the Champions of the World. She wondered if the Sox wives were feeling the same way right now. She closed her eyes and silently prayed there would be no blood to scrape off the dirty uniform tonight.

Suddenly a "Hello, Essie" interrupted her thoughts. She looked up to see Belle Moran sitting in the box next door (140)[9] with her own retinue including Mrs. Grover C. Alexander and Mrs. Bill Killifer. Mrs. Moran continued, "By the way, congratulations. Pat said that Edd clinched the batting title in the Cubs game. You must be very proud."

Essie thought, "You're darn tootin' I'm proud!" But she said politely, "Yes, thank you, Belle."

They chatted a few more minutes until the arrival of other wives required new topics of conversation. The new entries were the two "Rubys" (Groh and Rariden). Essie greeted her two friends warmly. She smiled and nodded at Ruby Groh, quickly assessing her outfit for the day—from Giddings department store, no doubt. Essie liked Ruby well enough but was a bit jealous of her stylish clothes. But Essie was proud of the new hat she was wearing today. Her sister Tina had sent it last week. It was that new "mustard" color with a lovely black feather sitting jauntily on the right side of the black hatband. She wondered if her friends would notice.

As Kate Sallee, Alice Fisher, Ethel Ruether, and Mattie Mae Wingo joined them, Essie was glad she was not particularly adept at "wives' talk." She wanted to observe the drama unfolding before her. The new bleachers looked swell, she thought. And there was the familiar billboard that she had seen so many times above her husband's head in the outfield—

"Make it a Hit with Puritan." Looking at the box of Puritan candy on the billboard always made Essie hungry around the middle of the game. And there were the new American flags on top of the press box and the eighty-two-foot flagpole in center field. She mused over the image of Edd wrapping his body around it to make one of his incredible "circus catches."[10] Essie relaxed; she was home.

With only officials with passes circulating in the ballpark this early, it was quiet. Some of the men would come over and "pay respects" to the wives. The first was Matty Schwab, Redland Superintendent and Groundskeeper.[11] He was a nice, quiet fellow and well liked by players and wives. He came over to say "hello" to the boss's wife, Mrs. Moran. Essie thought he was fishing for compliments because of the new scoreboard he had built in right field for the Series. Belle Moran complied by saying, "The new scoreboard is grand, Matty. And the field looks very nice. Thank you."

Next in line was a group of three well-dressed businessmen who must have been Reds Boosters to have entered the park early. As they approached the wives' box, Essie recognized Jimmy Widmeyer. Jimmy gushed over Essie, taking her gloved hand in a gallant gesture. He then introduced his "associates," Fred Mowbray and Dan Moul. Essie remembered Mowbray from the Business Men's Club dinner and was pleased with the opportunity to thank him for the lovely Rookwood vase. Mowbray responded cheerfully, "We intend to see our boys win big today!" Little did Essie know that he wasn't just making a shallow prediction. He had good reason to believe he would win a lot of money.

As Jimmy and his friends moved on, Essie glanced up at the press box behind her. There were so many reporters. It seemed more like New York than Cincinnati. She remembered what Edd told her about the one local sportswriter—Jack somebody.[12] Edd said he was a drunk and they had to wake him up at game time. As she looked up, she thought she recognized that nice young sportswriter who had dinner with Edd at the end of the season in New York. His name was Fred Lieb.[13] She didn't know that at that moment, Fred and his colleague, Dan Daniel of the *New York Morning Sun*, were reviewing Fred's prognostications syndicated by the Al Monroe Elias Bureau. Fred had given the Series to Chicago in six games.

As Essie took in the movement around her, she recognized Christy Mathewson just a couple of rows away. She hadn't seen him since he returned from the war. He was walking toward

1919 WORLD SERIES SOUVENIR PROGRAM
WITH REDS MANAGER PAT MORAN ON THE COVER

the press box with a small, older man wearing a floppy fedora with a press pass sticking up. Somehow, the hat looked out of place on him. He looked more like a university professor than a reporter. Matty towered over the man, and the pair seemed involved in a serious conversation. Whereas the other reporters were shaking hands and enjoying the morning, these two stood apart studying the program booklet with frowning faces.

GAME ONE

The weather was unseasonably warm with a temperature over 80 degrees when the Reds stepped onto the field at 12:20. The crowd roared. The White Sox, entered the grounds at 1:10. The band struck up the song "Hail, Hail, the Gang's All Here." Then they played a popular song of 1919 titled "I'm Forever Blowing Bubbles." Both teams took pre-game warm-ups, with movie cameras on the field filming the crowd and players. Celebrities such as Senator Warren G. Harding, Cincinnati Mayor John Galvin, and entertainer George M. Cohan settled into their box seats. Federal Judge Kenesaw Mountain Landis, later to be named the first commissioner of baseball, was in attendance, as were five former Reds managers: Clark Griffith, Hank O'Day, Joe Tinker, Buck Herzog, and Christy Mathewson. Two Cuban newspaper editors were on hand to watch their native son, Adolfo Luque, Reds relief pitcher.

During batting practice, young boys in the temporary bleachers raced out to grab balls that went past the infielders. Cincinnati policemen were stationed at five-yard intervals around the barriers. They didn't stop the boys from collecting their souvenirs. In fact, a policemen or two picked up a ball for himself.[14]

As game time approached, managers William "Kid" Gleason and Pat Moran met on the field and shook hands for the photographers. The band played "The Wearing of the

Green" in honor of the two sons of Ireland. As the players on both teams gathered around the plate for photos, Ray Schalk walked over to Edd and shook his hand. They had been friends for a brief time in 1913 when Edd had his stint with the Sox, before being sent to the minors. Edd remembered the kindness of Schalk in that difficult rookie season. He was delighted to see the little catcher again.

The band, directed by Walter Enberger, played "The Star-

Thomas Bressler Family Collection (son of Rube Bressler)

ABE ATTELL STANDING BETWEEN REDS PLAYERS LUQUE AND ELLER, OPENING DAY OF 1919 WORLD SERIES[16] NOTE: INSET PHOTO OF ATTELL FROM *CHICAGO TRIBUNE*[17]

Spangled Banner."[15] Then John Philip Sousa came on the field to conduct the band in a rendition of "The Stars and Stripes Forever." As the band played the patriotic music, the players on both teams stood solemnly while newsmen flashed cameras in rapid succession.

At this moment Jimmy Widmeyer recognized the owner of the mysterious "gambler voice" from the night before. He was looking down at the Reds bench when he saw him. It was the same fellow who had been taking bets in the Sinton lobby the day before. He was out there *on the field*, standing right with the Reds players in front of their bench. What sheer audacity! The man was flaunting the secret for all the world to see."

Or, perhaps, there was another reason for Abe Attell to be standing with the Reds as Game One was about the start. Could this have been a signal to a cohort, perhaps someone in New York who needed to know "the fish were caught"?

As Edd Roush jogged out to center field, home plate umpire Charles "Cy" Rigler and his fellow arbiters Billy Evans, Ernie Quigley, and Richard Nallin took up their positions. Rigler and Quigley were employed by the National League, and Evans and Nallin were from the American League. Dutch Ruether completed his warm-up tosses to Ivey Wingo.

At 2 p.m., Cy Rigler called "Play Ball!"[18]

Ruether's first pitch to leadoff hitter Shano Collins was a fastball for a called strike. Collins then singled to center. With two batters out, "Weaver lifted to left field. Roush raced over from his position in center and made a remarkable one-hand catch, retiring the side."[19]

Belle Moran winked at Essie. She exhaled long and slow. She was thankful now that she and little Mary had tiptoed around their apartment early that morning. This gave Edd the extra hour of sleep that was so precious to him. Throughout his life, Edd would insist that he "needed nine hours of sleep a night" to be at his best the next day.

Ruether shut down the Sox in the first inning without a run. In the press box, Matty smiled as Hugh showed him his score sheet with no circles on it. No suspicious plays noted. Whatever Ruether's evening of pre-game celebration had been, it did not appear to affect him on the mound.

In the bottom half of the first inning, Eddie "Knuckles" Cicotte took the mound. Cicotte specialized in a knuckleball, hence the nickname. He also threw a shine ball. The Reds' shine ball artist, Hod Eller, may have learned from Cicotte when he went to spring training in 1916 with the White Sox. Both the knuckleball and the shine ball were difficult to deliver and often got away from the pitcher.

Cicotte's first pitch was taken by second baseman Morrie Rath for a called strike. Cicotte's second pitch was to become the most discussed (and cussed) pitch of the Series. The pitch plunked Rath in the back, giving him first base. The play seemed to surprise Cicotte. He took the time to walk along the first base line with Rath, talking to him and asking if he was hurt.

As rumored, was *this* the signal to the gamblers that the fix was on?[20] Or was it merely a knuckleball that got away from Cicotte? In his own defense, he would later contend that hitting Rath was not planned or intentional. The misplay shook him up and he was never the same after that.[21] It was possible that the "misplay" was the result of the emotional ambivalence of a man with a conscience who was about to throw a game. The fact that he had $10,000 of bribe money sewn into his clothes was a tangible reminder of the ugly promise he had made. Seller's remorse?[22]

Up in the press box, Hugh and Matty looked ominously at each other. Were the Sox rumors true? Was this the beginning of the end?

First baseman Jake Daubert, who might have been expected to lay down a sacrifice bunt, instead singled Rath to third. Heinie Groh came to the plate. Many believed Heinie was the game's best at his position. He still used the old batting style of facing the pitcher. He described his stance: "By standing with your face towards the pitcher, you can see both foul lines, watch the pitcher's windup motion better, and follow the ball better."[23] From this frontal perch, Heinie used his short, fat "bottle bat" to bunt or swing effectively. Groh followed with a sacrifice fly to Joe Jackson in left, bringing Rath in for the run.

The crowd shrieked with delight as Edd walked to the plate for the first time. While watching from his box seat, George Wright may have felt a kinship with Edd as he remembered such applause for himself, the first great hitter for the Reds in 1869.[24]

Edd moved around in the box to confuse Cicotte. He strained to find a ball with his name on it, but Cicotte wisely refused to engrave one for him. Edd walked to first base, then promptly stole second. Pat Duncan, the recently acquired left fielder, grounded out to shortstop to end the inning with the Reds leading 1-0.

In the second inning Chicago scored its only run of the contest. Shoeless Joe Jackson led off with a ground ball to shortstop Larry Kopf. His wild throw allowed Jackson to reach second base. Happy Felsch sacrificed him to third. (Many writers after the Series disagreed with manager Gleason's many decisions to have Felsch bunt rather than swing the bat.) Jackson scored on Gandil's bloop single into short left field.

Edd opened the fifth inning, flying out to deep center field. In this inning the Reds broke the game wide open, with what seemed to be a little extra help from Eddie Cicotte. Pat Duncan singled over Eddie Collins's head into right field. On Kopf's ground ball back to the box, Cicotte seemed to hesitate before throwing to shortstop Swede Risberg. Duncan was forced out but the Sox were not able to complete what seemed to be an easy double play. Neale and Wingo singled, with Kopf scoring on Wingo's hit.

Matty and Hugh shared quizzical looks. Was Cicotte doing it all by himself? This time Hugh circled the play on his score-card and Matty headed down to the fence to get a closer look. When he arrived he could tell that the Sox catcher, Ray Schalk, was hopping mad. He could only guess that Cicotte was refus-ing to follow Schalk's signals. Matty knew that Schalk was a bad man to cross. His short, 160-pound frame was wound tight with a blazing desire to win. He was a little man with strong emotions, a twin brother of Abe Attell in another life.

Pitcher Ruether delivered a blast to the left-field fence that was good for three bases, Neale and Wingo scoring. Ruether was a good-hitting pitcher. When he came to the majors with the Cubs two years earlier, he was occasionally used as a pinch hitter. There was discussion then about converting him to play first base to utilize his hitting talents, but Moran had polished the pitcher in him to a fine gloss.

Morrie Rath doubled in Ruether, and Daubert completed the scoring, singling to right field with Rath scoring the fifth run of the inning. At this point Kid Gleason, disgusted with Cicotte's performance pulled him from the game, replacing him with Roy Wilkinson. "For the rest of the afternoon the Sox played like a beaten team, beaten not only for this game, but the Series."[25]

Matty was down at the fence when Gleason pulled Cicotte. He turned around and looked up at Hugh. Simultaneously they mouthed the same word from a distance, "Cicotte."

The Reds scored two runs in the seventh inning and one in the eighth to end as victors with a blistering score of 9-1. Dutch Ruether was the uncontested star of the game, provid-ing excellent pitching and two critical triples. Edd would later say, "Dutch never played so well before or after that game."

Tom Swope would write of Ruether, "He's Cincinnati's hero all right, and entitled to a big head."[26] This line was humorous since, in fact, Ruether was endowed by nature with an unusually large head.

As he ran off the field, Pat Moran acknowledged the fans as he shouted, "You all helped…helped a lot. And thank you." After the game Gleason spoke what turned out to be prophetic words. "Cicotte hit Rath in the first inning, and he was not himself thereafter. I could have taken him out then, but I trusted that luck would enable Eddie to regain his control."

Others, from places like Des Moines and Manhattan, saw it differently as they walked away calculating their winnings. Just in time too. The odds reversed to 10-7 in favor of the Reds for Game Two.

Some remembered Moran's prophetic words, "If we win the first game…"

In the showers, the Reds were elated about their win. With towels, they slapped each other on the behinds and laughed uproariously. Ruether received an extra affectionate flogging for his fine performance. Wingo, who always started the singing at the brewery, initiated a rendition of "Root, Root, Root for the Reds!" Edd threw his towel over his shoulder and added his tremulous bass to the chorus. He was feeling particularly good about his performance that day. Although he hadn't gotten the hits he wanted, his fielding had been superb. He had notched eight putouts.

Sixth Inning: *"Roush killed a hit for J. Collins with a long run and a fine catch in deep left."*

Eighth Inning: *"Roush ran over into right field and robbed E. Collins of a hit."*

Ninth Inning (one out): *"Felsch tried desperately to launch the Sox off in a belated rally, driving the ball far into center, but the greyhound Roush raced back and made a glittering corral.*

Roush's great catch took whatever little starch was left in the White Sox ."[27]

In the next day's papers, the writers would describe those saves in glowing terms.

> "Mr. Rousch seems to have caught Mr. Felsch's fly while facing Kentucky....if he hadn't have of (Felsch) would have tied up the game."
> – Ring Lardner, *Syracuse Herald*

> "They're talking about just two guys here today, Eddie Roush and Walter Ruether. There may be swell fielders in the National league, but Roush showed them all up yesterday. Some player that boy."
> – Tad, *Syracuse Herald*

> "The Sox to-day [sic] might have had the services of one of the most brilliant players of all time (Rousch) if only..."[28]
> – Jim Corbett, syndicated.

None gave quarter to Cicotte.

> "Cicotte's last three games in the regular season had been bad and this was the fourth."
> – Tris Speaker, interview reported by Mathewson

> "...it appears that Moran's Reds will win in seven games at the outside."
> – Christy Mathewson, *New York Times*

> "There is no excuse whatever for the ace of

the White Sox."
– Hugh Fullerton, *Atlanta Constitution*

As the workers picked up the strewn Crackerjack boxes and peanut sacks at Redland Field, crowds of people gathered in downtown Cincinnati to celebrate. The *Cincinnati Enquirer* said it was the largest crowd the city had seen since the armistice was signed ending World War I. Eddie Cicotte, the losing pitcher, was carried in effigy on a stretcher by boys of the 9th Ward. A trumpeter and drummer pounding on an available washtub led the parade.

> The gin mills became drain pans as the Queen City aficionados celebrated with alcoholic gusto, as if they knew in their hearts that this was an unusual windfall not apt to occur again in the Series. It was a case for drink, for tomorrow the Reds would probably die in the next five straight games. At the Peruvian Club, Garry Herrmann threw a stupendous victory party at which each guest received a take-home gift of a barrel of pickles.

The celebration lasted long into the night, but the Roush family was sleeping soundly in their Gilbert Hill apartment. Essie slept with a smile on her face, cuddled warmly next to her hero.

---

1   Sinton Hotel Ledger, September 30, 1919. HOF BSS/AL files.

2   Fred Lieb would describe Fullerton as "Mr. Baseball Writer," the best-known writer in the first twenty-five years of the 20th Century. *The Sporting News*, 1964.

3   Author's Note: More on Matty's leadership of the Reds in 1916 ad 1917 chapters.

4   Interview with Fullerton. *The Sporting News*. October 17, 1935.

5   John Lardner. *Saturday Evening Post*. April 30, 1938. Victor Luhrs. *The Great Baseball Mystery*. A.S. Barnes & Co, 1966.

6   Lardner's story was confirmed by Reds manager Pat Moran the same night. Moran told Fullerton that "Chicago gamblers were out to get his pitchers drunk." Hugh Fullerton, *The Sporting News*. October 17, 1935.

7   Al Stump. *Cobb*. Algonquin Books, 1996.

8   William A. Cook. *The 1919 World Series*. McFarland & Co., 2001. The final player bonus for the Reds came to $5,207.01. *World Series Encyclopedia*. Thomas Nelson & Sons. 1961

9   *Cincinnati Enquirer*. September 2, 1919.

10   Lee Allen. *The Cincinnati Reds*, Putnam, 1948.

11   Matty Schwab would take excellent care of Redland/Crosley Field for 69 years, retiring in 1963.

12   Jack Ryder. (See 1918 chapter for more information.)

13   Author's Note: Fred Lieb and his wife, Mary Ann, became lifelong friends of the Roushs.

14   William A. Cook. *The 1919 World Series*. McFarland & Sons, 2001.

15   First recorded instance of the playing of the "Star-Spangled Banner" at a baseball game was in 1862 when Cammeyer opened the Union Grounds. Robert H. Schaefer. "Biography of Lipman Pike." SABR Bio web site: www.sabr.org

16   Author's Note: Had anyone recognized Attell in this photo, it could have proven the case against him when he was brought to testify for the Cook County Grand Jury on the Black Sox Scandal in 1920. He admitted being in Chicago on Oct. 3, but denied being in Cincinnati during the World Series. Likely due to Rothstein's power, no one came forth to disprove him.

17   Inset photo of Attell from *Chicago Daily Tribune*. May 14, 1921.

18   Game descriptions contributed by Jim Sandoval, SABR historian and 1919 WS expert.

19   *Spalding's Official Baseball Guide of 1920*.

20   Eliot Asinof. *Eight Men Out*. Henry Holt & Co., 1963. Note: Edd Roush would later say the pitch was a knuckleball that Cicotte lost control of.

21   After the game, Cicotte claimed he was "unnerved" by this play. He said, "...when I hit Rath it seemed to have a strange effect on me. I felt so badly...I lost all control of the ball in the fourth inning." Frank Menke. *The Syracuse Herald*. October 2, 1919. Two years later, Judge McDonald would recall his first conversation with Cicotte in which he said, "I intended to walk the first man. Instead, I hit him. It hurt my conscience and I realized I was doing wrong." *New York Times*. July 26, 1921.

22   Cicotte would tell reporter Ed Bang, "I pitched the best ball I knew how after that first ball in Game One. But I lost because I was hit, not because I was throwing the game. *Cleveland News*. September 29, 1920.

23   F.C. Lane. Batting. SABR Publication, 2001.

24 Wright was an original member of the 1869 Red Stockings, the first professional baseball team. The team was undefeated in 81 games. Rhodes
& Snyder. *Redleg Journal*. Road West Publishing, 2000.

25 *Spalding's Official Baseball Guide of 1920.*

26 *Cincinnati Times-Star*. October 2, 1919.

27 Ibid.

28 Author's Note: Corbett's quote refers to the White Sox sending Roush
back to the minors in 1913 after a brief trial.

On a sad note, the excitement of the first game win may have been too
much for one fan. A *Cincinnati Times-Star* story said that Joseph W. Pugh
former chief of police of Covington, Kentucky "died from the excitement
of the opening ballgame of the World Series. Coroner Bauer said that his
death was from a stroke of apoplexy, brought on by the game he had just
witnessed. Pugh suffered the attack while driving his automobile home
after the game. Victor Luhrs. *The Great Baseball Mystery*. A.S. Barnes &
Co. 1966

9

Deep Throat

...Cincinnati was getting ready to tear down the fountain and get a statue of Pat Moran in the public square of Porkopolis....
– Edd Roush, 1983

OCTOBER 2, 1919
METROPOLE HOTEL   CINCINNATI, OHIO

The euphoria of the day was finally beginning to wear off as Edd stood outside the Metropole Hotel at 6th and Vine Street in the evening of October 2. As he looked up into the orange-streaked sky, he gave thanks to that Greater Being who had granted his one wish for this day—that he wouldn't get one of his famous charley horses during the big game. As he leaned against the building he crossed one foot over the other and allowed himself a few moments of pride as he relived his one-handed catch in the sixth inning. He lit one of his favorite cigars and recalled the glorious events of Game Two...

The first three innings were uneventful. Neither side pushed a run across. One scary moment resulted from a great liner by Schalk that looked dangerous when it left the bat, but Edd stopped it cold.

In the bottom of the fourth inning, Sox pitcher Lefty Williams opened the door to the Reds victory. Rath walked and was sacrificed to second by Daubert. Groh walked to put runners on first and second. As Edd moved into the batter's box he psyched himself up for the lefty. He looked hard at Williams and thought, "This is it, you busher. I'm not walking this time. You haven't got anything, and you're playing *our* game now."

With a 2-1 count, Edd lined a hard single into center field, scoring Rath and moving Groh to third. Duncan was up next, and Williams took him to a full count. Edd cooled his heels on first, then got ambitious. He was on a roll; he knew he could steal second. He'd have to slide hard, and he could already taste the dirt in his mouth. He ran for second with all his might, but the little dynamo squatting behind home had seen it coming. In two seconds it was over. Schalk threw to Eddie Collins and Umpire Nallin yelled, "Out!" Schalk and Collins, two future Hall-of-Famers, had made that play a thousand times before. It felt good to make Roush the goat this time. The Sox still had something left.

If Edd had looked up at the wives' box at that moment, he would have seen Essie look down with embarrassment and pretend to adjust the collar of her blouse.

With Groh remaining at third, Duncan walked, and Kopf tripled to the fence in left field, scoring both teammates. Neale grounded out to second base, ending the inning with the Reds ahead 3-0.

In the top of the fifth, Slim Sallee retired the Sox in order. They had been hitting Slim, but, as Fullerton would note in his column the next day, "It's not hard to hit Sallee until hits mean runs." The old pitcher was worth his salt.

In the top of the sixth inning, the Sox seemed to come alive. Collins and Weaver both got hits. Then Sallee stared down Joe Jackson and struck him out.

Edd remembered many times the strange thing that happened next. He couldn't believe his eyes. Sallee balked! To all appearances he simply started to wind up for delivery, making no effort to throw Weaver out at second, then he just stopped dead. Edd would later say, "It was as if he just blacked out." Larry Kopf, at shortstop, yelled, "Hey, Slim!" But it was too late. Umpire Evans moved Weaver to third. A mysterious gift from big Slim.

That was enough to rejuvenate the Sox. Happy Felsch came up next and hit a long beauty to center that had "home run" written all over it. Now it was up to Edd. If he missed it, the Sox rally might win the day. He marked the ball within the first second of its departure from the bat. Then, he turned his back on the ball and ran for all he was worth toward the center field wall. He turned and leaped upward and "plunk!" The ball landed flat in the middle of his little glove. The stands went wild. The fans who were watching the game outside the field on the hilltop of Fairview Heights were seen doing a snake dance.[1]

Essie would remember that she lost all sense of decorum and jumped out of her seat and screamed. Edd would remember that catch as long as he lived.

The Sox battled back, hitting Sallee for two runs in the seventh, but the game ended with the Reds victorious 4-2. They now led the Series two games to none as the teams prepared to move on to Chicago for the next three contests.

After the game the local newspapers raved over Edd's fielding.

> Roush took thirteen flies in the first two games, several of them catches of such sterling beauty that the crowd could hardly believe their eyes. This series, if nothing else, is stamping Roush as the greatest center-fielder in the game—he has no rivals.

In his column, "Wake of the News," Jack Lait wrote,

"Many a noble hit went down into the cold records of time with its modest tombstone inscribed 'Flied out to Rousch [sic]' or 'Out, Kopf to Daubert.'" Then, he waxed poetic.

> Hail Rousch [sic], the Reaper of Reddingham,
> He spears home runs wherever they am,
> While Kopf, the capper of infield bingles,
> Makes dogmeat out of White Sox singles.[2]

Even Sox manager Kid Gleason would say, "Fielding like that only happens once in a lifetime and robbed us of enough runs to win. Roush is a marvel in the outfield and my players give him all the credit for his work."[3]

The New York Tribune said if Felsch's flyer had touched the ground it would have been a home run. Although it hurt him to do it, Hugh Fullerton wrote, "Roush made one of the greatest catches ever seen in a World Series. The Reds showed more fight, more punch and more spirit than the White Sox."[4] Ironically, Fullerton had predicted the Williams and Sox loss in Game Two when he originally "doped" the Series, 5-3 Reds. He was still smarting from Cicotte's loss he had predicted as a close win, 4-2 Sox.[5]

To the delight of Edd and Essie's hometown, Damon Runyon wrote, "Wherefore is Oakland City, Indiana, now a sort of little sister to the proud, old Queen City of Ohio, linked by the bond of the baseball greatness of their favorite son."[6]

Federal Judge Kenesaw Landis was quoted as saying, "The Reds are the most formidable team I have ever seen!"[7]

Edd remembered Essie's pride as she kissed him goodbye at the Findlay Street entrance. She would not be coming to Chicago for the next three games. This decision, like most, was made jointly by husband and wife. The reasons were twofold: Mary had been slightly ill for the last week and a rheumatic

NOW WHAT HAVE YOU, MISTER GLEASON?

CARTOON RECAP OF GAME 2

fever scare was rampant; Edd thought it was safer for Essie to stay at home. The emotion of the Cincinnati fans had been extreme and, if this were also true in Chicago, it could be dangerous. And, to Essie, there was always fear of that "element"—big-city negroes. Since the team was leaving immediately for the train, they only had a few minutes to say goodbye. As he pulled away from her embrace, she held him firmly by the shoulders and said with a smile, "You played well today, my Beauty! I love you, Edd." This would warm him through the night as the train headed northwest to Chicago.

ENTER DEEP THROAT

Most of the fans had dispersed. Essie was home on Gilbert Hill by now, and the players were standing around smoking cigars and chatting in small groups. They were dressed in their blue traveling uniforms for the trip. (The Sox wore the same uniforms home that they had played in that day.)[9] The Reds were waiting for their taxis to take them to the overnight train headed for Chicago and Games Three, Four, and Five of the Series. In the

FOUNTAIN SQUARE, CINCINNATI, OHIO, CIRCA 1919.

dusk with the streetlights twinkling around them, the scene looked like a Van Gogh painting of the sidewalk cafe in Arles.

As Edd glanced down to Fountain Square, he noticed the familiar Widmeyer newsstand on the corner. It was just about closing time. Jimmy saw Edd and nodded to him. Then, he paused a minute. Should he tell Edd the secret?

He left his newsstand and solemnly walked toward Edd. Jimmy's voice trembled with excitement as he delivered the lines he had been rehearsing in his head. There was no formal greeting. The message was too urgent.[10]

"Roush, I want to tell you something," Jimmy said. "Did you hear about the squabble the White Sox got into after the first ballgame?"

"No, what about it?" Edd said.

"Well, the gamblers has got to them, and they're supposed to throw the Series to the Cincinnati ball club."

Jimmy paused to calculate the impact of his words.

Edd frowned. Gossip! As he would later say, "You hear anything around a World Series." He turned to walk away.

Jimmy was dumbfounded. How could Edd walk away

when he had just told him the biggest secret in the world—the secret that Jimmy had been living with for days now? Edd Roush didn't care?

Jimmy decided to give his friend the benefit of the doubt. Perhaps more evidence was required, so he followed Edd and continued. "They didn't get their money after the first ball-game, and they had a meeting up in Cicotte`s room last night. They had a heck of a go-around up there."

Becoming annoyed, Edd turned back and asked the logical question. "How the devil do you know this, Jimmy?"

The reply came swiftly and without hesitation. "The meeting was up in Cicotte's room. I have a room right next to theirs, and I heard everything they said. They didn't get their money, and they agreed among themselves to try to go out and try to win. Gleason knows about it. He was up there too."

"Well, I'll be dogged."

Edd didn't want to believe the story. He'd just played a hard game and certainly couldn't accept the idea that the opposing team had just let them win. Had he dreamed catching Felsch's long fly? If the Sox were throwing games, they had a weird way of showing it.

He decided that his friend had lost his mind. He didn't want to prolong the conversation. Somehow he felt complicity by merely talking about it.

Jimmy started to tell him more, "There was seven of them."

Edd cut him off. "Good night, Jimmy," he said, and walked away.

A crestfallen Jimmy stood in the dark. He had wanted to tell Edd what he had seen and heard last night. He knew who the conspirators were now. He had watched them enter Cicotte's room, one by one.

It had been close to midnight when the meeting began. Although he knew Cicotte and Felsch were in the room next door, it had been quiet for an hour or so. Then Jimmy heard sound in the hallway and jumped up on his chair to look through the transom. He recognized the three men—Weaver, McMullin, and Williams. A few minutes later, two more came. When Gandil and Risberg came into the room, an argument instantly ensued. Jimmy slid off the chair and picked up his glass to listen through the wall. He was more cautious than before because he'd read Pat Moran's statement in his newspaper today that called the Sox "two-fisted fighting gents."[11] He was about to see this first hand.

Like the night before, he couldn't make out whole sentences, but he got the gist of the conversation. It seemed that everyone was mad at the last two men who entered, Gandil and Risberg. He heard, "You lying bastards!" Then, somebody hit the wall where he stood, and he almost lost his balance. Were they fist-fighting? He cautiously placed the glass back to his ear. As best he could make out it was all about money. He caught phrases, "…cheated us…welched…deal…twenty grand." He heard one high-pitched voice yell, "never…I'm OUT!" Another thud vibrated against the wall.[12]

Then there was another knock at the door. He scrambled back up on the chair just in time to see the back of Kid Gleason's head go into the room. He wondered if Gleason had been standing out in the hallway listening before he knocked. Once the manager was in the room, Jimmy strained to hear. Now there was only one voice. It was low but the anger in it emanated through the hotel wall. Jimmy got words like "betrayal…choke….kill…take an iron to you." Then, everything got quiet.[13] Jimmy figured Gleason had heard the rumors and was giving his best shot to straighten out his team.

About fifteen minutes later he heard the door open again. Back up on the chair. He saw Gleason standing in the doorway. Each of the conspirators shook the manager's hand as they left the room, one by one. He noticed that big, blond truculent Swede Risberg hesitated before he took Gleason's hand. When he did, Gleason said, "Good boy, Swede." At 25, Swede was a "boy," one of the youngest members of the Sox. Before he left, Gleason turned back into the room and said, "This will all be behind us now, Eddie." The door closed and the room went silent again. The show was over for tonight.[14]

The fix was off, or so it seemed.

Based on what he had heard, Jimmy decided not to bet on Game Two. In fact, he decided not to bet on any more individual games. He would keep his $20,000 winnings and reinvest his original $10,000 on the Reds to win the Series. Although he knew the reputation of the Sox, he felt in his heart that the home team was better.

He waited an appropriate amount of time and scooted back upstairs to his room. On the way, he passed two other Sox players, Eddie Collins and Ray Schalk, coming home from dinner with their wives. The couples were next to each other in rooms 702 and 704.[15] Jimmy put his head down and hurried past them. He didn't want to get caught. That big, blond Risberg had a vicious look in his eyes, and Jimmy's boxing skills were long gone.

When he reached his room, he closed the door and leaned against it, glad to be in a safe haven. He remembered his brother Harry's comment that "Jimmy's got more nerve than a burglar."[16] He smiled, thinking Harry was right. Maybe that would be a good sideline, if his bets on this Series went sour.

Moments later, Jimmy slammed his own door, walked down the hall to the elevator, and went to the lobby to make a phone call. This was big news; it couldn't wait. As he passed the hotel bar, he noticed two men and a woman having a drink together. He didn't know the man with the pock-marked face or the woman, but he knew Ben Levi, the fellow he'd introduced to

Roush last summer. Must be the Des Moines contingent. He made no sign of recognition as he passed. Better to be on the safe side. He knew Levi was also Mowbray's deep throat for the fix. He couldn't help but wonder how a gambler from New York and a gambler from Des Moines had gotten together.

When he got to the phone carrels, they were full. As he waited he saw Abe Attell talking fast in one of them. If his hunch was right, the party on the other end was the big man in New York. Jimmy's pulse quickened with the thought— Rothstein. He wondered if they knew what he knew. Had Cicotte told Attell the fix was off? Now *that* would take major balls. He didn't envy anyone who would cross Rothstein; even famous ballplayers would be in danger for their lives.

A phone came open and Jimmy called the private number for the Mowbray estate. A maid answered. While he waited for Fred, he thought it sounded like there was a party going on in the background. "Sure," he thought, "here I am doing the shit work while the millionaire is having fun." He felt like hanging up, but he didn't.

When Fred got to the phone, he sounded inebriated. He must have been celebrating his winnings of the day. When Jimmy told him the news, the line went silent. After digesting the bad news, Fred simply said, "Moul is here now, so I'll tell him. We'll tell the others." He started to hang up, then quickly added, "Thanks, Jimmy. Good work."

As Jimmy was waiting for the elevator to go back to his room, he picked up a piece of conversation between Ray Schalk and Hugh Fullerton. They were standing a few feet from him. He noticed that the catcher was red-faced and distressed. The sportswriter said to him, "Keep your mouth shut. You can't prove it and they would ruin you."[17] When they saw Jimmy, they stopped talking.

When Jimmy got to his floor, he stopped and tapped softly on the door of Horace Schmidlapp.

Horace, age 36 was Jimmy's closest friend. While the Schmidlapp family was the upper crust of Cincinnati, Jimmy was the bottom of the loaf. Horace was the oldest son of one of the most powerful men in Cincinnati, financier Jacob Godfrey Schmidlapp. Jacob was a German immigrant who founded the Union Savings Bank and Trust in 1876. He was a close associate of Taft, Rockefeller, Guggenheim, Schwab, and Carnegie, served on several high-level policy committees during World War I, and was offered, but rejected, the U.S. Ambassadorship to Russia in 1909 by President Taft. In 1919, Jacob was paying little attention to his offspring since he was in the process of a major bank merger to establish the Fifth Third Bank of Cincinnati. He would pass away in December, 1919, soon after this merger.[18]

Horace was the black sheep of the Schmidlapp family, overshadowed by his successful younger brother, Carl, vice-president of Chase National Bank. Horace's problems had begun early in life when he was a runty unathletic boy who seemed an unlikely offspring for his tall German parents. When he was a boy, he may have felt envy when he heard the stories of the poor Negro folk who were treated well and hidden in the basement of his family's "safe" home. He was never good in school and would remember the echo of his mother's voice throughout his life, ""Just do your best, Horace." Through college at Cornell he was rebellious and always in trouble at the Sigma Chi fraternity. Not knowing what to do with Horace, Jacob set him up with a generous trust fund and gave him the empty office of president of the Monitor Stove Company.[19]

To make matters worse, Horace was estranged from his wife, Jean, and their four young daughters. At 5'9", Jean was taller than her husband, and she was the daughter of a prominent local attorney, Lawrence Maxwell. When rumors circulated about

Horace's infidelities,[20] Jean settled into their estate at 1135 Grandin Road and Horace moved downtown. Once a month, Jean would dress up the girls and take them to the Sinton Hotel to visit Daddy. After she filed for divorce and sued the Schmidlapp estate for $2,000,000, the family closed ranks. The children were never permitted to discuss their father again. It was as if Horace was dead to his family.[21]

In 1916, Horace found solace in his new friend, Jimmy Widmeyer. It was an unlikely match, but Jimmy was skillful at ingratiating himself with others, and they became great friends. It was Horace who helped Jimmy make his money by giving him stock tips. Jimmy invested the $5,000 he had saved from his newspaper business based on his friend's advice and started to realize big money for the first time in his life.[22]

By 1919, Horace and Jimmy both lived in suites at the Sinton Hotel. This was not an uncommon practice for businessmen of the time. They shared a love of adventure, and as Jimmy's wealth increased (with Horace's help), they became traveling companions. While Horace arranged their diplomatic passports, Jimmy was adept at getting seats at the captain's table for dinner. Little did customers know that when Jimmy was absent from his open-air newsstand office in the bitter Cincinnati winters, he was on safari in the Belgian Congo or riding a camel in Egypt with Horace. It was reported that he went around the world three times from 1915 through the 1920's.[23]

But then the adventures came to an abrupt halt. Two circumstances contributed to the end of this globetrotting duo: one of their own doing, and one beyond their control. In an embarrassing moment in the Far East, an inebriated Jimmy publicly announced that he and Horace would buy China. Jimmy saw a deplorably poor and primitive country, and he thought it could benefit from some American "know-how." As Jimmy told the story, Horace became enraged at his traveling companion's social blunder and called him a "so-and-so" news-boy. As Jimmy was prone to do, he socked little Horace in the nose on the spot.[24] Horace picked up his hat, walked away, and sailed home the next day. He never spoke to Jimmy Widmeyer again…as the story goes.[25]

But the end of the Widmeyer/Schmidlapp relationship was not to come for another decade. In 1919 they were like brothers.

Horace had been expecting Jimmy and came to the door in his silk nightgown. He offered Jimmy a scotch in return for his detailed description of the night's sleuthing. Jimmy much pre-ferred Horace's suite in the Sinton to his own. It was much more elaborate with all the family antiques, ornate moldings, and damask draperies. Although there were family pictures dis-played, Jimmy had never seen the family. He was always reminded that Horace was several rungs above him on the lad-der of life. He hated him for it, but he also needed him. The money was rolling in from his stock investments suggested by Horace. Pretty soon Jimmy would have enough to buy that big house in Mt. Washington close to the prestigious Taft family. But he'd never give up the newsstand. From 8 a.m. to 6 p.m. that was his true home.

As he got into bed, Jimmy pondered the events of the evening. He had certainly ruined the rest of Mowbray's night. The winner of tomorrow's game would be anybody's guess. No inside info from now on.

After his unexpected encounter with Jimmy, Edd walked into the Metropole and crossed the lobby. At this moment, with Jimmy's words ringing in his head, it seemed to Edd that the men standing around in the lobby all looked like New York gamblers. He wondered if Jimmy knew these guys. Flashes of the 1918 season passed through his mind—Lee Magee throw-ing the Boston game, that damned Hal Chase in New York.

Edd smirked as he remembered how Greasy Neale had beat the "living daylights out of Magee."

Then he thought of Jimmy again, and he remembered Essie's diamond. He'd always wondered how a newsstand owner was able to acquire a three-carat diamond in a few days. What connections *did* Jimmy have? Was Jimmy just listening in the room next to Cicotte, or was his information coming from another, more sinister, source? Was Jimmy actually talking to big-time crooks who were trying to "fix" a World Series? Was Jimmy one of them?

As he walked across the lobby, he noticed a clump of men dressed differently from the usual array of out-of-towners. Their hair was slicked back with grease. They wore big shirt collars high and stiff, and the silk bowties were the clincher. They looked like gamblers. He saw one man pull out a wad of thousand-dollar bills to cover a bet on the Reds at 13 to 10 for a Cincinnati fan who had raised the money in a pool. He didn't know Joe Art was one of the twenty-two Texas oilmen (friends of Harry Sinclair) who had bought out the top floor of the Metropole and held the first four rows of seats at the ballpark.[26] This was not typical behavior in the Cincinnati Edd knew.

He passed within inches of Des Moines gambler David Zelcer without knowing who he was. He did think he recognized one man in the group. He was a small, older fellow. He was out of place, Edd thought. In his mind's eye, he saw himself with this guy out on the ballfield, but then thought that couldn't be right.

A thought entered his mind. What was he doing in the lobby alone? He was, after all, a recognizable person in this city. Had others seen him talking with Jimmy outside? Would *he* now be accused of colluding with gamblers?

He was 26 years old, playing in his first World Series, and now he'd been thrown a hot potato. He wanted to get rid of it fast. He put his head down and hurried outside the hotel just as the taxis were pulling up to take the team to the train station for the 10 p.m. train.

OCTOBER 2, 1919
TRAIN TO CHICAGO

All the way to Chicago Edd's mind raced. Was Jimmy lying? He'd never known him to lie before. Had Jimmy told anyone else on the team? He looked around the observation car. His teammates had taken turns coming over to Edd and congratulating him on his great catch. Now, the guys were chatting, playing cards, generally relaxed and looking innocent. He thought not.

Then logic emerged and he wondered what Jimmy was doing with a room at the Sinton where the Sox were staying. Jimmy lived around the corner at 5th and Walnut in the Gibson, not the Sinton.[27] Did he move to be close to the action? Was Jimmy sent there to eavesdrop on the ballplayers for some big-time crooks? Was he some sort of "inside sleuth" for them? Worse yet, was he working alone?

Edd's thoughts raced back over the games of the last two days. There were Sox mistakes, yes, but this was true of the Reds too.[28] Edd winced thinking of that Risberg fly he missed by an inch. As he thought about it, it did seem that the Sox were mad and constantly screaming at each other on the field.[29] He remembered that Schalk kept making that loud, shrill whistle on the field in the first two games.[30] Gandil hated it and yelled for him to "shut up."

Jimmy had mentioned Cicotte. At 35, Cicotte was an old man by player standards. Maybe he felt his days were numbered and saw this as his last chance to cash in. Who else was in on it? Joe Jackson? Surely not Joe. He'd been fielding and hitting well. Maybe Gandil? Not Eddie Collins. He was a man of integrity and no friend of Cicotte, from all Edd had seen on the field. Couldn't be Schalk. He was hopping mad at Cicotte for ignoring his signals yesterday. Everyone on the field saw it. Gleason had to see it, because he pulled Cicotte in the fifth inning. He remembered then that Jimmy said Gleason was at the meeting. Maybe that was why he pulled Cicotte. He knew the secret too.

It all added up. Something was wrong out there. A passing thought made Edd mad: They know they can't beat us so they're starting a rumor that it's fixed to steal our glory! Then he placed the old guy in the hotel, the one who looked familiar—the guy had been with Jimmy and Fred Mowbray one day at the ballpark. He was sure of it. He vaguely remembered that day. They were walking around meeting the players. He also remembered thinking it was odd that Jimmy was friendly with Mowbray. Mowbray was a respected man in town, involved in Boosters, Business Man's Club, and all that. But what was that old guy's name? Something Jewish. Maybe Jimmy was connected to something bigger than he knew. Maybe Jimmy was over his head. Was the meeting in front of the hotel a cry for help?

He felt angry now. After all, he was out there *on* that field. If the opposing team were throwing the game, wouldn't he know it? Were they all just puppets on that field being manipulated by some powerful forces? Why even go out there? He'd just tell Moran he wasn't going to play tomorrow. He wanted to get off the train and go home.

Then he remembered Jimmy's words: "They didn't get their money and agreed to go out and try to win." He thought hard. If that happened last night then today's game was on the level. Okay, that made sense. Cicotte had seemed really off his game yesterday. But, they'd hit Williams hard today and Edd was sure they'd won it fair and square.

As the train clacked its way north, Edd sat alone. His thoughts moved to God, and all of his Masonic Lodge training.

He wondered what he should do. What was the "right thing" to do? Should he walk to the next car where the guys were shooting craps in the men's room and blurt it all out? Should he find Moran and tell him privately? Should he whisper it to an umpire. *Crazy*. Evans and Rigler would throw him out of the game. They'd all want proof! What real evidence did he have anyway—the word of some gambler friend in Cincinnati?

This last thought gelled. The whole thing was absurd. He didn't know anything for sure. He would keep his mouth shut. He decided to put it out of his mind and get some rest. He had an important game to play in Chicago tomorrow and, yes, he believed his performance would make a difference. If only he could get a triple or two tomorrow. He realized that a lot of his anxiety was also coming from his own disappointment about his hitting slump in the games. He vowed that tomorrow he'd do better.

He didn't make it to the Pullman car. He slept all night sitting up.

One can only surmise how the history of the 1919 World Series might have been rewritten had Edd Roush, star player for the Reds, "blown the whistle" after Game Two.

Edd fell asleep on the train to Chicago thinking he carried a heavy burden known only to him. He would have been shocked to know how many other people knew the "secret" of the World Series fix. It was shared in hushed voices all over the country. It was passed around in trains, taverns, pool halls, golf courses, and private men's clubs. It was even whispered in the back pews of churches. It had no allegiance to rank or station in life; rich man and poor man alike shared it. It was earmarked for one audience—gamblers—from the most effete gentlemen piker to the cheapest thug. Just a knowing wink and one word was all it took: "Reds!"

The editor of the *Reach Official American League Guide*

would later print: "Probably no Series preceding the remarkable Cincinnati–Chicago 1919 Series has been attended by so much public and private betting as the 1919 Series."[31]

At the time Edd was trying to sleep, a midnight train full of gamblers traveled in the same direction. Jimmy Widmeyer sat with the Cincinnati boys including Phil Hahn, racetrack betting commissioner, Horace Schmidlapp, and Charley Marqua. Jimmy had brought two quarts of his favorite scotch, but he was drinking from Horace's bottle. He would return from Chicago with those same bottles, if he was lucky. And Jimmy *was* lucky.

Although ten coaches had to be amassed for the Reds' Rooters group, Fred Mowbray, Dan Moul, and Dick Williams were enjoying the sausage covered with puff pastry being served in the private car of Reds' owner Garry Herrmann. Of course, hard-boiled eggs were present at any Herrmann party.[32] The wealthy backers of the Redleg organization sipped their scotch with Julius Fleischmann and Louis Kahn.

The Des Moines connection was there too—Nat Evans, the Levi brothers, David and Abe Zelcer—along with Abe Attell. It's likely that none of them noticed the well-dressed man sitting on the end in the last compartment scribbling in a little notepad.

GUILTY KNOWLEDGE

It seemed that only the Reds were in the dark as the menace swirled around them. So, what about those with the power to stop it? Did they know the "secret?"[33]

Yes, many did. Matty knew. So did just about every other major sportswriter covering the Series including Fullerton and Lardner. Earlier that very night, Ring Lardner and some drunk friends had created a song at one of the Kentucky roadhouses and then walked through the Sinton lobby singing it on the way home.[34] It was a parody of the popular song "I'm Forever Blowing Bubbles."

> I'm forever blowing ballgames,
> Pretty ballgames in the air.
> I come from Chi
> I hardly try
> Just go to bat and fade and die,
> Fortune's coming my way,
> That's why I don't care.
> I'm forever blowing ballgames,
> And the gamblers treat us fair.

Yes, other Sox players knew. That night Ray Schalk reported to Kid Gleason that in Game One, Cicotte had pitched balls with "nothing on them when he had signaled for shiners or curves." He claimed that in Game Two, Williams had crossed him "four times." Rumor had it that Shalk was so furious he had to be pulled off of Williams after the game. Captain Eddie Collins would later say he knew "after the first two plays of the first game."

Sox manager Gleason had to know. He not only had the report from his catcher, he had seen Cicotte fold in front of his eyes. Hugh Fullerton had to intervene in the Sinton lobby that night when Gleason verbally attacked Cicotte and Risberg, calling them "bushers" and "sonavabitchs." One report said that Gleason had tried to strangle Chick Gandil under the stands after the game.[35]

If, as Jimmy reported to Edd, the Sox had decided to win after Game One, their manager's threats may have strengthened their resolve. They knew they were "under suspicion."[36]

The magnates, owners, and league officials also knew. John McGraw was told personally by Arnold Rothstein. Rothstein felt indebted to McGraw over past dealings, and he fancied that if he "warned" McGraw, it would appear that Rothstein was not involved in the fix. He suggested to McGraw that he might want to pass the rumor on to Kid Gleason. In an effort not to be snared in the scandal, McGraw later denied this, calling Rothstein "several kinds of a liar."[37]

Gleason told his boss, Charles Comiskey, owner of the White Sox. Comiskey had received numerous tip-offs before the Series started. One credible source was a well-known Chicago gambler named Mont Tennes who became alarmed at the high volume of betting on the underdog Reds. Tennes was reportedly once seen as a visitor at Comiskey's north woods retreat. His inner circle was called the Woodland Bards. Tennes was motivated to report the rumor to Comiskey not least because he had a $100,000 wager on the Sox to protect. He was also angry that he hadn't gotten the word ahead of time. How could the Chicago syndicate have been left out of the fix?

Also, the night before the Series started, Comiskey had a visit from his star player, Joe Jackson. Joe was feeling guilty and nervous about dealing with the gamblers. He asked his boss to take him out of the lineup the next day. He said, "Tell the newspapers you just suspended me for being drunk, or anything, but leave me out of the Series and then there can be no question."[38] Comiskey refused to grant his request, but saw the pressure his players were under from the gamblers.

As the story goes,[39] at 3 a.m. the night of October 1, a separate meeting occurred in the Sinton on a floor above the players. Comiskey went to John Heydler, National League President, to tell him the secret. Both men went to the room of Heydler's counterpart in the American League, Ban Johnson. They woke him up and told him they had evidence that some Sox players were attempting to throw the Series to the Reds. His response is now famous in baseball circles. Looking at Comiskey, he grunted, "That is the yelp of a beaten cur," and promptly went back to bed.

Many reasons have been given for Johnson's flippant response. Most historians agree that his reaction was due to a personal feud with Comiskey. (This is also the reason Comiskey went to Heydler first, outside of his chain of command.) However, according to writer Fred Lieb, Johnson was in a drunken sleep at the time he was awakened, and the statement was a result of his irritable mood.[40]

Hugh Fullerton also reported in his memoirs that he, personally, informed both Comiskey and Johnson in Cincinnati *before* the Series began. He said that Johnson "scoffed" and said it was just "Comiskey squealing." Comiskey angrily refused to take action. Fullerton called them "whitewashing bastards who were letting a bunch of crooks get away with it because they were afraid of losing money."[41]

Regardless what Johnson said or didn't say to Comiskey or Fullerton, he saw the implications of a crooked World Series for organized baseball. The public was the customer and if the rumor went public, it could kill the goose that laid the golden eggs for him and all his colleagues. Doubtless, this was his primary motivation when he called his old friend, Cal Crim, private investigator, the next morning.

---

1   William A. Cook. *The 1919 World Series*. McFarland & Co., 2001.
2   *Cincinnati Times-Star*. October 3, 1919.
3   *Chicago Tribune*. October 3, 1919.
4   *The Philadelphia Inquirer*. October 3, 1919.
5   Hugh Fullerton. *Atlanta Constitution*. October 3, 1919.
6   Hugh Fullerton. *Syracuse Herald*. September 30, 1919.
7   *Cincinnati Enquirer*. October 3, 1919.
8   *Evansville Courier*. October 3, 1919.
9   *Cincinnati Enquirer*. October 3, 1919.
10 Ibid. October 4, 1919.

11 Earliest recorded interview in which Roush described encounter with Widmeyer was given to sports columnist Dan Daniel in St. Petersburg, Florida, during spring training, March 2, 1937. Daniel quotes Roush saying, "Well, I'm going to tell you something I have kept under my hat for eighteen years. Since I've never told anyone, it never has been printed."

12 *Syracuse Herald.* October 2, 1919.

13 Author's Note: The player most likely to fight was Swede Risberg, partner of Gandil. Based on testimony given to Cook County Judge McDonald, Joe Jackson asked for protection of the court because he thought Swede Risberg had threatened to "bump him off" if he testified. *L.A. Times.* September 21, 1920.

14 Just before he died, Gleason gave an account of this meeting to reporter Harvey Woodruff. He claimed he struggled over whether or not to start Williams in Game Two. He was "crushed and heartbroken" over the situation and warned the men. *Chicago Tribune.* January 6, 1933.

15 Hypothetical conversation based on Black Sox trial testimony and later reports. Gandil was the go-between with the gamblers who didn't give the players the money they promised after the first loss. Risberg was a violent character who likely got physical in the meeting. Weaver claimed to "want out." Reports indicated that Gleason talked with the conspirators early in the Series to dissuade them from the fix.

16 Sinton Hotel Ledger. HOF BSS/AL files.

17 Author interview with Widmeyer nephew, Jimmy, and his wife, Betty. Kentucky, 2004.

18 Hugh Fullerton Memoir. *The Sporting News.* October 17, 1935.

19 Jacob Schmidlapp, philanthropist, was a major contributor to the Underground Railroad in the 1800's.

20 Horace's company was sued for filing a fraudulent tax return in 1918.

21 News reports connected Horace to Rose Krier, 26, a telephone operator, when her roommate, Ethel Goodwin, was found dead with her head severed from her body in 1923.

22 Author interviews with granddaughters, Barri Schmidlapp Mapes and Clarinda Schmidlapp, 2004.

23 Widmeyer was later known as the "Million Dollar Newsboy" of Cincinnati. He parlayed his original investment into $1.8 million, losing most of it in the 1929 stock market crash. *Cincinnati Enquirer.* May 14, 1950.

24 *Cincinnati Post.* December 31, 1949.

25 Marvin Arth. *Cincinnati Times-Star.* 10/10/52. And author interview with Widmeyer cousins, Jimmy and Betty, October, 2004.

26 Horace Schmidlapp died suddenly (and rather mysteriously) on board the Santa Barbara steamer off the coast of South America in 1929. His body was taken ashore at Callao. *Cincinnati Enquirer*, January 29, 1929.

No mention was made of his traveling companion, Jimmy Widmeyer, being present that night.

27 *Sandusky Star Journal*. October 3, 1919.

28 Author's Note: Edd was unaware that Jimmy had moved from the Gibson Hotel to the Sinton in early 1919. Jimmy's move may have been motivated by Horace Schmidlapp, who kept a suite in the Sinton.

29 In the final tally, both Reds and Sox committed twelve errors in the Series.

30 Observation of Sox bat boy reported by John Sayles, director of the movie *Eight Men Out*. "Conversations with Filmmakers Series." MSU Press, 1999.

31 "Pepperpot" Schalk was famous for whistling at teammates when he thought they were getting careless or loafing. *Evansville Courier*. September 26, 1919.

32 As Edd would later say he didn't know what to believe about what Jimmy said, noting: "You can hear anything during a World Series." Taped interview with author, 1978

33 *Reach Guide*, 1920. p. 165.

34 Author's Note: Hard-boiled eggs were said to have been "invented" in Cincinnati. Jack Casey, *Pittsburg Chronicle Telegraph*. October 3, 1919.

35 Account of events based on articles by Hugh Fullerton after the series. *Atlanta Constitution* (October 29, 1919 through January 20, 1920) and Fullerton Memoir, *The Sporting News*. October 17, 1935.

36 Hugh Fullerton. *Atlanta Constitution*. October 3, 1920.

37 "*Black Sox Scandal of 1919*." Eastland Memorial Society. 2004.

38 Harvey Woodruff. *Chicago Tribune*. January 6, 1933.

39 "Thirty-Four Years in Baseball." Ban Johnson as told by Irving Vaughn. *Washington Post*. February 24, 1929.

40 Interview with Jackson entitled "This is the Truth!" Furman Bisher. *SPORT Magazine*. October, 1949.

41 Eliot Asinof. *Eight Men Out*. Henry Holt & Co., 1963.

42 Fred Lieb. *Baseball as I have Known It*. Tempo Books, 1977.

43 Hugh Fullerton Memoir. *The Sporting News*. October 17, 1935.

10

Red October

Many a noble hit went down into the cold records of time
with its modest tombstone inscribed, "Flied to Rousch," or
"Out, Kopf to Daubert."

– Jack Lait, "In the Wake of the News,"
Chicago Tribune, *Oct. 3, 1919*

OCTOBER 2, 1919

OFFICES OF CAL CRIM DETECTIVE BUREAU

TRACTION BUILDING   CINCINNATI, OHIO[1]

David Calvin Crim sat behind his imposing mahogany desk with his morning coffee and a copy of the *Cincinnati Times-Star* from the Widmeyer newsstand. It was 7:22 a.m. when the phone rang. (He made a note of it, as he always did.) Since the secretary wasn't in yet, he answered it himself.

"Crim Bureau."

"Hello, Cal? Ban Johnson…er, B.B."

"How are you, B.B.? How are the fellows working out at Redland?" Among other things, the Crim agency provided qualified guards (often retired police officers) to augment the Cincinnati police force at major events such as the World Series.

"That's not why I called."

There was a pause on the line. Cal decided to make it easier for his old friend.

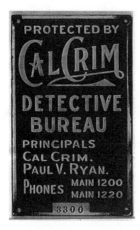

DETECTIVE CALVIN
CRIM (RIGHT)
1919 LOGO OF CAL
CRIM DETECTIVE
BUREAU (ABOVE)

Randy Hollensbaugh
President, Calvin Crim Inc., Cincinnati, Ohio

"I thought you might call today."

"I guess you've heard." Johnson sighed, as if under a heavy burden. "I need you to investigate these rumors going around. I don't know if they're true or not, but, it's coming from all directions now and I can't ignore it." He waited to see how much Crim already knew.

Crim obliged. "If you mean the rumor about your players throwing the World Series, yes, I've heard it."

A thought crossed Johnson's mind. "Is this line secure?"

"Yes, but if you'd rather meet somewhere...."

"It's worse if I try to go out. They swarm me."

Another long pause, and Cal broke the silence. "What do you want me to do, B.B.? Say the word, and it's done."

Johnson sighed again. "I need you to find out where all this is coming from—Cincinnati, Chicago, Boston, where? Come up for the Series tomorrow. I'll pay expenses, of course. I'll set you up in the Congress Hotel on Michigan Avenue."

"I already have a reservation, made it a month ago. Just had a feeling I'd need to be there. I'm on the midnight train."

"What do you know?"

Crim hesitated. He didn't have anything definite, just a lot of notes that were pieces of a puzzle that hadn't yet formed in his mind. There were the gamblers talking to the Reds at the ballpark and the all-night sessions at roadhouses across the river. There were some out-of-town gambler types who seemed to have local connections. He planned to start there. But he said, "Nothing yet…nothing hard, at least. I have my suspicions."

Johnson asked, "So you think it's true? Are the Sox throwing?"

"Can't say for sure, but my gut says yes."

Another long pause as Johnson's mind raced through the implications and the impact on his life in the months to come. "This assignment is on my personal tab, for now. I don't want the commission knowing about it yet." Then he said, "Well…just between us…I want to get there before Commy does. Understand?" This was spoken as an order.

Oh yes, Cal understood perfectly. He had been there at the beginning.

MAY 8, 1893[2]
TEN MINUTE CLUB
VINE STREET, CINCINNATI.[3]

It was to be a celebratory drink after work, just four young guys getting together to celebrate a buddy's promotion. The problem was they were all drunk now. The big guy, B.B., mused in slurred speech, "You're supposed to order a drink every "ten minutes," that's the name of the tavern." Commy, Hugh, and Cal had heard the joke a million times before, but laughed anyway.

Commy sputtered, "It's a rule here."

Cal said, "I'd have to arrest you fellas if you didn't follow the rules." They all laughed. There was one cop, one baseball player, and two newspaper reporters, all solid Midwesterners. They shared one quality among them: they were smart men just beginning their careers. Each would climb his personal mountain and reach the pinnacle of his chosen profession.

On this spring day in May, the four were toasting the promotion of Cal to Chief of Detectives for the City of Cincinnati. At age 28, the cop had already climbed several mountains in his short life. Calvin Crim had been a 14-year-old orphan in Oakland, Maryland, when he jumped a freight train and headed for Cincinnati in search of his only known kin, a long-lost sister. He arrived in Ohio barefoot because his shoes had fallen between the cars of the train. He was discovered hovering on the streets by a kindly policeman from the Hammond Street Police Station. Thomas Ryan and the entire station brigade adopted the waif and became the fathers he never knew. They got him a job as a bellboy at the Galt House for eight dollars a month, and he shined shoes for extra money on his off hours. Finally, the policemen found his sister, and he had a real home. Cal's education was completed on the streets of Cincinnati.

As a natural outgrowth of his life experience, Cal dreamed of becoming a policeman. In 1886, Colonel Philip Deitsch pronounced him a full-fledged officer in the old city stables of the Oliver Street Station. To Cal, looking back at a life full of accomplishments, this would be his most exciting moment.

Cal would go on to enjoy a national reputation as a detective. Articles would be written in *Front Page Detective* about the famous cases he would solve. The Pearl Bryan murder case of the headless body is still a classic in law enforcement. In 1901, he would be shot twice in the chest by an outlaw called "Foley the Goat." The entire city of Cincinnati prayed for his life as he lay desperately wounded. When he survived, he and his wife, Clara, were given a home on Menlo Avenue in Hyde Park as a reward for his heroism. It was paid for by donations from the grateful citizens of the city.

Cal would establish his own detective agency in 1913. With his partner, Paul Ryan, he would eventually have hundreds of employees and branches in twenty-five cities, including Chicago.[4] He would protect six U.S. Presidents during their inaugurations and would be instrumental in the formation of the World Association of Detectives. Throughout his life, he would donate time and money to the local Shrine, to the Knox Presbyterian Church in Hyde Park, and to every program that helped wayward boys in Cincinnati.

Commy and B.B. considered Cal their hero and had brought him into the mix after his heroic efforts to control the riot at the Reds' League Park on July 11, 1886. B.B. had been covering the Reds–St. Louis game when rowdy fans had gotten out of control. Cal was the policeman who had saved umpire George Bradley when a barrage of beer mugs and debris thrown from the stands almost killed him.[5]

B.B., Byron Bancroft "Ban" Johnson, was the unofficial leader of this brotherhood. At age 30, he was the sports editor for the *Cincinnati Commercial-Gazette*. He was a big man who seemed to enjoy towering over smaller, less significant creatures—particularly Hughie, who was his employee at the newspaper. B.B. saw Hughie as a necessary annoyance, like a fly on his shoulder, but Hughie was a smart up-and-comer, and B.B. fancied himself as Hughie's mentor. Commy was his closest personal friend and they would be inseparable for years, until they became bitter enemies over a disagreement in 1917.

Ban Johnson was born in Avondale, Ohio, the fifth child of a strict school headmaster. From the time he was a little boy, Ban dreamed of being a baseball player. He was a varsity catcher for Oberlin Prep School in 1880, but his father would not allow his son to pursue such a frivolous occupation. He was born to be a Presbyterian minister.

There was one problem: Ban hated school. It was too slow for his quick mind. He attended Marietta College, but after one year he quit. He had found something he was good at. His literary instructor told him he had a future as a writer. He encouraged young Johnson to keep journals and to write letters in order to hone his skills. Ban found the perfect mix of his writing skills and his love for baseball as a sportswriter.

But he had another talent that was latent in his early years; he was a true leader of men. He had always been a creature of strong opinions with the ability to express himself articulately. All he needed was a cause. He would find that cause in the emergence of the American Baseball League at the close of the nineteenth century. He would become its president and remain at the helm for almost three decades. He would take his friend Commy with him on this journey.

At age 32, Charles A. Comiskey was the player/manager of the Cincinnati Reds. He was born to a poor family in Chicago and began his career as a pitcher for the Dubuque (Iowa) Rabbits, making fifty dollars a month. He knocked around the minor league circuit for a while, and by 1882 he had found a solid berth at first base with the St. Louis Browns. He captained Chris Von der Ahe's Brown Stockings to four consecutive World Championships. Like B.B., he was a leader and was asked to join management as a player/manager with Cincinnati in 1893. Also, like B.B., Commy's style with employees was aloof and imperial. When he became a team owner, he treated his players as if they were serfs allowed to inhabit his fiefdom. He was stingy at contract time and rarely had a friendly word for players. Once successful, he forgot his own modest beginnings.[6]

He would become a millionaire through his relationship

with baseball and, in particular, with B.B. It was B.B. who would acquire the funding for Commy to own the St. Paul franchise of the Western League. B.B. would invite Commy, along with Connie Mack, to the home of his attorney, Henry Killilea, in 1899 for that very special meeting in which they would found the new American League. Commy would achieve his lifelong dream of returning to his hometown of Chicago as the owner of a team he called the White Stockings.

It was Commy who gave the first big break to the fourth member of the friendly tribe, Hughie Fullerton.

At 19, Hugh Stuart Fullerton was the youngest member of the gang. Fullerton was also the best educated, with a degree from Ohio State. Like B.B., he was from a Presbyterian family. His grandfather, the original Hugh Fullerton, was a minister. Hughie was a small, wiry fellow with indefatigable energy and a sharp mind for details. This quality would bring him to the top of his profession. In a decade, he would become a respected sportswriter for the *Chicago Herald Examiner*. His column, "On the Screen of Sport with the Major Leagues" would become so popular that it would be syndicated throughout the nation. As mentioned in an earlier chapter, Fullerton gained fame by developing a system of analyzing player data to predict the outcome of games. He called it "doping." He would later be a founding member of the Baseball Writers Association of America.

Hughie had a knack for analyzing statistics and a nose for athletes in trouble. He was a good judge of character and could sense when a boxer was fading or an eager rookie pitcher was about to blow out his arm. Hughie had one problem: he talked too much. He was an honest, forthright Midwesterner who never learned to play politics even though he was exposed to B.B., a master of the art, early in his career.

In 1893, Hugh was a cub reporter for the *Cincinnati Commercial Tribune*. He stood in awe of B.B., the sports editor. Ban intimidated Hughie with his air of self-confidence that was magnified by his large, six-foot frame. Hughie called it "B.B.'s look of disdain." Hughie had gained entry into this group through Commy, who had taken an instant liking to the young reporter and granted him exclusive interviews. This suited B.B. fine since he expected his reporters to bring home the scoops while he was busy with his favorite pastime—politics.

Hughie had developed another talent that balanced his otherwise serious personality. He was the best joke-teller in town. This talent helped him enter the nooks and crannies of the famous and the wealthy. One of his favorite "sparring partners" in the future would be the quick-witted Ring Lardner. Hughie could keep Commy in stitches for hours. Of course, compared to the others, Commy was the dullard of the group. But, Hughie would always feel a strong allegiance to Commy, a fact that would be important in how the media reported the events of the 1919 Series.

On this particular night in 1893, the conversation of the brotherhood centered on the man they loved to hate—John T. Brush, owner of the Reds. In print, B.B. consistently criticized Brush's neglect of his ballpark. One of B.B.'s most firmly held opinions concerned the state of the game. He disliked the fans having free reign to be drunk and rowdy. When he finally had the power of the Western League behind him, he gave great amounts of energy to elevating the role of the umpire as the sole arbiter of the game. A decade later, he helped Cal Crim set up a branch of his agency in Chicago to do background checks on American League umpires.

Although Brush was Commy's boss, there was no love between them. Brush was, after all, a Hoosier, and Ohioans had a natural dislike for Hoosiers. With some inexplicable notion of superiority, they looked down their noses at the "ridge-runner" farmers and coal miners of the neighboring states of Indiana and Kentucky.

From a long diatribe against Brush, the group quickly moved to another hated faction in Cincinnati—the political machine run by "Boss" George Cox. The ten-minute boys all agreed that the Republican machine was corrupt and had a stranglehold on the good people of Cincinnati. Although B.B. was most vitriolic in his criticism of Cox, he admitted to liking one of his henchmen nicknamed "Garibaldi."

He said, "That fellow is on the square."

Garibaldi was the boyhood nickname of Cincinnati native August Herrmann. August later became "Garry" when he worked in a type foundry[7] and the name stuck. In 1902, Garry Herrmann would join with Cox and the wealthy Fleischmann brothers (Julius and Max) to buy the Reds from John Brush for $150,000.[8] A consummate politician who trained at the feet of Cox, Herrmann would become an important ally for Ban Johnson on the National Baseball Commission in 1919.

As the four continued their discussion into the night, they could not have known how their lives would again intertwine around the "scandal" of the World Series of 1919. As middle-aged men, B.B. and Cal would be instrumental in discovering the truth about the fix. Hughie would shine the light of the media on that truth. In the process, all three would make their unique contributions to the destruction of the great Chicago White Sox team and, with it, a great loss for their friend Commy.

OCTOBER 3-6, 1919
CHICAGO TRIPLETS—GAME THREE

The city of Chicago was dumbfounded that those Ohio "hicks" called the Red Stockings had snatched Games One and Two away from their champions. People surmised that some under-handed business had gone on. Had their boys been drugged?

Had Kentucky Derby gamblers bought out the umpires? Well, they were back home in Chi-town now. Go Sox!

On Friday, October 3, Game Three matched rookie left-hander "Little" Dickie Kerr and Reds veteran Ray Fisher. Kerr, a Texan, was a favorite of the oilmen in the stands. Fisher had pitched in the American League with New York for eight seasons. He was familiar with the White Sox and they with him. Among the interested spectators were General Leonard Wood, Commander of the Central Department of the Army, with some of his staff members. Five hundred rooters were in attendance from Cincinnati.

The rooters would be disappointed. In the shortest game of the Series, lasting exactly ninety minutes, the Sox dominated with their first win, 3-0.

The real story of the game was Kerr's masterful pitching performance. He befuddled the Reds with an assortment of fastballs, "corking" curve balls, and exceptional control. Hugh Fullerton wrote, "Richard Kerr, 'de lion-hearted' ...the tiny Texan stood the Reds on their heads."[9] Cincinnati's Fisher was no slouch, giving up only three runs on seven hits.

Kerr allowed only three hits, one base on balls, struck out four, and shut the Reds down without a run. The three hits were Duncan's bloop single to right field in the second inning, Fisher's swinging bunt in the third that Weaver was willing to let roll foul and Kerr slipped upon fielding, and Kopf's sharp grounder, to right field in the fifth. After Kopf singled, Kerr retired the last fifteen batters. The man who would have pitched the game if he hadn't had a sore arm coupled with a serious flu was the first to reach Kerr to congratulate him. That was Urban "Red" Faber.

As good as Kerr was, it should also be noted that the entire Sox defense was alive and battling throughout the game. It seemed as if the two teams had switched uniforms because the

Sox looked like the Reds of the two prior games.

The one bright spot for the Reds was the performance of Heinie Groh at third base. He made two one-handed catches on hard-hit balls. The first came in the second inning from Leibold, and the second was a drive by Felsch in the third. In the seventh inning, Groh ran in front of shortstop Kopf to bag a Risberg grounder.

Possibly the most exciting action of the game did not appear in the box score. Eddie Collins, the White Sox captain, lost his composure. Jimmy Smith, backup infielder for the Reds and premier bench jockey, was applying the needle. According to Gleason, Smith had been shouting mercilessly at Collins from the bench. On his way back to the bench Collins walked toward Smith with fists clenched. Smith sprang to his feet. Players and umpires crowded between the two men to break it up.

In the sixth inning, Joe Jackson swung so hard he fell down. Later Jackson snarled at Ray Fisher when a pitch came a little too close to his head. He then dumped a bunt toward first base, hoping Fisher would cover. Fisher refused the bait and the bunt rolled foul, ending the row. Standing in his crouch position in center field, Edd laughed out loud. This was the type of smart play he loved.

Nemo Leibold had a few choice words for Pat Duncan as they passed in the field. In the eighth inning Moran put Cuban pitcher Adolfo Luque in the game. When he struck out Leibold, Heinie Groh yelled "Leo the Bold." Leibold lost it and came charging up the third base line with bat in hand, but Gleason was coaching third and intercepted him to prevent further trouble.

Cincinnati writer Tom Swope would blame the brawling on his home team. He wrote, "All the Reds chattered away at the White Sox like a bunch of monkeys, telling them how punk they were as a ball club."[10]

There were those who were happy about the Sox win and those who were miserable about it.

The Sox were ecstatic. Gandil practically knocked over little Dickey Kerr, slapping him on the back saying, "Good game, Dickey." It was the first time he'd spoken to Kerr in weeks. Kerr was in the *other* camp—with Schalk and Collins, the know-it-alls.

The city of Chicago was avenged. Their boys just needed the home field advantage. The Series would be theirs.

In the upper stands directly behind home plate were the seven rows of reporters relegated to a tight squeeze in the White Sox press box.[11] Matty and Hughie closed their books, satisfied that today's game was on the square. Fullerton would write that the "men of destiny" were losing and got a "bit peevish" over it.[12] W. 0. McGeehan, in the *New York Tribune*, said the Sox looked like white rabbits in Cincinnati and snappy white bull terriers in Chicago.

When Arnold Rothstein came into Lindy's in New York that night, he was no doubt smiling. The Sox victory would let the rumors die down. Everything was going as planned. The idiots who bet the Reds to sweep five in a row, well, they were just idiots. His money was on the Series, not each game. He was safe.

So, too, were Jimmy Widmeyer and his merry band. They had inside information on the game *inside* the game. They were no fools. Mowbray and his deep throat, Ben Levi, were especially happy. Levi had told Mowbray he had a "hunch" on this one, so they both bet the Sox and cleaned up nicely.

But there were those who were not so happy.

The Reds were shaken up. After the first two games they had believed the Series would be a cakewalk. But today was a different story. Jack Ryder would print the story the next day: "There was no hope for our boys at any stage, for Kerr had the stuff....Not a Redleg got past second base in the nine fast rounds.[13]

Edd was despondent over his inability to connect with the ball. He had only one hit in the three games. While it was true that the Sox pitchers were trying to walk him every time, he'd faced that before and still been able to get a solid hit out of a bum throw. What was wrong? It reminded him of that day in 1913 when his entire hometown had turned out to see him play in Evansville, Indiana. In front of the 300 "Roush Rooters" that day, he didn't get one hit.

CARTOON OF SOX PITCHER KERR IN GAME THREE

Hundreds of fans were seen tearing up little pieces of paper at the end of the game. These were pool hall tickets. They came in little envelopes, sealed or sewn up. Some bettors left several dozen around their seats. Discarded fifty-cent tickets, lost dreams of a thousand-dollar pay-off. It was reported that Cincinnati "businessmen" lost $60,000 that day.[14] Thanks to Jimmy Widmeyer's sleuthing and Ben Levi's "hunch," that list would not include Fred Mowbray and his compatriots.

Some of the professional gamblers hadn't gotten the word.

They expected a five-game sweep. Bill Burns and Billy Maharg had bet every cent they had on the Reds in Game Three. The loss cleaned them out. They were furious and felt double-crossed. They were headed downtown to find Abe Attell.[15]

Not all the Sox were happy. On his drive home, Eddie Cicotte was a bundle of mixed emotions. Although part of him was glad they had won, another part was scared. He rationalized that the gamblers hadn't paid off, so what did they expect? They broke the string first, not the players. As he passed by the homes of his neighbors, he hated himself. Many of these good people had bet money they didn't have on him, their hero. He couldn't tell them the truth. But he would be pitching tomorrow. It was time to win this thing for Chicago, for his friends, for *himself*. To hell with gamblers!

For Edd's part, he was thankful that so few balls had broken through to the outfield in the game. He was tired from the fitful sleep of his train ride the night before. As he ran off the field, he couldn't help but wonder if Jimmy was wrong. The Sox had been a different team today. Maybe this "fix" thing was all rumors started by the Sox to cover their failures in Cincinnati. Or maybe they were double-crossing the gamblers. If so, how would the underworld reciprocate? The thought both excited and repulsed him.

Then he saw Heinie and Ray Fisher in front of him. He ran up between them and threw one congratulatory arm around Heinie and another arm of condolence went around Ray. He said, "One game does not a Series make."

OCTOBER 4, 1919, CHICAGO, GAME 4

Cal Crim and his associate, Ora Slater, came into Comiskey Field through separate entrances. After the call from B.B., Cal knew he was officially on the job. He opened a file and marked it Case 2002.[16] At the last minute, he decided to bring in his best detective and, conveniently, Slater was in the Chicago office that month working another case. That case would have to wait. B.B. came first.

Ora Slater was Operative number 4 in the Crim agency after Paul Ryan and Jack McDermott. His career began as Sheriff of Dearborn County, Indiana. During World War I he had been chosen to assist the federal government as an agent for the Bureau of Investigation, Department of Justice (forerunner of the FBI) in Cincinnati. As Slater's reputation grew, he took on high-paying special assignments for individuals such as the Governor of Kentucky and the Crim Bureau.

Slater would become famous in the 1920's as the first detective to use an artist's sketch to find a criminal. When he was working on the Don Mellett murder case in Canton, Ohio, he found a telegraph operator who was the lone witness to see the murderer. After interviewing the witness, Slater walked outside and found himself in the middle of a street carnival. Along the side was a caricaturist drawing likenesses of carnival goers. He asked the artist if he thought he could draw a man's face from a verbal description. The artist thought he could. He was immediately dispatched to the telegraph office and the resulting drawing became the major factor in apprehending the killer.[17]

The two detectives could not have been more dissimilar. Ora was husky, deep-chested, broad-shouldered, and very soft spoken. Cal was thinner, flamboyant, and affable. He smoked cigarettes with a long, ivory holder that he would wave around when telling one of his favorite stories. Like most men of the time, Ora enjoyed an occasional Cuban cigar.

Cal and Ora had carefully planned their strategy. Like the day before, they would sit in different locations in the stands. Cal would be positioned over by third base where many of the gamblers sat, while Ora would sit near the Cincinnati businessmen and the Reds Boosters. He had memorized the photos of the men Cal suspected since he didn't know them by sight. They planned to reconvene at B.B.'s office downtown after Game Five on Sunday night.

Eddie Cicotte was on the mound for the White Sox against Jimmy Ring the hard-throwing right hander of the Reds. Jimmy was psyched. He was pitching in his first World Series. He thanked whatever gods there were for Moran's belief in him even though he had been 10-9 for the season. In the locker room, Heinie and Greasy encouraged him to "stay cool now," knowing Jimmy's tendency to let his emotions interfere with his play. Ivey Wingo would catch him since they'd practiced together most frequently. Ivey was good at spotting when Jimmy started to throw wild. He was also good at calming him down. But those skills wouldn't be necessary today. Jimmy would throw a great game, shutting out the Sox with only three hits—the best pitching performance of the Series for the Reds.

Cicotte was psyched too, but for a different reason. He wanted this one. He had to make amends for his poor performance in Game One. He vowed to himself that he would do his best. And he did.

Gleason had thought long and hard about putting Cicotte in for his second try, but his choices were limited. He also considered delaying the announcement of the day's pitcher until right before the game, but this was not common practice at the time.

If such a policy had been in force then, the gamblers would have had a more difficult time with their "sure bets."[18]

In the second inning, the crowd cheered as Cicotte came to bat. He got a piece of the second pitch, but Rath made a beautiful running stop behind second. In the fourth inning, they started hitting him in earnest. Rath, Daubert, and Groh found daylight in succession. This time, Cicotte was thankful for teammates Jackson, Schalk, and Collins, who saved each one in order.

As Cicotte walked out to the mound for the top of the fifth, he must have had an ominous feeling. They were hitting him now; he had to do better. He was psyching himself up when Edd came up to the plate. He threw a low knuckler that grounded to Collins. One out. Duncan was up next and shot a drive right back at Cicotte's face. Reflexes kicked in, and he lunged for it, then fumbled. In a frenetic attempt to save the play, he heaved it toward Gandil at first, but the ball headed wildly in the direction of the grandstand. Duncan took second on the error.

Kopf was next and slammed a hard one past Weaver at third; Duncan tagged third and started home for the score. The fans went wild as Edd joined his teammates yelling to Duncan, "Run!" As Duncan sped for the plate with all his might, Jackson raced after the ball and heaved it home. In the heat of play, Gandil saw it was another wild throw slanting left toward first and yelled to Cicotte, "Cut it off!" At the same time, Schalk saw the ball was heading off course and yelled something Cicotte couldn't hear.[19]

With the crowd roaring in the background, Cicotte had two confusing messages hitting him. He tried to catch the errant ball. He strained with all his might, but the ball nicked his glove and glanced off, rolling between him and Schalk. Cicotte didn't see it as he ran around the mound desperately trying the find the illusive orb. Schalk did see it and threw off his mask in hot pursuit, but Duncan scored first. The Reds bench started to chant, "Bushers...Bushers...Bushers." This play and the one preceding it would be analyzed by baseball historians for years to come as examples of Cicotte throwing the game.[20]

In the press box, Matty and Hughie went crazy drawing circles on their scorecards. That was it! Cicotte was definitely throwing the game. No question about it now. Hughie was convinced he had been right all along.

In the stands, Ben Levi turned to shake brother Lou's hand. Behind them, Abe Attell was literally jumping up and down and slapping Ben on the back. Just behind Attell, Cal Crim scribbled in his notepad. He recognized Levi as the man he'd seen with Mowbray at the ballpark in July.

Then the most amazing thing happened. He saw the profile of a man who had been partially hidden from his line of sight behind the bodies of Levi brothers. He was seated next to them and chatting amiably. He was a well-known person in Cincinnati. Crim himself had chatted with this friendly fellow many times as he'd stopped to buy a newspaper from him. What was his name? Cal combed his mental files. Widmeyer …that was it! What the devil was Widmeyer doing sitting here with these crooks? Coincidence maybe? Maybe not. Cal scrawled a big circle around the word "Widmeyer?" in his notepad. He would be checking this out, for sure.

Over in the Reds Boosters section, Fred Mowbray was cheering loudly as he nodded with a knowing wink thrown in Dan Moul's direction. The wink didn't go unnoticed. Ora Slater caught it. He recognized Mowbray from the photos.

When a shaken Eddie Cicotte returned to the mound after two devastating errors in succession, he saw big Greasy Neale in front of him. He tried to shake it off, but he had nothing left. Too many batters, too many fields, too many years—it all became a blur. He didn't remember throwing the ball. Neale doubled to left, driving Kopf in to complete the scoring, the inning, and the game. Ring completed the 2-0 shutout and the Reds went up three games to one.

In the end, Cicotte gave up only five hits, but two of them became runs. That's where the Reds excelled. They didn't leave players on bases to die. What rang in the their ears was

Moran's voice drilling into them, "get the man home, whatever it takes."

Tom Swope's review of the famous fifth-inning play the next day explained that Cicotte was "trying hard to redeem himself for his one-sided defeat in the first Series game."[21] Jack Ryder referred to "Jackson's long throw to the plate" as a "rank misjudgment on Jackson's part" since he should have thrown to the Sox shortstop to stop Kopf.[22]

But, Hugh Fullerton wrote it as he believed it to be: "There is no alibi for Cicotte." In the next lines, he said, "The rumors of crookedness of fixed games and plots are thick. ...There are three different lies going the rounds equally ridiculous."

Ban Johnson read his old friend's column the next morning. He wondered to himself, "*Three* lies? What did Hughie know that he didn't? Worse yet, if Hughie knew, then so did Commy." It was good to have Cal on his side now.

As was pre-arranged, Edd called home from the Sherman Hotel that night. Essie reported that Mary was much improved and eager to see "Daddy" play when they returned to Cincinnati the next night for Game Six. She said the entire city was elated that the Reds were now up three games to one. She had gone to the Sinton that day to watch it on the electric scoreboard and said it was so crowded that they had to turn people with tickets away. Many fans had to pay the twenty-five-cent admission to go to the Cincinnati Gym at Shillito Place to watch it there. Essie was pleased that the officials at the Sinton scoreboard had given her, Eddie Roush's wife, a seat up front so that she could see well. She said the crowd whooped and yelled so loudly when Duncan scored in the fifth that the Sinton Hotel actually shook.

Then Essie said, "Your brother and I were almost arrested downtown today!" She chuckled as Edd went silent on the other end of the phone. Then she explained what had happened. Edd's brother, Fred, had accompanied Essie to the Sinton. The trouble had started when they left the hotel on their way to the celebration at the river. At 6th and Vine Streets a police officer spotted Essie and Fred and waved them over to the curb. He ran over to them looking pale and highly distraught. He directed his emotional comments to Fred. "What's the matter, Eddie? Tell me the truth! Why aren't you in Chicago? I've bet everything I have on the Reds!"

Fred and Essie laughed and explained the mix-up to the great relief of the policeman. A few blocks later, the mistaken identification happened again, except this time, the confused party was Edgar Freiberg, stockholder in the Reds. He would later tell reporters, "I was frightened to death when I saw Eddie Roush walking downtown with his wife today! Just imagine the Reds playing the White Sox without Eddie!"[23]

Edd had a good laugh. Then he told her how the Chicago fans had gotten to their feet and cheered him when he took the field for pre-game practice before Game Three.[24]

Neither mentioned the obvious—Edd had not gotten a hit in the game.

OCTOBER 6, 1919
CHICAGO, GAME FIVE

Sunday, October 5, broke with a heavy downpour that didn't let up all day. The fifth game of the 1919 Series was postponed to October 6. When Moran knocked on the door and told Edd and his roommate, Heinie Groh, the news, they both grunted, turned over in their beds and slept another hour. Edd, Heinie, and Bill Rariden met for a late breakfast and talked about the Series. Rariden had an inside track on the Sox since he had done most of the catching for the Giants in the 1917 World

Series against the Sox and had an opportunity to study their batting styles. He had given Edd tips on when to play deep in the outfield based on his knowledge of the Sox hitters.

While at breakfast, they ran into some of the hometown fans from Indiana. Edd was delighted to see some of the guys he had played with in Evansville and Oakland City eight years ago. There was a contingency from Bedford, Indiana, to see Rariden. They passed the rainy afternoon reminiscing with old friends.

Edd would later tell Essie that this "day off" had been a godsend. Both teams were exhausted from the pressure of the Series and the tiring travel required to play in both cities. October 5 was a much-needed gift. He hoped he'd be able to start hitting the next day. His clumsiness with the bat was not going unnoticed. His hometown newspaper said, "Eddie's defensive work is the talk of the Series. He has not had but one hit."[25]

However, not all of the Sox spent their day off relaxing. As the story goes, Nat Evans handed over the last of the payoff that the dirty Sox would see. Sport Sullivan, the player go-between, received it and delivered it to Chick Gandil. He promised the rest after the succeeding games. (Sullivan never made good on his promise.) Of Rothstein's remaining $30,000, Gandil gave four players $5,000 each, echoing Sullivan's promise that each would get his remaining $15,000 later. The players were Swede Risberg, Happy Felsch, Lefty Williams, and Shoeless Joe Jackson.[26] Buck Weaver and Fred McMullin received nothing. Cicotte's $10,000 was all he would see. Gandil kept the rest for himself.

And what of the gamblers who had been double-crossed by Rothstein and Attell and lost big on the Sox win in Game Three? There was only one way left to make money—the Reds. If they could arrange a counter-fix with the Reds pitchers, they could clean up on one or two games. The odds were now in favor of the Reds. A bet against them could pay a healthy profit. Ruether and Sallee were likely to return to the mound if the Series went to Games Six and Seven. Would they like to ride into the sunset with a little something extra in their saddle bags?[27]

ONE MORE

The Series resumed the next day with Horace "Hod" Eller and Claude "Lefty" Williams on the mound. Eller had slipped on the tile floor in the hotel corridor the night before. Although his left arm had been bruised it was not "swollen to twice its normal size" as the newspapers reported.[28] Eller's start meant the Reds became the first team in World Series history to start five different pitchers in the first five games. The feat showed the great depth of the Reds' staff. Generally a team's ace pitcher returned to start in the third or fourth games.

Game Five belonged to Hod Eller. He was dominant, setting a World Series record by striking out six White Sox in a row in the second and third innings. Even the Chicago players applauded Eller when he returned to the bench after his feat.

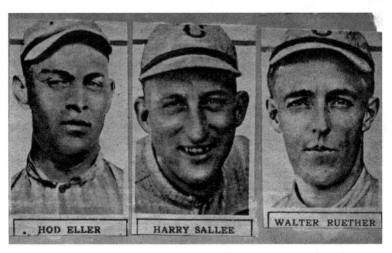

HOD ELLER   HARRY SALLEE   WALTER RUETHER

REDS PITCHERS: HOD ELLER, SLIM SALLEE, AND DUTCH RUETHER

Before the game, Christy Mathewson predicted, "Eller tomorrow will cut loose a shine ball far beyond anything Eddie Cicotte ever knew in the way of shining the pill." Matty knew what Hod could do.[29] In the fifth inning the fans roared when Bill Rariden fouled one off behind first base and a fan caught the ball in his megaphone.[30]

Eller received a standing ovation when he walked to the plate to bat in what was to be an exciting sixth inning. He responded by rapping a double. He continued on to third base on Felsch's bad throw. Rath promptly singled to right, scoring Eller for a 1-0 lead.

Daubert, as he had done many times throughout the season, sacrificed Rath over to second. Groh walked. Then up came Edd Roush. Edd was desperate for a hit. He suspected Williams would dust him again so he yelled at him, "Pitch the ball through here and I'll knock it down your throat." He did just that.

Edd broke the game open with a triple to deep center. Happy Felsch misjudged the ball and grasped wildly for it before it squirmed out of his glove. Rath scored for a 2-0 lead, and Groh was right behind him, sliding hard into home on a close play.

When Groh was declared safe, Sox catcher Ray Schalk jumped up and threw his body against umpire Cy Rigler's chest protector. As Schalk screamed at the umpire, fiery Reds pitcher Jimmy Ring exploded off the bench to enter the fray. Schalk threw his catcher's mask at Ring's knee. Rigler deflected it and ordered Schalk out of the game. Schalk stood defiantly until Rigler chased him to the bench. It was later reported as "the first time a player was chased by an umpire in a World Series."[31] It was the second time a player had been put out of a World Series game.[32]

Heinie Groh would later observe, "I was sorry to see Ray

Schalk who, with Buck Weaver, has been hustling hard through the Series, something I can't say of all the other Sox. But Schalk didn't tag me and should not have kicked so much.[33]

The rest of the game belonged to Edd and Pat Duncan. Pat ended the scoring with a sacrifice fly to left, and Edd scored on a great slide. The Reds added an insurance run in the ninth. Edd reached base on an error by Eddie Collins. Duncan walked and both moved up on Kopf's sacrifice bunt. Edd then scored again on Neale's ground out.

The final score was 5-0 and the Reds now led the Series four games to one. In previous years that would have been enough victories to win the Series, but because the Series had been extended to best of nine games that year, the Reds would have to win one more to clinch the World Championship.

The excitement in the Reds' clubhouse after the game was overwhelming. A chant went up that was repeated throughout the night, "One more, settle the score!" The guys were surprised by a visit from some of the Chicago Cubs who came in to celebrate with them. The Cubs had always hated Comiskey's "golden boys" who got the lion's share of the publicity in town. Heinie Groh said that Bill Killifer and Grover Cleveland Alexander were so happy they were crying.[34]

Pat Moran telegraphed home to say it was time to measure the flagpole at Redland Field for a World Championship flag.[35] Moran had a friendly battle on his hands to choose the next day's pitcher since one by one they each begged him to give them a shot. Rube Bressler was wild to get out there and so was rookie Eddy Gerner, the young southpaw who had only pitched one game in the regular season. Adolfo Luque had a one-inning taste and begged for more.

But the happiest Redleg of all was Hod Eller. The White Sox had cast him off four years earlier and beating them today with such a resounding victory was the dearest wish in his heart.

As a footnote to the story, Claude "Lefty" Williams delivered a credible performance as the losing pitcher for the Sox. He held the Reds scoreless until the sixth inning. If Williams was "throwing," it wasn't evident in Game Five.

With the Series sitting at 4-1 in favor of the Reds, Hugh Fullerton could only pull his oversized hat down and slip onto the train to Cincinnati.

Twelve special trains with Pullman cars were required to transport the teams, officials, newspapermen and fans returning to Cincinnati for Game Six. The writers were on the 11:30 train, following the team by one and a half hours.

CARTOON BELITTLING FULLERTON'S DOPE

There was only one thing on Edd's mind all the way home—Essie on Gilbert Hill. At least he'd gotten one hit today, but that was still miserable. Heinie wasn't doing much either. Was there some kind of jinx on the "heart and soul" of the Reds They had both excelled in defense, but they *had* to start hitting.

---

1   Author's Note: Descriptions of detective Cal Crim based on local news-paper articles (1901-1953) and author interviews with retired detective and Crim Bureau partner Claude E. "Bert" Hinds. October, 2004.
The author is indebted to Jim Sandoval, SABR researcher and 1919 expert, for the "lead" that led to the discovery of the role of Cal Crim in uncovering the baseball mystery of 1919.

2   On this date in Oakland City, Indiana, Laura Roush gave birth to twin boys—Edd and Fred.

3   Author's Note: Description of Johnson's and Comiskey's early years in Cincinnati drawn from various sources including Eugene Murdoch's biography of Johnson, *Czar of Baseball* (Greenwood Press, 1982), and articles by Earl Obenshain, Hugh Fullerton, and Douglas Linder. Conversation is hypothetical but true to the spirit of the lives of the characters and the times.

4   Still in existence after 92 years, and renamed Cal Crim Security, Inc., the present owner is Randy Hollenbaugh. Interview with author, Cincinnati, 2005.

5   Greg Rhodes and John Snyder. *Redleg Journal*. Road West Publishing, 2000.

6   Future Hall of Fame catcher Ray Schalk referred to his boss, Comiskey as the "Old Roman" and reported that he had been in his employ for two years before the boss deemed him worthy of a handshake. The *Evening Telegram* (Portland, Oregon). November 19, 1913.

7   Author interview with William A. Cook on August Herrmann, September, 2005.

8   John Saccoman, biographer. Tom Simon, Editor. *Deadball Stars of the National League*. SABR publications, 2004.

9   *Atlanta Constitution*. October 3, 1919.

10   *Cincinnati Post*. October 4, 1919.

11   Ibid.

12   Ibid.

13   *Cincinnati Enquirer*. October 4, 1919.

[14] John Lardner (son of Ring Lardner). "Remember the Black Sox?" *Saturday Evening Post*. April 30, 1938.

[15] Burns would testify in the Cook County Grand Jury in 1921. Many thought he was willing to snitch because Attell had double-crossed him.

[16] Case Report #2002 is included in the papers of Ban Johnson. HOF BSS/AL collection.

[17] Based on author interviews with Jonathan Slater, grandson, and Marilyn Barrow Smith, cousin, of Ora Slater. Cincinnati, October, 2004.

[18] Tris Speaker initiated the policy of announcing pitchers fifteen minutes before a game began in 1921 with the Cleveland Indians. Ban Johnson endorsed Speaker's decision and sent an official letter to all AL managers ordering them to adopt this system. *New York Times*. April 27, 1921.

[19] This controversial play was described by Gandil (1956) and Schalk (1921). HOF BSS/AL files.

[20] The description of these famous plays is exactly how Edd Roush described them in later interviews. He claimed the throw was wild, an error on Joe Jackson. Cicotte strained with all his might to catch the ball in a genuine attempt to save the play. He contended that the sportswriters called the play differently because at this point they had become convinced of a "fix" and were gunning for Cicotte.

[21] *Cincinnati Post*. October 6, 1919.

[22] Jack Ryder. *Cincinnati Enquirer*. October 6, 1919.

[23] "Talk of the Town." *Cincinnati Enquirer*. October 5, 1919.

[24] "The bugs applauded in so vociferous a manner that Roush had to acknowledge his reception." *Cincinnati Enquirer*. October 4, 1919.

[25] *Cincinnati Enquirer*. October 6, 1919.

[26] Jackson's wife, Kate, testified in his 1924 trial that Williams had passed the $5,000 bribe money to Joe and she had deposited it their account in the Chatham Bank of Savanah, GA.

[27] There is no hard evidence to support a Reds counter-fix. However Edd Roush believed that for some reason unknown to him, Ruether and Sallee "slacked off" in Games Six and Seven.

[28] *Cincinnati Enquirer*. October 7, 1919.

[29] Mathewson's quote reported by Grantland Rice in his syndicated column, October 7, 1919. Mathewson recruited Eller when he was the Reds manager in 1917.

[30] *Cincinnati Enquirer*. October 7, 1919.

[31] *The News and Courier*. Charleston, S.C. October 7, 1919.

[32] Frank Chance was thrown out by umpire Tom Connolly in 1910.

[33] *Cincinnati Enquirer*. October 7, 1919.

[34] William A. Cook. *The 1919 World Series*. McFarland & Co., 2001.

[35] Charleston, S.C. October 7, 1919.

11

On The Square

...Cincinnati was getting ready to tear down the fountain and get a statue of Pat Moran in the public square of Porkopolis....
— Hugh Fullerton, 10/7/19

OCTOBER 6, 1919
OFFICES OF BAN JOHNSON
FISHER BUILDING, CHICAGO

As Cal Crim and Ora Slater entered the wood-paneled barroom on the first floor of the Fisher Building in downtown Chicago, they were slightly intimidated. John Burns, the manager, had greeted them at the door and was now escorting them into the private sanctum known as the "J.V.B. Club." (No one knew for sure what the initials over the mirror stood for. Some guessed it meant "Johnson Victory Bar.") For years this room had been the nerve center of the American League.[1]

Ban Johnson stood at the bar with his trusted secretary of many years, Will Harridge. They looked like Mutt and Jeff. Although overweight and suffering from diabetes, Johnson still cut an imposing figure. Harridge, by contrast, was a thin, timid man with a severe speech impediment. However, he was the most loyal of employees as evidenced by his presence in this meeting with the detectives.

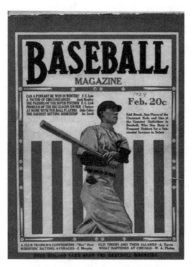

ROUSH ON COVER OF *BASEBALL MAGAZINE*

Johnson's face lit up when he greeted Cal, and his grip was warm as he shook the hand of the new man, Ora Slater. Any friend of Cal's was a friend of B.B.'s. He offered his guests a scotch and one of his favorite El Principe de Gales cigars. Ora accepted a cigar. Ban was a lavish entertainer. He drew a salary of $25,000 a year, and his "entertainment budget" was almost bottomless. He served at the pleasure of the American League team owners, and they expected only the best. Ban was relaxed, having played a round of golf that morning at the Edgewater Beach course overlooking Lake Michigan with his friend, Judge Charles MacDonald.

Since they all had a train to catch for Cincinnati that evening, the meeting would be brief. Cal reported their findings to date. They had no hard evidence yet, but through careful observation at the Chicago ballgames, they had some meaningful leads. As evidence, Cal gave Ban one name that night. It was a professional gambler named Ben Levi. Neither Ban nor Will had heard of him. Before arriving at Ban's offices, Cal had contacted a couple of friends who were detectives in the Chicago police force and made a few phone calls to his staff in Cincinnati. He had reviewed his notes from his summer observations at Redland Field and simply connected the dots. He planned to leave for St. Louis to investigate leads immediately after the final game of the Series.

Ban was surprised Cal's investigation would take him to Missouri instead of Boston, the "gambling center" of the nation at the time,[2] but he trusted his friend's sleuthing expertise. He felt no compulsion to rush to judgment until all the facts were in. The Series would be played out as planned. There was no need to stop it now; that moment had passed a week ago.[3] The objective now was to quell the rumors. No one wanted this to become some big "scandal" that could hurt baseball.

He had heard that Commy had hired detectives also, but he wasn't worried; that was just for show. If he knew anyone, he knew Charles Comiskey. He knew Comiskey would protect his investment above all things. Unless a great deal of pressure was applied, much more than just the current rumors, Comiskey would do nothing. There was too much money involved. This nine-game World Series was bringing big bucks into the Sox treasure chest.

Cal understood the situation. B.B. wanted the inside track as insurance against the future, and, in particular, against Commy. If this thing exploded into a scandal, and Commy tried to blame B.B., he'd have his ammunition ready. It was Cal's job to get the evidence before Commy did. Both were betting on the whole thing blowing over. Of course, if it didn't, it had to be Commy who would fall.

Cal understood the way B.B. thought. What a shame it would be if Comiskey lost his empire, and B.B. had to step in and pick up the pieces. Why, B.B. might have to assume the ownership of a struggling baseball team in his own hometown. What neither

Ban nor Commy were counting on was the tenacity of their old friend, Hughie Fullerton, the one who "talked too much."

OCTOBER 7, 1919
GILBERT HILL, CINCINNATI

It was early morning and still dark by the time Edd reached the door of their Gilbert Hill apartment after the train ride back from Chicago. Essie was awake. She had put Mary to bed late that night hoping she'd sleep in and let Edd rest. He never slept well on the train and often grabbed another couple hours of sleep when he got home. Essie hadn't slept much either. She was too excited to sleep. She was elated that the Reds had won two of the three games at Comiskey Park and were now sitting on a 4-1 lead in the Series. She expected Edd to be in good humor and was surprised when he opened the door with such a sad look on his face.

He walked across the room like a man carrying a hundred-pound weight on his shoulders. He sat down next to her at the breakfast nook and said, to her surprise, "Got any beer around here, Mrs. Roush?" Minutes later they were across from each other at the table, Edd with a cold Hudepohl and Essie with her coffee.

For a few moments they sat silently at the table. Finally, Edd released his burden in slow, measured sentences. He told her the whole story that had been plaguing him for the last three days in Chicago: waiting for the taxis, the conversation with Jimmy, the gamblers in the hotel.

To his surprise, Essie was not surprised. She'd never really trusted Jimmy as Edd did.[4] She asked him the most important question: "Do you believe it, Edd?"

He gave her the only answer he could, "I don't know what to believe," followed by, "and, I don't know what to do about it." Essie realized the impact of the information on Edd. The implications were staggering. She could see that Edd didn't want to believe Jimmy. He wanted to believe that his team was winning legitimately.

She also suspected that the real reason for Edd being so upset was his own failure to live up to his reputation as a star hitter in the Series. Although they didn't discuss it, she knew deep down that he was feeling himself a failure. She didn't tell him that the *Enquirer* had written about his triple in Game Five, but also mentioned he had only gotten two hits up to that point—both off of Williams.[5]

They talked a bit longer until exhaustion began to creep around Edd's eyes. He pulled himself up from the table, shuffled into the bedroom, and fell asleep with his clothes on.

Essie went in and nestled next to him. She stroked his hair across his forehead with great tenderness, and as the sun rose, she closed her eyes and whispered the nightly prayer from her childhood: "Thank you, God, I humbly pray, for all you've done for me today. If I should die before I wake, I pray to God my soul to take." Then she added, "Please, God, help Edd to do the right thing." And then an afterthought: "And please let him get a home run today."

GAME 6
REDLAND FIELD, CINCINNATI

This was to be the day the Reds won the World Series. Thousands of fans who were unable to get into Redland Field swarmed around newspaper office bulletin boards downtown. Those who had their lucky seats in the grandstand believed they were about to see history.

As Essie took her seat, she was confident the Reds would win the game, and she would have her husband back for the winter. The story Edd confided the night before reinforced her confidence in a victory. She thought, "If the Sox want to lose, let them lose. That suits me just fine!" She looked around the wives' box wondering if anyone else knew about the rumor. If so, no one said anything to her. It was probably all baloney anyway, she thought. That darn Jimmy Widmeyer shouldn't have upset Edd like that.

Before the game, a group of Texas oilmen presented a gold watch to Lone Star State native Dick Kerr. Such a watch was a perfect accompaniment for the vests that were stylish at the time.[6] This special attention may have inspired the diminutive hurler to pitch brilliantly on the day the city of Cincinnati expected their Reds to become World Champions. Dutch Ruether hurled for the Reds for the second time. After the game, Moran would face stiff criticism for choosing Ruether.

Edd was feeling good since he had finally gotten a few hours of sleep, and he'd released the burden he had been carrying by telling Essie. He was ready to play ball.

Cincinnati looked like a sure winner by the end of the fourth inning. The Reds scored two runs in the third and two more in the fourth for a 4-0 lead. In the third, Jake Daubert singled and then stole second base. Edd followed Jake and was hit hard on the third pitch from Kerr. Essie gasped in the stands. She had seen those bruises on Edd before.

Pat Duncan doubled in Edd and Jake. In the fourth, Greasy Neale tripled and scored on Ruether's double. When Greasy got back to the bench, Edd and Heinie were the first to congratulate their friend. This was Greasy's third triple of the Series. He was having a great Series and would end up with the highest batting average among the Reds.

Rath then grounded to Risberg at shortstop. Ruether made an attempt for third base on the play. Risberg's throw hit Ruether in the back as he was running. This allowed him to score the fourth run for the Reds. Rath moved up to second on the play. Rath then stole third. Jake Daubert lifted a fly to left field, with Rath attempting to tag up and score. Joe Jackson saved the run by firing a strong throw to the plate, nailing Rath and ending the Reds scoring for the inning and for the game.

The White Sox began their comeback in the fifth—with a little help from Dutch Ruether. Risberg and Schalk both drew bases on balls, with Kerr singling to load the bases. Greasy and Edd shared fearful looks in the field. In the stands, Essie's hands were tightly clasped together. Bases loaded, Sox.

Edd made two critical plays in the fifth that slowed the Sox rally. Shano Collins hit a solid drive into center field, and Edd picked it off easily. More importantly, he followed the catch with a strong throw home preventing the runners from advancing. Eddie Collins hit another one directly to center. It was dead in Edd's glove, but this time he was not able to prevent Risberg from scoring.

Edd swore under his breath and glanced up at Essie. He couldn't see her face, but he knew that she shared his pain. It felt good to have her there again. He had missed her in Chicago.

On the play, Kerr made a base-running mistake. Thinking that Schalk would advance to third, he ran for second base. Schalk, however, had stayed at second. Edd rallied to take advantage of the situation and fired directly to Heinie Groh in the infield. Kerr froze on his way to second while Heinie ran across the diamond to tag him, ending the inning.

As the Reds started back to the bench, Heinie slowed for Edd to catch up with him. He said, "What's with Dutch? He looks all out today."

Ruether had a decent start on the mound, but after five innings the Sox had scored four runs. In the sixth, the Sox rallied again, putting three more runs on the board. Weaver started the damage with a bloop double to left, and Jackson singled him in.

Hap Felsch doubled in Jackson. Heinie glanced back at Edd and both men were of a single mind. *What was wrong with Dutch?*

As Edd came into the bench he saw Rariden throw down his catcher's mask. It was unlike phlegmatic "B'gosh Bill" to get riled. Edd wondered if Dutch shaking off Bill's signals, or was Rariden merely upset with the turn of events?

Had the gamblers gotten to their pitcher? He remembered how they had to drag Ruether out of the bar the night before the opening clash. Moran had said, "Some piker-gambler tried to get one of my pitchers oiled up with hooch, but I found out and stopped it."[7] Edd thought it was a little odd that Moran had been unusually angry about it, since he was known to tip a few himself.[8] Edd guessed it was the presence of the gambler that upset his manager. Did Moran overhear the gambler pressuring his pitcher to throw a game? Why had he gotten drunk on the night before he was to pitch? Now he was blowing the game.

At that moment, Pat Moran had seen enough and motioned to the bullpen. As Ruether hung his head and took the bench, the look on Moran's face was one of sadness more than anger. The team knew how Moran had taken pride in his development of this young pitcher. It hurt him to see him fail.

Jimmy Ring, the Game Four starter and victor, entered the fray. Ring was able to produce two outs, but Ray Schalk singled through shortstop Kopf to score Felsch for the third run of the inning. The game was now tied going into the seventh inning, 4-4.

For the next three innings, the united citizenry of Cincinnati held its breath. Ring was beginning to throw wild, but his teammates were saving him. The fans were perplexed. What was going on? This was supposed to be the championship game. Come on, Reds—put those uppity Chicago boys to bed!

In the top of the eighth inning, the Sox rallied again. Ring walked both Jackson and Gandil. Risberg then fired a solid low liner to center field. Edd was playing back and had to run hard to get there. The ball was just about to hit the ground when he scooped it up off the top of his shoestrings. The crowd roared as the Sox retired. The band struck up their "Roush song." They had a song for every player now and would stop between choruses and shout out the player's name. "Pack your troubles in your old kit bag...(ROUSH!)...and smile, smile, smile... (ROUSH!)" Essie loved it.

The game remained tied until the tenth, when Buck Weaver doubled to left. Duncan couldn't quite reach it. Jackson bunted and beat catcher Bill Rariden's throw to first, putting runners on first and third. Now the Reds were in trouble. Ring took a deep breath as he faced Gandil. The crowd put up a mighty roar. Out in the field, Edd couldn't hear anything but the crowd. He frantically waved his arms to try to quiet them. When Essie saw his desperation, she yelled "shush" to everyone in the boxes around her, but they were stomping their feet now and refused to stop.

Gandil hit the second offering for a slow, high bounder that should have been an easy infield catch. It wasn't. The crowd was screaming so loudly that the infielders couldn't hear each other's signals, and the ball went between them. Weaver scored: 5-4, Sox. With thousands of dollars of gambler money in his pocket, Gandil got the winning hit.

In the bottom of the tenth, the Reds had one more chance. Edd came to bat. He was praying now. In the stands, Essie crossed her fingers, her toes, and every other part of her body she could think of.

In the final moments, Kerr was masterful. He refused to give Edd anything to hit. Edd had to resort to the technique he used for outside pitches. His bat was heavy but also shorter than most, but he could get a piece of an outside pitch by loosening his grip as he swung.[9] The bat slid through his hands and automatically lengthened a few inches, just enough to reach the ball. Edd tried this approach on Kerr's fifth pitch, but his hit was weak. Eddie Collins grabbed the wobbly grounder and put Edd out at first. The same fate befell Duncan and Kopf.

The White Sox won a hard-fought 5-4 victory. Jimmy Ring pitched the last five innings, giving up only one run but taking the loss. Kerr went the distance for the Sox, allowing four runs and earning the win. Ruether allowed the four hits that had sealed the fate of the Reds.

Many said it was the most exciting game of the Series. Hugh Fullerton thought otherwise. He called it a "slow, unemotional game" played in front of "a semi-hysterical crowd." He said the Sox had given up in the beginning with a "We're licked" attitude. He said any team could have beaten them in the beginning. He attributed the Reds' loss to the lousy pitching of Dutch Ruether who was "far from the fellow who won the first game of the Series." Hugh gave one plaudit to the Reds.

> The Reds outfield performed much better than that of the Sox...much advertised as superior. ...what glory was coming belongs to Roush, who certainly stalled off that defeat for a long time. He made one of the most remarkable catches ever seen in a ball game, a driving scoop of a line drive that would have given Chicago a huge majority.[10]

On the way home, the fans were shell-shocked. What had happened to their team? How had they lost the momentum they'd had a week ago, even on the home field? Overnight the odds changed back to even money again.

At home, the *Enquirer* noted: "Ruether who had allowed only two hits in the first four sessions grew careless and with his lack of control went the super confidence of the team behind him."[11]

Writer Frank Menke described the feeling in the city: "…a chill of fear pulsed in the bosoms of those who disport the crimson hue of Rhineland."

OCTOBER 8, 1919
GAME SEVEN, REDLAND FIELD

Essie sat down next to Ruby Rariden a few minutes late. After making the usual pleasantries around the wives' box, she took a deep breath and looked up. She couldn't believe her eyes. Where were all the people? The grandstand was a ghost town and the game was about to begin. It was ominously quiet in the stands as a chill ran through her. Were fans boycotting the game? Had JImmy Widmeyer told everyone in town? Had the entire city of Cincinnati been listening to the conversations between she and Edd in their breakfast nook? She shuddered.

Essie hadn't had time to read the newspaper that morning, or she would have known about the column in the *Cincinnati Times-Star*. "There is a story going the rounds to the effect that the Reds threw the game Tuesday on account of the gate receipts. The remarkable thing about the story is that a considerable number of Cincinnatians think it is true." Were the people of Cincinnati insulted by the thought that Garry Herrmann, the owner of the Reds, was manipulating the Series to line his pockets?[12]

After the fact, more rational voices attempted to explain the phenomenon. *The Spalding Guide* said the falloff was "due to a misunderstanding concerning the sale of tickets." *The Sporting News* speculated that the Reds "didn't make the arrangements that should have been made for the tickets."[13] Fans had been able to buy three-game ticket strips for home games one, two, and six. When the Series unexpectedly went to a seventh game, single tickets had to be prepared and distributed.[14] Although some became available at Redland Field, its location in the West End was dangerous at night, perhaps keeping fans away.

Another explanation was that Sox fans had given up and not even come to Cincinnati. But, with primarily Cincy rooters, the park had been sold out the day before.

Whatever the reason, attendance at Redland Field dropped to less than half. Whereas 32,006 fans had turned out for Game Six and more than 10,000 had been turned away, only 13,923 fans showed up for Game Seven. It seemed the Cincinnati mindset had changed overnight. The massive celebrations after games one and two a mere week ago seemed a distant memory. The idea that something was rotten appeared to be the common perception.

The real shame of the empty stands was the effect it would have on the home team in Game Seven. Just twenty-four hours before, there had been 30,000 people in love with every player wearing a Reds cap. They had become a raging mob ready to come on the field and devour the opponent. They breathed with the players as one. When they went away, it seemed to the players that their beloved city had withdrawn its support, as if those Red boys were bad children who needed to be punished.

Edd would later say, "I didn't blame the fans. We should have won that game the day before." When the Sox took the field at 1:15, they saw the empty stands. They heckled the Reds mercilessly, telling them their fans had given up on them. They couldn't have said much that would make Edd feel worse. He needed a good hit today.

Game Seven began as a match up of two veteran pitchers who had faced each other twice in the 1917 Series. Slim Sallee was then a member of the New York Giants, along with current teammate Bill Rariden. Cicotte, who had lost two previous games in this Series, was determined to get into the win column with a victory this time. Ivey Wingo would catch Sallee. He had been Sallee's teammate in St. Louis during his rookie year of

1911. Sallee had spent almost a decade with the Cardinals before being traded to the Giants in 1916.

The White Sox jumped out to an early lead that the Reds were not able to overcome. In the first inning, Shano Collins singled to center and was sacrificed to second by Eddie Collins. Scoring a run in the third and two more in the fifth gave Cicotte a lead he would not relinquish. Sallee looked like an old man on the mound. Gone was the wily spark of Game Two. Edd just shook his head watching the Sox score. He wondered what had happened to the pitchers, first Ruether and now Sallee, two friends on the team. Two bad days in a row; it seemed fishy. Had Herrmann told them to slack off to prolong the Series and make more money at the gate?

Finally, Moran pulled Sallee, and Ray Fisher completed the inning. But he was no better. Luque was snapping at the bit in the bullpen, so Moran gave him his chance. Dolf Luque pitched four shutout innings of relief, fanning five. Many wondered if Game Seven would have ended the Series if Luque had started instead of Sallee. Luque's career was just beginning. He would go on to make baseball history with the Reds in the next decade.

There would have been more scoring by the Sox if it hadn't been for the exceptional play of Reds infielders Rath and Kopf. This was their best game of the Series—and Edd's worst.

The Reds had a brief flurry in the sixth when Heinie Groh belted a double over the temporary left field fence near the foul line. Edd was up next, and Essie gritted her teeth as he took the plate. She knew that Edd needed this one desperately. He was increasingly upset about his failure at the bat. He'd only gotten one hit yesterday and nothing today. It was getting embarrassing.

He was at 2 and 2 when he connected with a mediocre slap at the ball. Essie jumped up and screamed, but her joy was short-lived. The ball dribbled toward Cicotte and Edd was out at first. However, Groh moved to third on the out, and Duncan singled him in. As Essie sat down, she was sorry for Edd, but, she was still hopeful. She didn't know that Groh had put the only Reds run of the day on the scoreboard. Final score: 4-1, Sox.

Kid Gleason had been quoted as saying that if they could beat Sallee in Game Six the Sox would come back to win the Series. It was starting to look like that was a possibility.

Hugh Fullerton wrote about how Cicotte had redeemed himself that day, but the pitcher did more than that. Cicotte would later say (under oath), "I didn't care whether or not I got shot out there the next minute. I was going to win the ballgame and the Series. I didn't care for the money after that. I lost too many friends there at baseball, friends that look up to me, and everything depended on it and I couldn't stand it."[15] Only a handful of Sox players would ever know what it felt like to be on a baseball field in front of thousands of people praying you wouldn't get shot in the next minute.

Fullerton also lambasted Moran for his choice of pitchers: "...he should have used anyone excepting Sallee today." His words described perfectly the feelings of the city of Cincinnati: "Tonight the Red Rooters are in a panic."[16]

Edd Roush was in his own little panic at the end of Game Seven. He felt that his poor hitting was responsible for his team's losses. Even Heinie had gotten a double today, but under Roush the box score would say "0." He was playing worse than he'd played all season. In fact, he was sitting at a miserable .130 (3 for 23). The Sox strategy for the Series seemed to be to avoid giving Roush or Groh anything to hit. Let the other Reds beat them if they could, but don't let the two stars do it. Given the lack of hits from Edd and Heinie, the strategy appeared to be working. Without their bats, the Reds couldn't generate enough runs to win.

Pat Moran was both embarrassed and upset. It was bad enough that his star hitters couldn't produce, but what had happened to Dutch and Slim? He felt betrayed. Pat had figured Dutch was "gambler prey" that first night in the roadhouse before the Series began, but his performance the next day had erased that suspicion. Now, it reared its ugly head again. Maybe it was all coincidence, and the Sox had been on fire in their rally. Anybody could have a bad day.

What about tomorrow? Moran wondered if should he put Eller on the mound again. It would be his third game in a week. Would he be able to meet the challenge where his colleagues had failed?

For a second, he considered going to Herrmann but was afraid to relinquish the control that he had been given by the owner. If he talked to anyone, he would seek wise counsel from his friend, Jake Daubert. Finally, he decided to "keep it in the family."

But it didn't stay there. As baseball historian Gene Carney has noted, "There were rumors after games 6 and 7 that the Reds were losing on purpose, to extend the Series and bring in more revenue—or because they were bribed to lose by gamblers."[17]

But it was not just the fans of Cincinnati who were panicking that night. There were several people who stood to lose some *serious* money if the Sox won the Series. Among them were some of Cincinnati's finest, some of Des Moines' less desirable, and one man in New York who stood to lose an estimated half-million dollars. After Game Seven, Arnold Rothstein was not pleased. He made a call.

Someone else made a call that same night. It was Ban Johnson. After two days of watching the White Sox decimate the Reds, he was convinced that these "fix" rumors were just rumors. There was no need to pursue the investigation further, just a waste of money. It looked like the American League was going to be victorious and the rumors would be forgotten. He thanked Cal Crim for his services and asked him to send a final expense report. As they hung up, Cal closed the file on Case

2002. Then, he paused. He had that kind of premonition only an experienced sleuth would trust. He placed the file in the "Active" drawer of his cabinet.

A SHADOW IN THE NIGHT: ACT TWO

Was it coincidence, or was it the fated second act? It was the same scenario repeating itself with new dialogue. Edd was again standing outside the Metropole Hotel waiting for the taxis to take the team to the Chicago train for Game Eight. He was again smoking his cigar. This time Jimmy Widmeyer beckoned for Edd to come over to the side of his newsstand. The conversation was again succinct.[18]

"Edd, you know what I told you about the gamblers getting to the White Sox?

Edd replied with a "Yup."

"Well, they got to some players on your own ball club now!" Jimmy was adamant. "Some smart crooks, angry at the double-cross by the New York gamblers, began figuring out a way to get even and recoup their losses. If they could get the Reds to throw a couple games, they'd clean up because by now everyone figured the Reds were set to win. Looks like they succeeded."

Instantly Edd's mind raced back to Game Six and the Sox clobbering Ruether. "If that's true, I know damn well what it is." Edd said. "It has to be the pitching. It's damn sure not in the field." Then he remembered Sallee's balk in Game Two.

Jimmy said nothing else. He didn't deny Edd's allegations. Jimmy was going to keep this one to himself until he saw Edd standing there looking like he'd lost his best friend. Jimmy figured Edd was blaming himself for the losses, so he decided to tell his friend what he had heard.

Jimmy's message struck Edd to the quick. He looked into those wide eyes for a few long seconds, but Jimmy was done.

He'd said his piece. Jimmy started packing up his newsstand for the night.

Edd knew now what he had to do.

Although it was 5 a.m. when the team checked into the hotel in Chicago, Edd kept his promise and phoned Essie from the booth downstairs. She was waiting for his call. He wanted to tell her about Jimmy, but was afraid to say anything on the telephone. Edd remembered how his mother used to listen in on party-line conversations in Oakland City. Essie had thought he was unusually somber that morning but just figured that Edd was worried about the upcoming game. She knew the losses in Redland Park had hurt the team's pride, particularly after the stunning wins in the first two games there. If they lost tomorrow, they'd have to return to Cincinnati for Game Nine, and then they might lose the whole Series. She wished him luck, said, "I love you, Edd" and they hung up.

OCTOBER 9, 1919
GAME EIGHT, COMISKEY FIELD

At exactly 11 a.m. Edd walked into the clubhouse loaded for bear.[19] He had kept the conversation with Jimmy to himself all night on the train, but he had thought of nothing else and had not slept well. He had visions of Ruether drinking with the gamblers the night before Game One. Although Dutch had pitched well the next day, he remembered his lousy performance in Game Six when Ring was brought in to replace him in the fifth. Then Moran had to pull Ruether's pal Sallee yesterday in the sixth inning.

Edd stood at his locker and waited for his moment. He was still burning and committed now to bringing it all out into the open. Jimmy's words had cut deep. He knew Ruether was standing down the row and couldn't bear to look at him. Then he saw Hod Eller and remembered that he would be pitching today. Come to think of it, he wasn't sure about Eller either. And he'd been the one who recommended Eller to Matty back in 1917 when Eller was still playing semipro. He seemed honest enough then.

Who could he trust? The whole room seemed suspect to him. He knew it was irrational, but he couldn't help it. These rumors about gambling collided with his anxiety over the ballgame, and the emotions were poisoning him.

The moment neared. Moran was due to arrive any minute. He would come in and call a clubhouse meeting to go over the other team's hitters. That would be Edd's chance. Moran navigated his short, stocky body into the locker room. He looked like a pugnacious little bulldog. He had a temper, too, and it got worse when he was drinking. He was called by many descriptive nicknames through the years, such as "Dot Irisher" and "Old Whiskey Face." To his credit, he drank alone, never imbibing with his players. Five years later the alcohol would kill him.[20]

Moran cleared his throat and spoke loudly to his players: "We'll have a meeting today before you all—"

"I have something to say," Edd interrupted. He paused. "I hear someone on this club doesn't want to win today. I understand that the gamblers have gotten to some players on *this* ball club, and damned if I'm going out there and run myself to death trying to win a World Series if somebody around here is trying to throw it!"

No one responded. Edd looked straight at Dutch and Slim. He would later describe the scene with the phrase, "You could hear a pin drop." Receiving no response, Edd went on to say, "I'll be out in center field watching every move and nobody better do anything funny. No damn crook is going to rob *me* of my winning share of this Series."

Moran's steely glare scoured the room. Then he said,

"Jake, Edd," and motioned for them to join him in the shower room. As the trio left the locker room, the rest of the players remained silent. Moran told Edd to repeat what he had just said and he did. Jake looked dumbfounded. Then Moran cut to the chase, "Eller is our pitcher today. We need to talk to him." He nodded to Jake.

A somber Jake walked back into the open space of the locker room, where Hod Eller stood with his back to him.

"Moran wants you," Jake said. Hod followed Jake to the shower room.

"I want the truth right now," Moran said to Hod. "Did any gamblers offer you money to throw today's game?"

Hod didn't miss a beat. He raised his thick, black eyebrows and looked directly at his manager and said, "Yup. I had breakfast and went upstairs, and a guy got on the elevator with me. He got off the same place I did and followed me to my room in the hotel in Chicago. As I was unlocking the door, he said 'Wait a minute.' He walked right up to me and held up five thousand-dollar bills. He said 'These are yours if you throw the game tomorrow. And there'll be five more just like them for you after the game.'"[21]

There was a stunned silence. Somehow Moran had not fully expected the answer he got. Edd wondered later, was it because he didn't want to believe it, or because he didn't expect his player to tell him the truth? Moran asked Eller, "What did you tell him?"

Hod's natural backwoods honesty gleamed behind his eyes. He, too, had waited for this moment. He was exploding with the desire to tell his story. And, he knew he was blameless. He straightened his back and prepared to relive the event. "I told him to get out of my sight quick, or I'd punch him right square on the nose." His dark eyes flashed with anger. "And I would have, too. I don't have no use for those kind of guys."

No one could doubt the young pitcher, and Edd felt a surge

of pride in his teammate. He knew Hod spoke the truth. Hod's and Edd's careers had paralleled one another. Both were Hoosiers and both started in the Three-I League in the Midwest. When Christy Mathewson was putting together his team in 1917, Hod and Edd were both new members. He felt a slight pang of guilt at the thought that he had suspected him. Damn that Jimmy Widmeyer.

But Moran still had a job to do. All eyes were on the boss. Moran said, "Okay, Eller, I'm going to start you today. But if I see anything off-kilter, if they start hitting you, I'm gonna yank you. Understand?"

Eller responded with a simple "Yup." He walked back to his locker and continued to adjust his gear. He didn't seem the least bit upset. In fact, he looked relieved to have the story out in the open. Now it was time to play ball.

While Moran was having a heart-to-heart in one locker room, Kid Gleason was addressing his team next door. As he would confide to sportswriter Harvey Woodruff, "We've had a player's meeting. I told them the talk going round. They know they're under suspicion…. I'm crushed and heartbroken over what I fear is happening."[22]

Unfortunately, no one on the Sox was willing to be as honest as Eller. And unlike Moran, Gleason didn't need to ask for confessions; he *knew* who the culprits were. He could only pray they would keep the promise of their handshakes with him for one more day.

PLAY BALL!

Chicago fans filled the stadium. They were rabid for a win today. Some feared that a loss might ignite a fury so great that the fans might attempt to locate Mrs. O'Leary's cow again. October 9 was the forty-eighth anniversary of the great Chicago fire.

ROUSH SAFE AT SECOND BASE
WITH EDDIE COLLINS LOOKING ON

The final game of the 1919 Series in Chicago will be talked about as long as there is baseball. As the story goes, White Sox starting pitcher Lefty Williams was approached the evening before and threatened with the possibility of injury to his wife if he didn't lose the game.[23] Hugh Fullerton reported a year later that before Game Eight started, he was told by a gambler (likely Bill Burns), "Better get a bet on the Reds. You'll see the biggest first inning you ever saw in your life."[24] Had Rothstein's telephone call done the trick?

An examination of Williams's performance in the first inning lends credence to this story. But this was his third game in one week, and the Reds had his curves all figured out by this time. He didn't last through the inning. With the first six balls he pitched, he gave up five hits and four runs. With one out, Daubert and Groh singled. Edd later said that he "saw the curve coming" and whopped it for a double.[25] Daubert scored and Groh moved to third. When Pat Duncan followed with a double, Groh and Edd came in to score.

Gleason was horrified. If there was ever a time the Sox manager felt duped, it was the first ten minutes of the final game of the World Series. With anger, not sadness, he yanked Williams from the box. Bill James came in to pitch. He gave up a single to Bill Rariden and Duncan scored. (Duncan's run was charged to Williams.) The Reds scored four runs in the first inning. They scored single runs in the second (Groh) and fifth innings (Kopf tripled) and put the game away with three more (Eller, Rath, Roush) in the sixth.

By this time Gleason was livid. In desperation, he replaced James with Roy Wilkinson. Wilkinson hit Edd with a pitched ball in the eighth, and his teammates moved him around the diamond to home with little effort, completing the scoring.

Edd delivered an excellent performance in Game Eight. He finally connected and slapped out three hits in five at-bats, scored two runs, and drove in four others. He also made a spectacular catch in the ninth on a swat off the bat of Nemo Leibold. Leibold hit a fly to the right of Neale, who lost it in the sun. Edd rushed over and made the catch while sliding on his shoulders. Greasy Neale loved to recall that "Eddie did a *full somersault*," but came up with the ball safely in his hands. He said that Edd "never knew how to hit the ground and roll like a football player, so he often jammed his shoulder, generally the right one. But he played anyway, even when he could hardly lift a bat."[26] Edd loved to recall Greasy's hitting in the Series: "Greasy saved us in the '19 Series. He was on fire at the plate."[27]

The White Sox tried to come back, scoring a run in the third on Joe Jackson's home run, the only one of the Series. They put four runs on the board in the eighth, but Eller managed to hold back the onslaught with an array of fastballs and shine balls. His left pant leg was worn threadbare in the spot where he "shined" the ball on his left thigh. Eller finished the game and was awarded the win as the Reds beat the Sox 10-4. They clinched their first World Championship.[28]

> Six little White Sox, very much alive,
> Eller fanned one and then there were five.

Five little White Sox, hoping they would score,
Eller fanned one and then there were four.
Four little White Sox, chipper as could be,
Eller fanned one and then there were three.
Three little White Sox feeling very blue,
Eller fanned one and then there were two.
Two little White Sox, having lots of fun,
Eller fanned one and then there was one.
One little White Sox, standing all alone,
Eller fanned him and then there were none.[30]

FINAL BALL THROWN IN 1919 SERIES, SIGNED BY HOD ELLER[29]

The Sporting News later declared Edd Roush the fielding star of the Series.

> Critics concede (to Roush) the honor of being the star of the Big Games when it came to spectacu-lar fielding. In the final game he pulled another brilliant piece of work. (As) the White Sox were

making a desperate dying effort and every bit of
help that the hard-pressed Hod Eller could get
from his teammates was an item.

Sixty-five years later, baseball historian Stanley McClure
would remember the defensive prowess of Edd Roush.

> There have been several great catches by out-
> fielders in World Series games; Willie Mays in
> 1954, Sandy Amoros in 1955. But the World
> Series has never seen such great outfielding as
> that of Edd Roush in 1919. Roush made sever-
> al extraordinary plays in this Series, some in
> game-saving situations... little credit has been
> accorded to him. His efforts should be accepted
> and rated as one of the most outstanding..."[31]

In the eight games he had a record 30 putouts and a .943
fielding percentage. Edd also tied an offensive record of zero
strikeouts in more than 28 at bats.

Although there was no Most Valuable Player award in 1919,
years later baseball expert Bill Deane published his "What If"
awards and chose Edd as MVP of the National League and Joe
Jackson as MVP of the American League.[32] Bill James, using a
sophisticated statistical analysis, chose a Gold Glove winner for
each position in both leagues in the deadball era (1901-1919).
For 1919, James awarded the Gold Glove to two Reds: Groh at
third base and Roush in center field.[33]

When the dust cleared and the statisticians completed their
analysis of the 1919 World Series, the numbers didn't lie.[34] The
Reds posted a batting average of .255 with 64 hits and 35 runs in
251 at bats. The Sox averaged .224 with 59 hits and 20 runs in
263 at bats. The shaky games of the Series were One, Two, Four,

and Five, which were lost by the Sox primarily because two of their top hitters (Collins and Schalk) did not peform.[35] Both teams accumulated 12 errors each. The outstanding hitter for the Reds was Greasy Neale[36] with a .357 in 28 tries, whereas Joe Jackson pounded .375 (32 at-bats). (Strange tally for a man trying to throw games.) The two top hitters for the Reds in the regular season had poor showings: Roush at .214 and Groh at .172.

Years later Edd and Heinie were still reliving those dramatic moments. They were the motivators, the hustlers, the never-say-die guys on the team. They would sit outside the Roush trailer in Bradenton and chastise themselves because they didn't deliver at the plate.[37] They'd try to make each other feel better. Heinie would recall Edd's smashing a triple in Game Five, and Edd would remind Heinie of the doubles he got when they counted. Heinie agreed when Edd said, "We had something to prove. The dopers had called us the underdogs."

The difference, according to many baseball experts, was the X-factor: the 1919 Reds played as a team. J.H. Lanigan, sports editor for the *Cleveland Plain Dealer,* said it best:

> Perhaps there are many of those who predicted the White Sox would win, did so through a sympathy for the American League and hope that their predictions would come true. They feared a team made up of so-called 'misfits' would blow in the pinches. They counted not the great total strength and ability of the Cincinnati aggregation.[38]

HEROES HOMECOMING

The first city to ever field a professional baseball team had finally won a World Series. The hearts of Cincinnatians swelled with pride and beat as one. Congratulations poured in from many directions. Gleason said he was glad that, if the Sox couldn't win it, Moran and Herrmann were victorious. He also said that the Reds had the better ball club *this week*.

John Galvin, the Cincinnati mayor, said he would graciously abdicate if Moran wanted the job. What pleased Moran most was a telegram from Fitchburg, Massachusetts, saying "Congratulations" and simply signed "Dad." The minute he got back to his wife and two sons in Cincinnati, he fired off a return telegram to his father, a mill worker, that read, "Proud of my Daddy and Proud to be your Son. This moment was the highlight of Pat Moran's short life. He had taken the underdogs that nobody thought had a chance and made them world champions.

Fountain Square filled up with joyous fans. In streets and hotels, crowds congregated. The superintendent of schools declared a holiday. A check for $117,157.35, the winning share of receipts for the Reds, was handed to captain Heinie Groh at the Reds offices in the Wiggins Block Building. The check was drawn on the new Fifth Third National Bank of Cincinnati[39] in which majority interest was held by the family of Horace Schmidlapp. Each of twenty regulars received $5,207.01 apiece, whereas partial shares were given to Frank Bancroft, business manager, Matty Schwab, groundskeeper, Doc Hoskins, and players See, Schreiber, and Duncan. (Duncan's performance in the Series warranted more the half share, $2,612, that he received.[40]) Pat Moran received a well-earned manager's bonus of $5,000.

Unlike modern times when players receive an elaborate ring clustered with diamonds, the Reds of 1919 expected no more than their bonus money. However, in an unexpected gesture of generosity, Garry Herrmann decided to give each of his players a personal gift. (Herrmann could afford to be generous with a gate receipt total of $722,414 for the Series.) In keeping with the fashion of the times, Herrmann awarded diamond stickpins to each Reds player.

The unique design on the circular head of the stickpin featured a baseball diamond in relief. Engraved in the outer circle were the words, "Worlds Champions— 1919." A small one-third carat diamond was placed in the center, in the middle of the pitcher's mound. (The symbolism may not have been intended, but the depth of the Reds pitching staff was certainly a critical element in their success.) Each player's name was engraved on the back, but the Reds joked that the engraver must have been drunk. The head of the pin was so small that few names came out right. Edd's stickpin read "dd J Rous". (At least the engraver got the double "d" on it.)

There was another award that may have served as an incentive for the Reds in the final game in Chicago. An anonymous wealthy Cincinnatian sent word to Herrmann that he would award a $500

1919 SERIES
CHAMPIONSHIP
ENGRAVED STICKPIN

gold pocket watch to the Reds player who "contributed the most to the final game victory." On the train home to Cincinnati, Herrmann called Edd into his private car. When Edd entered the car, Fred Mowbray stood and led the guests in an enthusiastic toast, "Here, here…all hail Roush!" Then Herrmann added his personal congratulations to Edd for his fine performance of the day and informed him that the mystery donor had chosen him as his "personal MVP" for Game Eight. He handed him a small square box. Edd thanked him and, feeling uncomfortable among the magnates, Edd politely took his leave. As Edd sat down in his Pullman berth, he opened the box. Nestled in the center of purple velvet was an exquisite Patek Phillipe pocket watch that chimed on the quarter, half, and full hour. Edd smiled with pride and the anticipation of the look on Essie's face when saw this beautiful prize.[41]

Upon their arrival in Cincinnati early on the October 10, a large crowd, along with a band, filled the station to cheer the team. The train dispatcher at the station bent a rule by instead of placing the name of the train on the board announcing the arrivals he placed the following: "World's Champs due at 7:12. On time." The fans hollered out the names of players as they disembarked from the train. Edd was oblivious to the cheers, because he was looking so hard to find Essie in the crowd. She was not there.

The Reds were whisked away to a celebratory breakfast at the Business Man's Club. Standing at the door to greet the heroes were club president Henry Frost and Fred Mowbray. When Edd walked into the club he walked right past the two men. He was looking for Essie. A big smile broke over his face as his eyes met those of his wife. In a rare display of public emotion, the couple from Indiana hugged each other. Finally, it was over.

Edd and Essie had completed a difficult journey together. Edd had displayed courage in the face of adversity, giving an outstanding performance while shouldering the heavy burden of secret information that he didn't ask to know. He hadn't slept well since the first night when he had been haunted by shadowy whispers of a crime in the process. Essie had been his confidant, helping him through the dark and confusing days. They would not realize the true magnitude of their journey for months to come. For now, it was enough to be in each other's arms again.

---

1   Eugene C. Murdock. *Czar of Baseball*. Greenwood Press, 1982.

2   Author's Note: Boston would be eclipsed by Manhattan and, later, Chicago.

3   Comiskey would later lash out at Johnson for not stopping the Series

after Game One. "I blame Ban Johnson for allowing the (1919) Series to continue. If ever a League President blundered in a crisis, Ban did." Erik Varon, SABR researcher. www.1919blacksox.com. March 5, 2005.

4   Author's Note: In numerous interviews between this author and Essie, she was open and effusive in her descriptions of all the people in this book whom she knew. On several occasions, when asked about Jimmy Widmeyer, she would grimace and merely say, "You ask your grandfather about that man."

5   *Cincinnati Enquirer.* October 7, 1919.

6   Five years later (1924) Edd would be the recipient of a gold watch given by another Texan from Beaumont named Jerry Weiss. It was an exquisite engraved pocket watch made by Patek Phillippe in Geneva, Switzerland.

7   Mike Bass. *The Sporting News.* October 17, 1994.

8   Hugh Fullerton reported that Pat Moran was "wild with anger" about Ruether's drinking escapade the night before the Series began. *The Sporting News.* October 17, 1935.

9   Edd would later describe this batting technique to F.C. Lane. *Baseball Magazine.* August, 1926.

10   *Atlanta Constitution.* October 8, 1919.

11   *Cincinnati Enquirer.* October 7, 1919.

12   The gross receipts for Game Six had set a then single-game record of $101,768.12.

13   Gene Carney. "A Minor Mystery." Paper for SABR 34 National Convention, Cincinnati, 2004.

14   A more colorful explanation for the low attendance in Game Seven was written by Tom Swope years later. He said that Garry Herrmann had over-slept that morning and forgotten he had a suitcase full of tickets to be distributed to seller sites that day. Thus, the tickets were never made available to the fans.

15   Cicotte testimony in Joe Jackson trial. (Milwaukee, 1924)

16   Hugh Fullerton. *Atlanta Constitution.* October 9, 1919.

17   Gene Carney. *Burying the Black Sox.* Potomac Books, 2006.

18   Based on word-for-word account by Edd Roush given to this author and to sportswriter Dan Daniel in 1937.

19   Reds locker room event description recalled by Roush on author interview tape #3, 1978.

20   Moran died of Bright's Disease in 1924. Edwin Pope. *Baseball's Greatest Managers.* 1960.

21   Author's Note: The name of gambler was never revealed. Based on documented events after the fact, it was most likely Bill Burns.

22   Harvey Woodruff. "In the Wake of the News." *Chicago Tribune.* January 6, 1933. (Story printed by Woodruff after Gleason's death.)

23   Unconfirmed story told by Eliot Asinof in *Eight Men Out.* Henry Holt & Co, 1963.

24   Hugh Fullerton. October 3, 1920.

[25] Some descriptions of Williams's performance in Game Eight claim he did not throw curves. In an interview with John Devaney, Edd would later insist this was untrue. "I know what I hit—it was a curve ball." *The World Series*. Rand McNally & Co., 1971.

[26] Arthur Daley. "Report of an Eyewitness." *New York Times*. February 18, 1960.

[27] Author's conversation between Greasy and Edd in West Virginia, years later.

[28] Author's Note: This was the first Reds World Championship since the American and National Leagues became known as "organized baseball" in 1903.

[29] Hod Eller, dying of cancer, gave this ball to David Johnson, sports editor for the *Evansville Courier*, in 1960.

[30] L.C. Davis. Sporting News. October 16, 1919.

[31] *The Sporting News*. October 16, 1919.

[32] Stanley W. McClure. *Sports Collectors Digest*. May 11, 1984.

[33] *Total Baseball*. Thornton and Palmer. 2nd Edition. 1989.

[34] Jackson would hit .375 in the series and later tell Joe Williams, a Cleveland sportswriter, "On my mama's grave, I swear I played my best...if I had sold out and then hit like that, them gamblers would have had me killed long before this." *Cleveland News*. September 24, 1959.

[35] Bill James, SABR statistician. *Win Shares*. Bill James and Jim Henzler. STATS Publishing Inc., 2002.

[36] Full statistical summary of 1919 World Series in book Appendix.

[37] Statistical Analysis provided by SABR researcher David Karickhoff.

[38] To his credit, Hugh Fullerton predicted Neale's success: "He (Neale) is certain to do a lot of hitting in the coming series." *Syracuse Herald*. September 26, 1919.

[39] Author recalls these conversations in Bradenton in the 1950's.

[40] *Cleveland Plain Dealer*. October 14, 1919.

[41] Edwin Pope. *Baseball's Greatest Managers*. 1960

[42] Fifth Third Bank was formed by a merger of two banks and located on 5th and 3rd Streets. Just after the merger was complete, the entrepreneurial architect Jacob Schmidlapp passed away, endowing his sons Horace and Karl with large trust funds. Karl would follow his father in the business, whereas Horace would spend much of his inheritance on an opulent lifestyle.

[43] Pat Duncan (and Sammy Bohne) would be accused of game-throwing in 1924 and win a lawsuit against the Collyer Publishing Co. for the accusation.

[44] *Official World Series Records. The Sporting News*. 1975

[45] In the recollection of this author, Edd wore this fancy pocket watch on only a few rare occasions. One was his induction into the Baseball Hall of Fame in 1962. The home of this watch for 85 years has been a bank safety deposit box.

12

Scandal!

The full story never has been told and never will be, because
Johnson, Comiskey, Herrmann and Alf Austrian, the only ones
who knew it all, are dead.

– Hugh Fullerton, 10/17/35

If there had been real justice after the scandal of 1919,
Charlie Comiskey, the Sox owner, would have been the
one kicked out of the game.

– Studs Terkel "Nine Men In,"
New York Times *October 28, 2005*

The 1921 trial was not about justice, it was about image.
– Gene Carney, **Burying the Black Sox, 2006**

OCTOBER 9, 1919
CHICAGO, ACT 1

On the night after the final game of the Series, Dave
Zelcer met with his Midwestern compadres at the
Congress Hotel to make a final distribution of their
jackpot. It was later reported that Zelcer and Ben Levi "cleaned
up between $70,000 to $80,000 by the manipulations."[1] The
group celebrated by raising champagne glasses in toasts to the
brains behind the capper, Carl Zork. In one moment of serious
contemplation, they toasted the ghost of Kid Becker who had

given his life so they might succeed.[2] They wouldn't have guessed that they would all be back in Chicago sitting in a courtroom two years later.

As the gamblers celebrated their windfall, Charles "Commy" Comiskey sat in his ballpark a bitter man. He had begun his career as a penniless ballplayer. He was ending it as the millionaire owner of one of the greatest franchises in American history, a franchise that seemed about to collapse under the weight of a few filthy gamblers.[3] On either side of him sat two friends, Kid Gleason and Hughie Fullerton. None of the men doubted that the players had betrayed them. Comiskey had called Cicotte into his office after the game, but the pitcher left the park. Hughie would remember that day because in the midst of his pain, Commy struck the table with a clenched fist and said, "Keep after them, Hughie, they were crooked! Someday you and I will prove it."[4]

Fullerton took him at his word. The next day he wrote the first of several exposes that would be sneered at and degraded by his colleagues for months to come. He quoted what Commy told him that day. The headline read, "Fullerton Says Seven Members of the White Sox Will be Missing Next Spring."[5] Within days after the Series ended, Comiskey offered a reward of $20,000 (later reduced to $10,000) for information concerning gambling activity leading to the loss of the World Series by the White Sox.

The first "taker" was Joe Gedeon, second baseman for the St. Louis Browns. He told Comiskey and his lawyer, Alfred Austrian, what he knew about the fix. He fingered the St. Louis gamblers, Ben Frankel (called Franklin) and Ben and Lou Levi. This was no great news since Kid Gleason had already been informed by the owner of the Majestic Theater in St. Louis, Harry Redmon, about the Levi brothers. In fact, the day after the Series, Gleason traveled to St. Louis to meet Redmon. Hughie would later report that Gleason offered Redmon

$5,000 for information connecting gamblers and players, but Redmon refused to say more for fear he would be shot down like another St. Louis Series-fixer-wannabe, Kid Becker.

Comiskey, Gleason, and Austrian concluded that these were just small-time crooks. They couldn't possibly have fixed a World Series. They completely discounted the testimony of Gedeon and Redmon. This was also beneficial thinking since Comiskey wouldn't have to shell out the promised $10,000.

Then, on the advice of his attorneys, Comiskey clammed up. He took no further action and, as advised, ceased communication with Fullerton. He decided that the better part of valor was to protect his investment. He really didn't want to know if his expensive stable of players were crooks. He wanted them to continue to win ballgames and to pack his ballpark with paying customers.

As Ban Johnson had predicted, Commy would play-act an investigation but cover up the truth. Comiskey's first impulse was to hush it up; "only later would he adopt the role of outraged defender of baseball's purity."[6] The same analysis could be applied to Johnson himself.

Besides, both were distracted by the bitter political battle going on in the American League. The magnates were vying for power with Comiskey (Chicago), Ruppert (New York), and Frazee (Boston) attempting to unseat the powerful Ban Johnson. To them, the "scandal" was merely a pawn in this power struggle. Comiskey would issue statements to the press such as, "Mr. Johnson is endangering not only the value of our properties, but the integrity of baseball."[7] By December 10, the war would be over and B.B. would (again) emerge victorious.

But Hughie was tenacious. For the next four months, he would pepper his columns with commentary that ranged from sarcasm to anger to resignation. On October 21, he struck back at Commy for shutting him out by suggesting a cover-up due to "owner's greed." On October 29, he defended his original Series predictions by claiming the Reds could not have won without some "help." On November 12 he became really brazen by calling for the resignations of both Johnson and Herrmann. (Herrmann did resign from the National Commission two months later. He had learned from Cincinnati's Boss Cox how to stay away from a sticky political situation.) Always a company man, Herrmann's parting shot attempted to stave off further embarrassment for organized baseball: "Why start another investigation of moth-eaten rumors?"[8]

On October 24, Hughie released a diatribe on how gambling had left the racetrack and entered the baseball park. By November 29, his credibility was so shaken that his column was advertised as the "latest baseball gossip." Throughout December Hughie continued to attack the baseball establishment (B.B. in particular) and to defend his assumed protector, Commy. But Commy didn't come to his defense.

Nor did Matty. Matty jumped out of the controversy early in October by declaring that "baseball is clean." He did send a letter with his opinions about the fix and the circled scorecards that he and Hughie had made to the National Commission. The team owners immediately destroyed the scorecards...no paper trail, please.[9] Matty also refused to testify in the later trials, but he was also very ill by this time. According to Mathewson biographer Eddie Frierson, Matty died with sorrow over the "scandal" that demeaned his Reds. He always thought they would have won anyway.

Nor did Ring Lardner stick by his fellow scribe. He simply dropped out of the baseball sportswriter scene. He would later say, "Well, friends, I may as well admit that I have kind of lost interest in the old game,...the game which the magnates have fixed up to please the public."[10] Lardner moved to Great Neck, Long Island, where his neighbor and drinking buddy was author

F. Scott Fitzgerald. It is possible that the famous passage on "Meyer Wolfsheim" fixing the 1919 World Series that appeared in *The Great Gatsby* may have been a result of late night musings of Lardner and Fitzgerald on Long Island.[11]

Nor did any of the established baseball publications support Hughie. F. C. Lane's *Baseball Magazine* and G. Taylor Spink's *The Sporting News* called Fullerton a "rumormonger."[12] *Reach's Baseball Guide* said that anyone who suggested a fixed Series was "a menace to the game."[13] The magnates of the sporting press were circling the wagons.

Finally, on December 19, 1919, Hughie dropped the journalistic bomb, "Is Big League Baseball being Run for Gamblers, with Ballplayers in the Deal?" Although Hughie didn't identify suspected players, he did name some of the gamblers, such as Attell, Zork, and the Levi brothers. He also sacrificed his own source of information, Bill Burns. And then, he did the unthinkable. He fingered Arnold Rothstein. Although Fullerton was careful to say there was "no legal proof advanced against him," he couldn't resist adding "...he is the only man in the entire crowd who had money enough to handle such a deal." He later reported (in 1922) that he suffered two attempts on his life during this time.[14]

By the end of the year, it was generally accepted that something rotten had happened in the 1919 World Series. Sundry versions abounded about the particulars, but the consensus was clear. Newspapers from "neutral" locations tried to finalize the story. In Reno they reported that a St. Louis syndicate was responsible for influencing the White Sox.[15] In Los Angeles, Harry Williams wrote about the whole thing being a "joke" because "the Cincinnati club really figured to win the Series without any of the alleged help from the White Sox." He insinuated that the gamblers were misled by incorrect dope.[16] In South Carolina, on December 31, readers were reminded that

Comiskey's offer of $10,000 was "still open." They quoted a White Sox official as saying Comiskey's people had interviewed parties from St. Louis who told them "nothing we had not heard before."[17] End of story.

And then the curtain came down in the baseball theater's production of "Scandal in 1919!" Everyone raced to the theater next door to see the debut of the Yankees' new production of "Babe Ruth and the 1920 Lively Ball." Thus, the fickle public tucked those silly World Series rumors away and became enamored with the new season of the new decade and the new star—Babe Ruth, home run king.[18] B.B., Commy, and their respective retinues let out a sigh of relief.

Fullerton made one last stab in March, claiming, "Silencers put on Everybody." Although Fullerton had tried his best, the cover-up was working.[19] He would later say, "I was informed that I would be driven out of the game. The way of cleaning the sport seems to have been to banish reporters who dared to tell the truth."[20]

But that was only Act 1 of "Scandal 1919." In September 1920 the scandal broke, almost a full year after the infamous Series. And now the destruction of the Chicago White Sox and the humiliation of the Cincinnati Reds would begin in earnest.

SEPTEMBER 22, 1920
CHICAGO, ACT 2

Burlesque events occurred in quick succession at the grand jury investigation in the fall of 1920. Newspaper writers attended the theatrical performances and reported to the public with applause.

Sept. 22: Judge and Jury Jugglers

Cook County Grand Jury convenes to hear testimony concerning Cubs–Phillies game throwing of Aug. 31,1920. Presiding is Judge Charles McDonald, friend of Ban Johnson.

> Based on testimony of Charles Weeghman, owner of the Cubs, and Ban Johnson, the focus of the investigation moved quickly to the 1919 Series.

Note: *Weeghman was the first to implicate Arnold Rothstein.*

Sept. 23: Hoofer Headliner

> Rube Benton, Giants pitcher, gives testimony naming Bill Burns and Hal Chase as "fixers" and four Sox players as "throwers" (Cicotte, Gandil, Williams, and Felsch). Benton identifies Philip Hahn, betting commissioner of Cincinnati as his source.

Sept. 24: Flame-throwing Landlords

> Charles Comiskey issues a press release claiming he has done his own investigation with no cooperation from Johnson. He claims he will fire any dishonest players who are convicted by the jury.[21]

Sept. 25: Jury Foreman Striptease.

> Harry Brigham, jury foreman, informs the press that Arnold Rothstein was the primary "fixer" of the 1919 Series with Abe Attell and Bill Burns as go-betweens with the players.

<u>Sept. 26</u>: Olio Act behind curtain: The Money Lenders Walk Tightrope

Ban Johnson meets with Arnold Rothstein in New York. He reports later that he is convinced that Rothstein was not involved in the 1919 fix.

<u>Sept. 27</u>: Barbershop Quartet of Villains

The *Philadelphia North American* publishes the story of gambler Billy Maharg's confession to reporter Jimmy Isaminger. Maharg identified the primary fixers as Abe Attell and Bennett (David Zelcer) and Sox pitcher Eddie Cicotte. He claims that Rothstein refused to be involved.

<u>Sept. 28</u>: Victim Solo, "Curses…foiled again!"

Eddie Cicotte "spills the beans" with a full confession. After signing an "immunity waiver" with lawyer Alfred Austrian, he declares Hahn[22] the brains of the operation with Burns and Attell assisting. He names seven other players on the White Sox.

Note: *Cicotte's exact testimony concerning his own involvement is a matter of conjecture since his written testimony was later "lost."[23] However, the* Philadelphia Inquirer *posted one story one Sept. 29 in which Cicotte claims he did not play to win in the entire Series. The next day the same newspaper quoted him as saying, "The first ball I pitched I wondered what the wife and kiddies would say if the ever found out I was a crook. I pitched the best ball I knew how after that first ball. But I lost* *because I was hit, not because I was throwing the game."*

Sept. 29: Saints and Sinners Pantomime

> Joe Jackson[24] and Claude Williams confess. They tell similar stories to that of Cicotte, but focus on the fact that the gamblers had double-crossed them, and they didn't get the $20,000 they were promised. Williams identifies Attell and Burns, then adds two additional gambler names, Brown (Nat Evans) and Sport Sullivan.

Sept. 30: The Contortionist

> Comiskey suspends eight White Sox. By doing so he effectively forfeits the 1920 AL pennant to Cleveland.

Oct. 1: Star Magician and Sacrificial Lamb

> Nervous in New York, Arnold Rothstein issues a statement: "The unfortunate use of my name in this scandal was the last straw. I made up my mind to retire from the gambling business."

> Two weeks later, after consulting with attorney William Fallon, he came to Chicago in a bold move to testify personally. Afterward he issued a statement: "The whole thing started when Attell and some other cheap gamblers decided to frame the Series and make a killing. Attell did the fixing....I've come here to vindicate myself.

> Attell was sacrificial. It was only business, after all.

Day's later, attorney Fallon met with Rothstein, Attell, and Sullivan in New York. He ordered Attell to Montreal, Sullivan to Mexico, and suggested that Rothstein and his wife should take a slow ocean liner to Europe. With an estimated worth of four or five million dollars,25 Arnold would pay for everything, including Fallon's fee, of course.

ENTER: THE CRUSADER

After Rothstein's testimony, Ban Johnson claimed, "I felt convinced he [Rothstein] wasn't in any plot to fix the series." The American League attorney, Alfred Austrian, said, "Rothstein in his testimony today proved himself to be guiltless."[26]

Of course, Johnson failed to mention his "deal" with the "guiltless" millionaire crook. In return for Johnson's public statement absolving him of all guilt, Rothstein would give Johnson the Polo Grounds. Rothstein would convince his partner, Charles Stoneham, owner of the Giants, to transfer the lease on the ballpark to the American League. In return, Johnson would allow Stoneham to name the replacement for Garry Herrmann on the National Commission.[27]

Sweet deal. Now Johnson had to play out the courtroom burlesque, and his role was clear to him. He would be the crusader who would release his child from the evil grip of the gamblers. He would send his cry throughout the land saying, "I am determined that baseball shall be divorced from gambling."[28]

Then the fickle horse of politics galloped into the scene. In the November election in Cook County, Illinois, the voters replaced the district attorney, so the prosecutors who had championed the conspiracy case were gone. The trial would be delayed. Indictments had been handed down to seven White Sox players, exempting Fred McMullin. The indicted players were Cicotte,

Gandil, Williams, Risberg, Jackson, Felsch, and Weaver. No indictments were issued to any gamblers, including Rothstein. It would not be until June 1921 that the courtroom would hear more testimony on the 1919 conspiracy.

At the same time, the horse rode into baseball's ruling elite, the National Commission. Team owners had been jockeying for replacement of Ban Johnson for some time. The Johnson-Comiskey feud had become so volatile it erased any last vestige of faith the owners had in this ruling body. John Heydler, President of the National League, had lobbied for a singular independent commissioner. Johnson would be forced to step down from his perch at the top of the baseball power structure. As Johnson biographer Earl Obenshain would later write, "It was the action of Johnson in exposing the 1919 scandal and bringing the culprits to trial in a court of law that really cost him his throne as "czar" of organized baseball."[29]

On November 12, 1920, Judge Kenesaw Mountain Landis, age 53, became the Commissioner of Baseball. He agreed to a salary of $50,000 a year with the stipulation that he would be permitted to continue on the bench and subtract his federal salary of $7,500 from the total amount. Thus, organized baseball would pay him $42,500 per year.[30] He also demanded "full control" in his new job. The team owners would not grasp the full meaning of his request until Act 3 of the 1919 Scandal played out in August 1921.

Then, the "crusader" flew into action. Ban Johnson went to the new commissioner in his chambers at the Federal Building in Chicago within two weeks of his appointment. He wanted to know what progress Landis had made on the most pressing issue, the 1919 Scandal investigation. Landis said, "None." He further stated that he didn't feel this was his duty because the event had occurred prior to his tenure. He agreed with Johnson's request that the American League would now "take up the running."[31] It was after all the AL's mess; they would clean it up. The meeting was merely ceremonial, Johnson was already on the case and way ahead of Landis at this point.

He had already convinced the AL owners to grant him a $40,000 budget to "clean up baseball." The owners had approved the hiring of the Pinkerton Detective Firm to investigate the scandal. At first request, William Webster of the Pinkerton Agency in Chicago had turned him down, saying the agency had decided "not to have anything to do whatever with the investigation." This became the official statement that was issued to the public.[32] Newspapers across the nation published Johnson's explanation: "Two detective agencies refused to make a thorough investigation of those behind baseball gambling." He added a statement to give Commy a little jolt: "They feared it would reach too high in the official and public office."[33]

Privately, however, Johnson didn't take "no" for an answer and certainly not from some little bureaucrat in the Pinkerton Chicago office. So Johnson went right to the top. He enlisted the support of Allan Pinkerton, via the Los Angeles office, to clean up the gambling influence in the ballparks and to track down and provide protective services for witnesses (Gedeon and Burns) who would testify in court in Act 3. Johnson was afraid that Rothstein's men would locate and kill his witnesses. He wrote to his attorney, James Price, "It is highly likely that Rothstein and his henchmen will try to 'reach' Gedeon during his stay in New York."[34] The Pinkerton agency in Boston would identify a list of sixty well-known gamblers who frequented ballparks in both leagues. Their operatives would be positioned in the ballparks, ready to escort any known crook out of the park. They became known as the "Watchful Waiters for Gamblers."[35]

Johnson would also receive considerable help on his crusade from two AL owners, Phil Ball of St. Louis and Frank

Navin of Detroit.[36] Whatever one sleuth didn't turn up, perhaps the other would.

Of course, unbeknownst to the owners and never mentioned in public statements, Johnson already had hired his own most "private" detective of all—his friend, Cal Crim.

FLASHBACK TO EARLY SEPTEMBER, 1920
ACTIVATING THE "COLD CASE"

In the second week of September, Johnson decided he needed the services of the Crim Detective Bureau after all. The phrase "Black Sox Scandal"[37] had now invaded the newsprint and he had to take action. The minute he got wind of Illinois State Attorney Hoyne's intention to pursue the alleged fixing of the Cubs–Phillies game, he saw the writing on the wall; the 1919 Series fiasco would be next. He immediately called Cal and asked him to pursue the case they had discussed a year ago. Cal's intuition about Case 2002 had been right. Now B.B. needed him and he was ready.

Before Act 2 of the Scandal drama began playing out in the Cook County Courthouse in September, Cal Crim was busy in Cincinnati. His precious notepad was his blueprint. He knew exactly where to start: Fred Mowbray.

Cal's first call to the Mowbray-Robinson Lumber Company yielded no result.[38] Mr. Mowbray was not in. Would Mr. Crim like to set up an appointment for Friday? Cal thought, this is good. Give him some time to worry about why a detective is coming to see him. He made the appointment.

On Friday, Fred Mowbray greeted Cal with his usual affable smile and handshake. They had known each other for some years and worked together on various committees and city projects. Fred didn't suspect that Cal might be here on "official business," so he was taken aback when Cal's manner was curt and professional.

His voice had a sympathetic tone as he said, "Fred, I've come today to save you some embarrassment...if I can."

Fred's brain signaled "alert!" He thought of everything he'd done in his life that he could possibly be ashamed of. He said, with forced calm, "Okay, Cal, I'm all ears."

Now Cal's voice carried a slightly threatening edge to it. "I have a client in Chicago." He paused to see the initial effect. "We need to know everything you know about gambling in baseball both in 1919 and 1920."

Fred frowned and said with a tone of disbelief, "Gambling!" One look at Cal told him the "innocent" act wasn't going to work.

Cal pulled out the big guns. "Fred, this is serious. If you don't give us the information, a commission will be appointed by the Court of Cincinnati, and you'll be compelled to give a deposition under oath."

Fred knew Cal's history with the Cincinnati police force. He knew he wasn't making an idle threat. It crossed his mind to call his attorney, but he remembered he was out of town for the month. No use bringing some junior partner, clerk-type in on this. He could handle it himself.

Cal saw Fred's mind working. He added, "I'm sure you don't want the notoriety this thing could bring. That's why I'm coming to you personally."

"Okay, yes, I appreciate that," Fred said. "I'll be glad to tell you what I know." Better to tell the truth now, or at least enough of it to convince his interrogator.

He told Cal a couple stories involving the Reds Rooters organization. He told about making a $1,000 bet on the Reds against the Cubs that spring of 1920. It was the opening game of the season in Chicago, and he and his friend, Dan Moul of the Moul Lumber Company, had gone up for the game.

Cal just sat and nodded as if waiting for more. He wrote down Moul's name on his notepad.

Fred responded, "I told the guy I wasn't a gambler, that this was just a "piker's bet.""

Cal asked the obvious, "Who was the guy?"

Fred answered immediately, "Phil Hahn." This was credible because Hahn had a reputation for making side bets in his job as betting commissioner. Because of his inside information on the odds, he was able to make a tidy little income that way.

Nobody seemed to care. Fred guessed that Cal would know this. He did.

Cal wasn't satisfied. "What about the 1919 Series. Did you go to the games?" Cal had a note in his pad that Fred had been there.

The answer was honest: "Yes. I get tickets through the booster group." He added, "I get seats for Redland through the Business Man's Club." He hoped to pull a little rank on this detective.

Cal gave no sign of intimidation. He'd interrogated much craftier guys than Fred, and they were *real* criminals.

"Tell me about the 1919 Series. Did you bet on it? If so, did you bet on individual games or just the Series?"

"I just put a little money down on the Series, that's all." Wrong answer, thought Cal. The informed bettors just bet the Series, the pikers bet individual games. Fred saw his mistake in Cal's eyes. Of course, Fred didn't tell him that he had, in fact, done both and that both were lucrative bets based on inside information from Jimmy Widmeyer and Ben Levi.

Cal wanted to move on. There was one name he wanted to hear: the man he had seen Mowbray escorting around the practice field a month before the Series. He knew who the man was now, but he wanted to hear Mowbray say "Levi." He never did.

"Who took your money?" said Cal.

"I can't remember. Really...I can't remember! Maybe it was Hahn again." The lie didn't work. Now Fred would have to give him something big.

He decided to throw Cal a bone to gnaw on. This one was far enough away and remote enough that Crim would never find him.

"There was another guy who tipped me off about the Series, a fellow I met in New Orleans." He explained that his wife, Louise, was from that city, and he'd met this gambler at the racetrack there. Cal made a note.

"This fellow tells me he won $5,000 betting on the Reds in '19. I think his name was Borr, Ramey Borr. (Fred purposefully changed the name, but just enough to make it seem like an honest mistake later.)

Cal almost smirked. It wasn't working, but he wrote the name in his notepad and decided to play along. "How'd you meet this Borr again?"

Now Fred was caught. He had to give up a friend. Oh well, it was a safe bet that Crim wouldn't pursue *this* friend. He was too high up on the ladder for this little local detective to touch.

"The guy's a friend of Dick Williams. You know...the Williams Brothers stables and all?" He checked to see if his attempt at intimidation had been effective. Cal was poker-faced.

"I try to stay close to Dick to get information on horses." Okay, so he'd have to call Dick later and warn him, just in case.

Cal's comeback was too easy. "If you get the inside scoop on horses, you must get it on ballgames too."

"Nah, just what the Rooters get. The same old sharing of ignorance, I guess. Who's got a sore arm, whose wife is pregnant, all that. Nothing more." Feeling more confident but anxious to end the discussion, Fred said, "I've got a railroad guy from Kentucky coming in about now. Is there anything else I can help you with today, Cal?"

Cal called B.B. that night and told him what he'd learned. Johnson listened intently and made notes on Ramey Borr, Phil Hahn (again), Dan Moul, Dick Williams. He instructed Cal to investigate them, all except Williams. Ban knew of the Williams empire. He didn't want Cal snooping around that family. They were well respected in Ohio and Kentucky, and at the big races everywhere. It didn't make any sense anyway; the Williamses were horse breeders of the highest quality. They didn't need to dabble with chintzy gamblers. No...that was just a red herring that Mowbray had thrown at Cal. No reason to pursue that one.

As the winter of 1920-21 passed, Ban Johnson was on a tear. He was furious that Rothstein had duped him. He had kept his part of the bargain, but Arnold had not. There was no Polo Grounds lease forthcoming, and, moreover, Stoneham had supported Landis as commissioner. To add insult to injury, the incoming states attorney, Robert Crowe, informed him in January that all records of the 1920 testimony (Act 2) had been lost. This included the invaluable confessions of the Sox players Cicotte, Williams, and Jackson. Johnson knew of only one man who could have pulled off this theft.39 He would write his suspicions to Allan Pinkerton: "Recent evidence would indicate Rothstein was deeply involved in the World's Series scandal. It was always your contention he was the prime mover. I am prepared now to accept your version. ...the Grand Jury may indict him for stealing the records."40

Johnson was after Rothstein now. But, the only way to snare the Big Bankroll was through his lieutenants. He had turned on the charm for the Grand Jury, and they had completely exonerated him. Johnson developed a three-pronged strategic plan: (1) extradite Abe Attell from Canada, (2) locate and retrieve Bill Burns from Mexico, (3) gather evidence for indictments on the Western arm of Rothstein's gang.

He would succeed in two of the three prongs of his plan.

The third prong was capably handled by Cal Crim. A second visit to Fred Mowbray in March yielded the information he sought. Cal brought two of his operatives with him this time, Ora Slater and Jack McDermott. Learning that Slater was also an FBI agent, Mowbray caved in and told the whole story. He told of his long association with Ben Levi that began when he was a young boy growing up in Peru, Indiana. He explained that he had run into Levi in the lobby of the Sinton Hotel. He said Levi had asked a personal favor of him.

"Levi wanted me to hold a bet of $6,000 for him. [I] referred him to Harry O'Neal, clerk at the Sinton, who accepted this and held the money. Levi was betting on Cincy."

Mowbray went on to say he saw Levi again after the second game, and he now had $15,000 in winnings. "He asked me if I would accept the $15,000 in cash and give him my personal check for same, as he didn't want to carry the money back with him to Chicago. I gave him my personal check and deposited the money in a safe deposit box in the Sinton..."[41]

Mowbray stopped short of mentioning that he had earlier communication with Levi, which provided him and his cohorts with the inside information from which to bet on the Series. But Cal could read between the lines. After all, Mowbray and Levi had been friends since childhood in Indiana.

But Cal was satisfied with this windfall for now. He wasted no time in getting to the Sinton to interview O'Neal, who confirmed Mowbray's story and produced the Sinton safety deposit log, which confirmed the receipt of $15,000 cash from one Fred Mowbray on October 2, 1919. O'Neal remembered the little man with Mr. Mowbray and described Ben Levi to Cal's satisfaction.[42]

Cal reported his findings in a letter to B.B. on April 8, 1920. Johnson was not as pleased with this report as Cal had expected him to be. He shot a letter back to Cincinnati the next day.[43]

> I have turned it [Crim report] over to our attor-
> ney, Judge Barrett. The man who gave you the
> information in regard to Ben Levi, did not
> uncork all he knew about the World's Series fix-
> ing in 1919. It is my guess Levi gave this lumber
> man some information as to who would win the
> first two games. Don't you think it possible to
> give this individual the third degree, and make
> him tell all he knows?

Cal wrote back on April 11.

> ...Fred Mowbray, the subject, is in
> Arizona...will not be back until about May
> 1st. ...I thought it advisable to have Mowbray
> come to Mr. Bruce's office for the moral effect
> it would have, knowing he is an attorney con-
> nected with the American League. ...you will
> find me awaiting your command.

On April 22, Johnson wrote another letter which encouraged Cal to take strong action in the matter of Mowbray.

> We want to convict the Levi Brothers, and if
> Mowbray won't come through clean, then it
> may be necessary for us to indict him. ...It is my
> thought you should "treat him rough." ...It was
> in your city that the "sure-thing" gamblers made
> their great "clean-up."

By the end of May, Cal had produced the desired evidence

requested by Johnson. He identified the gambler called "Bennett" as David Zelcer of Des Moines, Iowa. He sent complete location information for indictments of the gamblers involved in the Western front of the fix conspiracy. His second report included a canceled check for $15,000 signed by Ben Levi as hard evidence to be presented to the jury. Cal never mentioned what techniques he employed to extract additional information from Fred Mowbray and Johnson never asked.

Cal's final contribution to the investigation was a telegram to Johnson dated May 23, 1921, in which he reported the location of one Remy Dorr [alias Ramey Borr], boxing referee in New Orleans, now at the Hotel Hamilton in New York City.[44] For some reason, Johnson chose not to implicate Dorr in the trial.

To their great amazement, Ben Levi, Carl Zork, David Zelcer, and Ben Franklin were indicted on March 26, 1921, by the Cook County Grand Jury. Each person received eight separate indictments charging "1- conspiracy to defraud, 2- obtaining money under false pretenses and 3- conspiracy to do an illegal act." Levi received his indictment in Kokomo, Indiana, and Franklin got his at his new address in Omaha, Nebraska. It was the habit of the gamblers to constantly change their residence.[45]

Ironically, Comiskey and his lawyers had received most of the names of the St. Louis gamblers from Gedeon and Redmon early in their investigation. For some reason, they chose to ignore what Ban and Cal chose to pursue. Fred Mowbray and his friends were never indicted or identified to the court.

The indictments of the Des Moines/St. Louis gang were based on the evidence provided to Ban Johnson by the Cal Crim Detective Bureau of Cincinnati. In return for Cal's excellent work on the investigation of the 1919 fix, B.B. gave his friend a gold lifetime pass to any major league game with his name engraved on the front. Cal cherished this gift all of his life and enjoyed pulling it out to show Cincinnati "disbelievers."[46]

THE LIFETIME MLB PASS ISSUED TO EDD ROUSH

It would have been similar to the lifetime passes issued to Baseball Hall of Famers.

As to the other prongs of Johnson's attack plan, he won one and lost one. Although he amassed an army of officials, Johnson was unable to extradite Attell from Canada for the final indictments in 1921. He would write to Harry Redmon, "Abe Attell, backed by Rothstein's money, is putting up a desperate fight against extradition."[47]

Attell did testify at the grand jury investigation in 1920 and, aided by the brilliance of his attorney, William Fallon, they got away with claiming there were *two Abe Attells*. The "other" Attell claimed he hadn't been in Cincinnati for the World Series. No one came forth to deny his claim.[48] The press later referred to Abe as the "Artful Dodger."

However, through great personal effort and some assistance from Billy Maharg and Mrs. Burns, he did bring "Sleepy" Bill Burns back from Mexico. In return, Maharg received an undisclosed amount of cash and state-of-the-art fishing equipment. Mrs. Burns became a personal favorite of Ban Johnson as they corresponded extensively. He referred to her as "that sweet woman." She received a set of fine luggage and some spending money for her efforts—small change in the larger scope of Johnson's investigation.[49]

JULY 18, 1921 CHICAGO

ACT 3

Burns was the prosecution's "star witness" in Act 3 of Scandal 1919. He testified on July 18, 1921, with an honest description of the events "from his perspective." He laid responsibility for the fix directly at the feet of Rothstein with support from his lieutenants, Attell, Chase, Bennett (Zelcer), Zork, Sullivan, and the Levi brothers. He implicated seven Sox players, exempting Joe Jackson. Burns had "lost everything he had on the Sox win in Game Three[50] based on what he now knew was a double-cross by Attell. He had an axe to grind and he was granted immunity in return for his testimony.

The Western Alliance of the Rothstein cadre was treated in a friendly manner by Judge Hugo Friend. Ben Franklin was excused by a letter from his doctor (C.A. Vosburgh). Friend dropped all charges against the Levi brothers. Carl Zork marched in an army of character witnesses on his behalf.[51] David Zelcer took the stand and conveniently forgot that he had shared a room at the Sinton Hotel with Abe Attell. His quiet, polite, and unassuming manner stood him in good stead on the witness stand. The prosecution readily admitted to reporters that Zelcer "was the only one of the gambler defendants to be deeply incriminated by the chain of evidence."[52] However, Cal Crim and Johnson knew that Zelcer had not acted alone. They had been on to the St. Louis/Des Moines gang for some time. Johnson wrote to Harry Redmon in St. Louis, "That pair of Des Moines crooks have been eating at the vitals of baseball for the last three or four years, and should not go unwhipped of justice."[53]

Hal Chase again escaped unscathed with the primary evidence against him being a series of telegrams he had sent to friends to tell them the Series was fixed. Fred Lieb would later claim it was really Hal Chase who was the "evil genius behind the Fix."[54]

On August 2, 1921, Judge Friend charged the jury with these instructions: "The state must prove that it was the intent of the ballplayers that have been charged with conspiracy through the throwing of the World Series to defraud the public and others, not merely to throw games." He made no mention of the gamblers.

In just under three hours, the jury returned at 11:22 p.m. with a total acquittal for everyone, players and gamblers alike.

The eight Black Sox were legally declared "White" again.

A great celebration erupted in the courtroom with jurymen and defendants departing to enjoy a celebratory dinner together at a local Italian restaurant. The happiest man in Chicago was Charles Comiskey. He had his team back, unscathed. His $230,000 investment[55] had been protected and he had weathered the storm of public scrutiny and emerged victorious.

The "clean" Sox were not happy. Teammates of the Black Sox had suffered two years of misery, often wondering if they would be the next to be accused. Ray Schalk would later say, "No one will ever know what we put up with all this summer....Hardly any of us talked to those fellows except on the ball field. I know there were many times when things were about to break into a fight, but it never got that far."[56]

Garry Herrmann was happy in Cincinnati. Indirectly, his team had been vindicated as well. Now everyone *had* to recognize that the Reds had won the 1919 World Series fair and square.

Hugh Fullerton was not happy. He believed there had been a fix and justice had not been done. As the courageous White

Knight who had ridden into the fray carrying the flag of truth, he now would be a laughingstock. His career was over.[57]

Ban Johnson was not entirely unhappy. Although he believed the acquittal was a miscarriage of justice, he was pleased with his performance as the Crusader. He had fought the good fight. He had brought the evildoers to justice. Although he had not succeeded in destroying his enemy, Comiskey, he could never again be accused of "covering up" the truth. Most importantly, his beloved baseball was now secure and washed clean of scandal.

BUT…there was one last scene to be played. It was not the expected denouement; it was the climax of the morality play.

THE CONQUERING HERO

On August 4, 1921, with less than eight months into his lifetime job, the new Commissioner of Baseball, Judge Kenesaw Mountain Landis, made a decree that completely obliterated the acquittal of the eight White Sox players. He banned Cicotte, Williams, Gandil, Felsch, Risberg, McMullin, Weaver, and Jackson from professional baseball for the remainder of their lives. His rationale for this decision was printed in every newspaper in the land.

> Regardless the verdict of the jury, no player that throws a ball game, no player that undertakes or promises to throw a ball game, no player that sits in conference with a bunch of crooked players and gamblers where the ways and means of throwing games are planned and discussed and does not promptly tell his club about it, will ever play professional baseball.

> Just keep in mind that regardless the verdict of juries, baseball is entirely competent to protect itself against crooks, both inside and outside the game.

The *Spalding Guide* editor would sum it all up in the 1921 edition.

> The gambler has done his worst again. He is the respecter of no game. …He will try again. The honest ballplayer need have no fear of any gambler. There are thousands and thousands of honest ballplayers. There is another small group— they were ballplayers once too—to be immured in the Chamber of Oblivion. There let them rest.

THE TAINTED TEAM

Although the events of the grand jury investigation of the Black Sox Scandal in 1920 were well publicized in national newspapers, Edd said that he and Essie took it all with "a grain of salt" at the time. However, Edd later admitted that the story did hurt the Reds of 1920. It undermined the morale of the team at the moment they needed to remember they *were* the World Champions. The Reds were in first place for 75 days in 1920. In the midst of the fix revelations in the newspapers in September, the Reds were just three games out of first place. When the headlines shifted from the pennant race to the "Scandal," the world began to believe that the Reds had won a synthetic victory in 1919.

The Dodgers dominated the final stage of the season, and the Reds laid down and died. The Reds were forced to forfeit their *tainted* crown and came in third. The next year was even worse, as Jimmy Ring and Greasy Neale were traded and Edd and Heinie held out for weeks into the season. The Reds spent most of the season in sixth place.[58]

More insidious than the losses the team experienced in the two years that followed the 1919 Series was the personal suffering. Since Edd would live the longest of any of his 1919 teammates,[59] he would be forced to relive the painful story of 1919 to sportswriters for 69 years, responding to questions again and again.

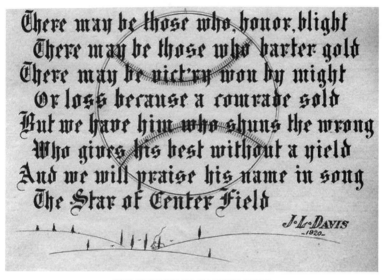

There may be those who honor, blight
There may be those who barter gold
There may be vict'ry won by might
Or loss because a comrade sold
But we have him who shuns the wrong
Who gives his best without a yield
And we will praise his name in song
The Star of Center Field

J. L. Davis
1920

FAN TRIBUTE IN CALLIGRAPHY

But the people of Cincinnati would not forget their heroes who were "on the square." In 1920 Edd would receive a personal tribute from one of the grateful fans.

He would also enjoy the personal support of the owner of the Reds, Garry Herrmann, throughout his remaining seven years with the team.

Roush never did a wrong thing in his life on the

ball field. No player ever lived who tried harder
all the time to win games than Roush. He had a
bad day, yes, but it was not due to any mistake
of the heart.
– Garry Herrmann *Cincinnati Enquirer* (10/21/26)

PITCHER GUILT?

Years later, this author, Edd's granddaughter, questioned him
incessantly about the 1919 World Series. He was free with
information about most of his teammates, save one, Dutch
Ruether. In an interview with the author in 1978 concerning
Dutch, Edd said, "I don't want to talk about Ruether. He's
dead and gone." When pressed, he added, "Well, we should
have won that sixth game in the '19 Series. Mighty funny
pitchin' goin' on out there." Without evidence to support a
case against his teammates, he did not want to present accusa-
tions to the public. He would say only, "I saw Ruether and his
buddy Sallee talking to gamblers all the time. You know, during
practice and and all. Ray Fisher backed me up on this. Hell,
everybody knew it!"

Two years later Bob Hunter, a sportswriter for the
Columbus Dispatch, interviewed both Reds who had played in
the 1919 Series and were still living, Edd Roush in Bradenton,
Florida, and pitcher Ray Fisher in Ann Arbor, Michigan.[60]

Hunter/Fisher interview transcript, 1980

Q: I recently talked to Edd Roush, and he told me that
before the 1919 World Series, the Reds had a meeting
about the possibility of some Reds players being involved
with fixing of the Series. Do you remember that?

A: No…I had thoughts. I saw guys around, but I wasn't near them and didn't know anything about them, but I just, you know, after things come out, I wondered about it.

Q: You don't really have any idea whether that was true or not then?

A: I just saw the guys around, and saw a couple of them together and wondered about it, you know what I mean? Not at the time I saw it, but afterwards when I knew what had been going on.

Q: Edd Roush mentioned Dutch Ruether and Slim Sallee as guys who…

A: Well, that's…I, I don't want to get my name in…

Q: Oh, I see…

A: But it's that same group…he saw the same group that I did, apparently.

Hunter/Roush interview transcript, 1980

Q: Do you think Ruether was throwing games in 1919?

A: I know damn good and well he was. He and Sallee were with those gamblers right across the street from the Metropole Hotel all the time. Now proving it, that's a horse of different color. But…you could pretty well tell if a pitcher was trying to throw a ball game."

In 1988, the year of his death, the *The Sporting News* would print the perspective of Edd Roush for the last time.

> Roush would contend in later years...the scandal was the result of Chicago players throwing the first game (9-1) and that at least four members of the Reds also were involved.
> – Roush Obituary. *The Sporting News* (4/4/88)

The sportswriter got it wrong. Edd Roush believed that in his career he had played on teams with four players who threw ballgames. The first two are matters of history—Hal Chase and Lee Magee, neither of whom played in the 1919 World Series. The other two were likely Reds pitchers (Ruether, Sallee) who were never formally accused and about whom no evidence exists. Edd took his suspicions to his death.

> Cincinnati was the place that first officially accepted money 'over the table' in baseball. How intriguing the suggestion, even if false, that they also got away with accepting it under the table." – Kelly Boyer Sagert, 2005[61]

---

1 The *Des Moines News*. September 28, 1920.

2 As mentioned earlier, Becker was shot in St. Louis in April of 1919. He was the original architect of the fix.

3 Author's Note: There is evidence that the 1920 Sox were also plagued by gamblers. Eddie Collins told Joe Williams (*Cleveland News*) that the Sox "practically lived with gamblers" in the 1920 season.

4 Hugh Fullerton. *The Sporting News*. October 17, 1935.

5 *Chicago Herald and Examiner*. October 10, 1919.

6 Martin Kohout. *Hal Chase*. McFarland & Co., 2001.

7 *The News and Courier*. Charleston, S.C. November 22,1919.

8 *Cincinnati Post*. December 20, 1919.

9 Interview with Eddie Frierson, Mathewson biographer and creator of the play *Matty*. 8/2005. Frierson claimed that Matty believed that all the Sox players were guilty including Joe Jackson (due to his poor fielding performance in the Series.) The exception was Buck Weaver, who Matty thought had gotten a "raw deal."

10 Quote written in Lardner "style." Donald Elder. *Ring Lardner*. University Microfilms, 1972.

11 Steve Klein. "Newspaper Coverage of the Black Sox Scandal." Academic Thesis, 1992.

12 Daniel Ginsburg. *The Fix Is In*. McFarland & Co., 1995.

13 Ken Burns and Geoffrey C. Ward. *Baseball: An Illustrated History*. Knopf, New York, 1994.

14 "Some day I am going to write the story of my personal experiences in that case [the B-Sox scandal]," writes Hugh Fullerton, "the attempts at intimidation, the *two* efforts to kill me, and several other things." *New York Evening Mail*, 8/1/22. Reported by Gene Carney in Notes from the Shadows of Cooperstown, #358, August 27, 2005.

15 *Reno Evening Gazette*. December 30, 1919.

16 Harry Williams. *Los Angeles Times*. November 14, 1919.

17 *The News and Courier*. Charleston, S.C. December 31, 1919.

18 Edd Roush would describe his first exposure to the "lively ball" of 1920: "Spring training had just begun when I noticed that several of our .200 hitters kept slugging the ball into the outfield. I was running like a jackrabbit out there. I asked Moran, 'How did these fellas get so good over the winter?' He told me about the new lively ball."

19 It was rumored that Ban Johnson pressured Colonel Robert McCormick, owner of the *Chicago Tribune* to stop publishing articles on the fix. The *Tribune*'s coverage of baseball in general was reduced by 73 percent between September 1, 1919, and the same date in 1921. Steve Klein. "Newspaper Coverage of the Black Sox Scandal." Academic Thesis, 1992.

20 *Atlanta Constitution*. October 3, 1920.

21 In fact, Comiskey and Gleason were well aware of the dishonest players, and Comiskey gave them salary increases for the 1920 season. Many considered it "hush money."

22 Philip Hahn testified and was released. He claimed merely to have spread the "rumor" to Billy Maharg on a hunting trip in South Carolina. There was no other evidence against him.

23 Most historians agree that the testimonies of Cicotte, Williams, and Jackson were stolen by court officials who were bribed by Arnold Rothstein. Ban Johnson would later say, "We learned that he [Rothstein] was responsible for the theft of the secret data." "Thirty-Four Years in Baseball." *Chicago Daily Tribune*. March 10, 1929.

24 When Jackson left the hearings that day, the famous "Say it isn't so, Joe" allegdly occurred. Most historians today agree that the story is untrue and was created by a reporter for dramatic effect.

25 Amount estimated and reported to newspapers by Abe Attell. Pietruzsa. *Rothstein*. Carroll & Graf Publishers, 2003.

26 Ibid.

27 Ibid. Recorded in diary of Harry Grabiner, White Sox secretary. *Hustler's Handbook*. William Veeck. Berkeley Publishers, 1967.

28 *Appleton Post-Crescent*. September 24, 1920.

29 Earl Obenshain. "The Life Story of Ban Johnson." *Oakland Tribune*. January 18, 1929.

30 J.G. Taylor Spink. *Judge Landis and 25 Years of Baseball*. The Sporting News Publishing, 1974.

31 Ban Johnson. "My 34 Years in Baseball." *Chicago Daily Tribune*. March 10, 1929.

32 Ban Johnson. *Baseball Magazine*. (December, 1920 – Volume 26.)

33 *Appleton Post-Crescent*. September 24, 1920.

34 Letter from Johnson to Price, June 4, 1921. HOF BSS/AL files.

35 Correspondence between Johnson, D.T. Green, WB Montgomery and Alan Pinkerton, 1920-21. HOF BSS/AL files.

36 In a private letter to Navin, Johnson admits, "Personally, I would like to have spared Cicotte on account of his children." May 25, 1921. HOF BSS/AL files.

37 The origin of the phrase "Black Sox" was attributed to their black (dirty) uniforms, not the game throwing of 1919. Gene Carney. *Burying the Black Sox*. Potomac Book, 2006.

38 Meeting between Crim and Mowbray based on Crim report to Johnson dated September 23-24, 1920. HOF BSS/AL files.

39 Rothstein was shot to death in 1928. Federal officials who cleaned out his offices after his death found in a file a payment of $53,000 to Boston lawyer William Kelly. The file included affidavits proving Rothstein bribed the White Sox and stole their confessions. Craig Thompson and Allen Raymond. *Chicago Daily Tribune*. (4/28/40).

40 Correspondence between Johnson and Pinkerton, May 4, 1921. HOF BSS/AL files.

41 Mowbray description of events located in Crim Report to Johnson. (September 23-24, 1920) HOF BSS/AL files

42 "Crim was instrumental in cracking the 1919 World Series fix by locating cancelled checks in a safety deposit box." Crim Obituary. *Cincinnati Times-Star*. May 31, 1951.

43 Segments of correspondence between Crim and Johnson. HOF BSS/AL files.

44 HOF BSS/AL files.

45 Ralph Christian, SABR researcher. "The Des Moines connection to the Black Sox Scandal."

46 Claude "Bert" Hinds, partner of Cal Crim in Cincinnati. Author interview, October, 2004.

47 Letter from Johnson to Redmon, May 23, 1921. HOF BSS/AL files.

48 Via the New York City News Association, Johnson put out an urgent bulletin requesting the appearance of any news writer who could identify Attell at the Series. None came forward—including Hugh Fullerton. Hugh may have avoided this exposure because his presence would support Johnson's case (Comiskey's enemy) or because he had received two death threats by this time. HOF BSS/AL files.

49 HOF BSS/AL files.

50 Burn's testimony in Black Sox Trial, 1921. HOF BSS/AL files.

51 One character witness for Zork was Sid C. Keener, St. Louis sports editor and future Director of the Baseball Hall of Fame.

52 Ralph Christian, SABR researcher. "The Des Moines connection to the Black Sox Scandal" and *Des Moines Evening Tribune*, July 27, 1921.

53 Letter from Johnson to Redmon, July 28, 1921. HOF BSS/AL files.

54 Fred Lieb. *The Baseball Story*. 1950.

55 Comiskey's own estimate of the worth of the eight "Black Sox." Comiskey would die in 1931 having lost this investment at the hands of his former friend, Ban Johnson, and Judge Kenesaw Landis.

56 *Chicago Daily Tribune*. September 29, 1921.

57 The 1919 Fix destroyed Hugh Fullerton's career. "He lost his reputation and livelihood by biting the hand of the game that had fed and delighted him." Steve Klein. "The Lone Horseman of Baseball's Apocalypse." www.BlueEar.com, 2005.

58 Greg Rhodes and John Snyder. *The Redleg Journal*. Road West Publishing, 2000.

59 Author's Note: Edd was the last living member of the 1919 Reds in 1988 when he was interviewed by John Sayles and actors playing roles in the movie recreation of the 1919 World Series Scandal based on Isaac Asinof's book *Eight Men Out*.

60 Interview with Ray Fisher is reproduced here with permission from Bob Hunter. November, 2005.

61 Author interview with Sagert, SABR historian and author of *Joe Jackson*. (Greenwood Press, 2004.)

13

Synthetic Champions

McGraw sent me to St. Louis so that Dr. Hyland could repair my
stomach muscles. I had the only transistor radio in the place, so
guys would come and listen to games. I remember there was this
one old guy—gangster-type guy—on the same ward with me. He
had lots of company. They used to sneak beer in. We got to talking about baseball and the '19 Series...

– Edd Roush interview with Author, 1978.

AUGUST, 1928

ST. JOHN'S HOSPITAL   ST. LOUIS, MISSOURI

E dd Roush was the most popular inhabitant of the west
wing of St. John's Hospital. It was not because he was
a famous baseball player for the New York Giants. It
was because he had the only radio[1] in the ward. His fellow
patients enjoyed coming in to listen to the ballgames in the
afternoons. Sometimes they even brought beer, which made
them very popular with Edd, if not with his doctor.

Having pulled the muscles in his abdomen on a running
catch at the Polo Grounds in late July, he had finally been sent
to St. Louis a month later. McGraw had forced him to play
with his injury. The team doctor had finally intervened and told
McGraw that Roush "wasn't faking," that he had a serious
injury and was truly in pain.

Edd's doctor in St. Louis was Robert W. Hyland, known as

the "Surgeon General of Baseball."[2] Hyland was used to pro baseball players; he'd operated on hundreds in his career.[3] When Hyland first saw the extent of Edd's injury, he admonished him, saying Edd should never have played with a severe stomach muscle injury. The muscle was torn clean from the bone. Edd responded angrily with, "You tell that to John McGraw!" Edd, who had always hated McGraw, had been traded to the Giants by Cincinnati that year. He had negotiated an incredible contract with McGraw for $70,000 over a three-year period (1927-29).[4]

Essie had accompanied Edd on the trip to St. Louis, but she went home after the operation when they found out he needed to stay in St. Louis for several weeks to recover. Edd was left to fend for himself, flat on his back in an unfamiliar city.

At 34, Edd was in the closing years of his baseball career. He was still a famous player and a definite "draw" for the fans. In 1926 he hit .323 (his lifetime average) and he had never fallen under .300 during the last decade. He was constantly featured in *Baseball Magazine* and *The Sporting News* and even gave a couple of interviews to local reporters from his hospital bed that August.

One of the other patients in the all-male ward was an older fellow whom Edd would later describe as a "gangster-type." He was short with square shoulders from which hung the sinews of a once muscular frame. His gray hair was thinning with streaks of red that looked like someone had painted them. His face was scarred with pockmarks.

The guy was from St. Louis and had many local friends who brought him beer. This was no small feat in 1927 during Prohibition, and it was real beer too, not the near beer available at the time. He'd share the beer with Edd in return for being able to listen to his radio. He also finagled a big electric fan for Edd's room, for which Edd was thankful. Edd grew to like the man, and they spent many long, hot St. Louis afternoons in conversation. Years later, when Edd would describe those weeks in the hospital and the friendship he formed there, he could never remember the man's name. Or, he chose not to share it.[5] Despite the man's generosity and good fellowship, Edd remained wary of such underworld types, even years later.

One afternoon, Edd and his new friend had just turned off a Browns game and were working their way through a fresh case of beer when the subject of the 1919 World Series came up.[6] Edd went off on his usual tirade about how the Reds were cheated and would have won the damned Series anyway. As his friend seemed unusually interested, Edd described the various games and some of his own fielding triumphs. His friend encouraged him to tell him more of the specifics. What was Groh really like? Was he a hot head? How heavy was that bottle bat he used?

Then the fellow asked about the pitchers. What did Edd think about Ruether...Eller...Sallee...Ring? Edd was surprised that the guy remembered the names of players from a Series played eight years before. At first he thought the guy was some kind of sports nut, and he went on to describe his teammates in detail. In the middle of Edd's description of the wild side of Jimmy Ring, his friend interrupted him.

He said, "I was there. I was in Cincinnati and Chicago ...saw the whole Series."

Edd squinted in disbelief.

The gangster added some evidence: "I saw you do that somersault catch in the last game in Chicago. That was something. I'll never forget that play."

Edd asked, "Do you go to all the World Series?"

The answer was quick: "Just that one." Then he added with a strange little twinkle in his eye, "I had a little business to do."

Edd remembered the newspaper reports that said some of

the gamblers involved in the fix had been from St. Louis. He blurted out, "Were you one of them gamblers who got to Cicotte?"[7]

The man just smiled and said, "Well, no...but I knew a couple of them."

"So, was it really fixed? The courts let them off. It was Landis who barred them for life."

"It was fixed all right. It started right here in little ole' St. Louie. A fellow name of Zork came up with the idea, but the money came from New York, from Rothstein."

The names came flooding back. They had been in the newspapers, but he hadn't really paid much attention to the details when it happened. He didn't want to know about it. He wanted to believe his team had won fairly.

"One thing I never could figure out," Edd said. "Why did it take so damned long to work out the whole mess?"

The fellow laughed. "Yeah, the magnates were our best friends for a while. They wanted to hush it up. And they did, until that suck-ass Harry Redmon decided to sing. He owns the Majestic Theater over in East St. Louie. He lost a lot of money and thought he'd cash in on Comiskey's $20,000 reward. Dumb ass. He and Gedeon practically got us all wiped out."

Edd noticed that he was now talking about "us" rather than them. "How did you guys get off scot free?"

"The magnates were in cahoots with the lawyers. They didn't want us. The whole thing was just a big show to prove to the public they were 'cleaning up baseball' and all that. There's always been gambling in baseball, always will be." The gangster looked out the slat of the open window for a few seconds, as if remembering it all. "We had Cicotte and Williams in our pockets all the way. That is until Cicotte grew a conscience and started playing to win. That was a double-cross, no question about it. He'd probably be dead now if Landis hadn't banned all of them. I guess New York figured that was punishment enough, taking away their livelihoods and all."

"What about Jackson? Was he dirty?" This question had plagued Edd for eight years.

"He took the money, didn't he?"

"But I heard he tried to give it back."

The man cackled with laughter. "He tried to give it to Comiskey! What a dumb ass."

Edd said, "What about Gleason? Did he know what was going on?"

"If he had two eyes, he knew it. He got the bum's rush in the whole thing. Really messed him up too. Shame." The gambler seemed genuinely sorry about the Sox manager.

Then Edd remembered the biggest shyster he'd ever known. Why not throw him in the mix too? "I played with Hal Chase in Cincinnati before they booted him out. He was the dirtiest player I ever saw. But he was good at it. Hard to catch him." Edd recalled specific incidents involving Chase. Then he asked, "So, was Chase involved in the fix?"

"What do *you* think?" His hospital mate's eyes were gleaming.

"I don't know. That's why I'm asking you."

"Never could have happened without him. He was the go-between for everyone...the East and the West. He even brought in Burns from the South. He had all the connections— the players, the gamblers, the magnates, even your buddy McGraw, by the way."[8]

Edd nodded. That didn't surprise him at all. He knew Muggsy had underworld connections. Who didn't know it? He bragged about his casino and his gambling wins all the time.

The gambler continued, "Yeah, that Chase is a piece of work. He's sneaky, but smart. I once saw him win a bundle in a dice game. When he left he handed me the dice. They were loaded!" They laughed together.

A thought crossed Edd's mind, something he'd read some-where. He said, "I understand those big Tammany thugs in New York are nothing to mess around with. Did anyone get roughed up over this thing?"

His friend nodded. "I just know what I heard. Rothstein went after your big magnate…Johnson. As I heard it, Johnson double-crossed the big man and made him come to Chicago to testify in the grand jury doings. He wasn't happy about it. Warned Johnson in the newspaper.[9] By the way, is Johnson still alive?"

They had a good laugh together, but the undercurrent was serious.[10] One of the St. Louis gamblers, Joe Pesch, had com-mitted suicide, and many others had gone into hiding for sev-eral years.[11]

Edd said, "What about *our* boys? Were they involved?"

The gambler's answer was light and cheerful. "Hey, you won it, didn't you? Who cares now?"

Edd said, "I want to know!"

The guy looked at Edd squarely. "The way I heard it, they oiled up Ruether and Sallee before the Series started—during the season. But I don't know for sure if any arrangements were made. Tried for Rariden and Wingo, but no dice. That was a problem with the Sox, too. We really needed the catcher, but Schalk wouldn't play."

Edd was shocked to hear his friend Rariden's name men-tioned.[12] He was not shocked that Bill had been on the square. As for Ruether and Sallee, it was much tougher to know, but he suspected they had not tried to win games Six and Seven. Edd said, "We saw those two talking to gamblers during practice lots of times. Groh and I talked about it. Fisher too. They were out there everyday." Then he remembered something else. "After the game when we'd all go down to the brewery, they'd go off with those gamblers again. Hell, everybody saw them."

The gambler offered a shrug and a quizzical smile. "Our guys here had nothing to do with the Reds. That probably was Burns.[13] He got double-crossed by Rothstein and sang at the trial to pay him back. He also walked away with a bundle of magnate money, as they tell it. He fingered us in St. Louis too. Then he disappeared. We're still looking for him."

As the late afternoon sun beamed through the slanted windows of the hospital room, it became a contest: Who could tell the biggest story? Edd said, "Now I'll tell *you* something. I knew one of your guys, a gambler in Cincinnati.[14] He told me all about it the night before the last game. I went straight to Moran the next morning." Edd told the story about Hod Eller, the bribe offered in the hotel, and the scene in the Reds locker room.

His friend seemed surprised. "That's a new one on me. We scouted the Reds pretty close...Eller wasn't an option. Our guys here didn't figure any of your team would take the bait."

"If you came to me. I would have punched you right in the nose," Edd said.

His friend laughed. "We knew you were one of the honest ones. Your team too. You all wanted to win too much to throw it."

This comment took Edd on a sentimental journey. He had loved the Reds. He was still hurting because his Reds had traded him back to the Giants. There was nowhere he'd rather be than Redland Field. That had been his ballpark, his team, his life. Always would be.

Then the nurse came in and stopped the conversation. With dinner trays in hand, she admonished the men for the beer drinking, as she had done so many times before. The hospital administration seemed to have a double standard when it came to patients who were professional ballplayers.

Edd never knew how much to believe of those conversations in St. Louis. Sometimes he felt the guy was telling the truth, was somehow "in the know." Other times, he wasn't sure. As long as he lived, Edd Roush he did believe that the Reds won the 1919 World Series on the square. As years passed, his teammates would take their turn with reporters and echo the same claim.[15]

"I was there. I saw them. Jackson and Weaver just couldn't be playing that way and not playing." – Adolfo Luque

"The Sox were playing for keeps in the two games I pitched." – Hod Eller

"I didn't realize it at the time. I couldn't believe it, although it was whispered around the hotels and gambling headquarters that something underhanded was taking place." – Slim Sallee

"There isn't any question but that there were some shenanigans in the first game, but remember the Sox who fell for the fixers weren't paid what they were promised. You can bet your life they were shooting in the next seven games." – Greasy Neale

"We didn't surmise a damn thing. I couldn't figure it out." – Larry Kopf

"I found [Cicotte's pitching] as hard to solve as any I had faced during the year…they seemed to be doing their level best to win. We attributed the stories heard around Cincinnati about the White Sox not trying to 'sour grapes' on the

part of American League sympathizers."
– Heinie Groh

"Well, maybe the White Sox did throw it. I don't know. Maybe they did and maybe they didn't. It's hard to say. I didn't see anything that looked suspicious. But I think we'd have beaten them either way; that's what I thought then and I still think it today." – Heinie Groh

"If they threw some of the games they must be consummate actors, and their place is on the stage, for nothing in their playing gave us the impression they weren't doing their best....It is an astonishing thing to me that [they] could get away with that sort of thing and us not know it." – Pat Moran

"I had no suspicions whatever of any wrong-doing." – Richard Nallin, Umpire

"Well, I guess I'm just a big dope. That Series looked all right to me." – Billy Evans, Umpire

"I did watch the games with particular care for evidences of crooked dealing, but I could see nothing." – Ban Johnson

"I have never given such a ridiculous question any thought. We won the National League pennant fairly and squarely, and we had to beat a team or two to do it that were stronger than the White Sox playing at their best and on the level. …what is more, we believe firmly that we would have beaten them had every man on Comiskey's team played the string out and on the level." – Garry Herrmann

"I didn't get a bingle off Cicotte, and every time I faced him he seemed to have a world of speed. I can't yet see how they could play the way they did and throw the games. It is a mystery to me." – Edd Roush

"I was reading a piece the other day in a book, *Eight Men Out*, where a fellow said Williams was just laying the ball in there, he didn't throw a curve ball. Now I know what I hit—it was a curve ball. …There were two men on in the first inning and I hit a curve ball off Williams—he was a left-handed pitcher and I was a left-handed hitter—and it went right over the first base bag." – Edd Roush

"Have I suspicions today? Yes, I have, about some of our own men who figured in those defeats in the sixth and seventh games. They are gone and forgotten, so why bring up any names?" – Edd Roush

"I don't know whether the whole truth of what went on there with the White Sox will ever come out. Even today nobody knows exactly what took place. Whatever it was, though, it was a dirty, rotten shame. One thing that's always overlooked in the whole mess is that we could have beat them no matter what the circumstances!" – Edd Roush

"Well, I'll tell you. They [the White Sox] didn't get their money after the first game. After that they decided to go out there and try to win it. We beat them fair and square. I'll believe that to my dying day." – Edd Roush

When Edd went to sleep that night in 1928, he must have wondered what was the actual truth about one of the most dramatic events he had lived through in his career. He would wonder for the rest of his life.

Whatever the whole truth is, we may never know entirely. As long as there are baseball fans in the world, the 1919 World Series will be a subject that stimulates emotions that range from heated argument to mythical dreams. Almost a century later, books and movies are still produced about that famous week in October so many years ago.

Edd Roush always swore to anyone who asked that the Reds were better in 1919 than the White Sox. Long after Essie passed away, Edd was still being interviewed about the Series. He would get angry when someone said the Reds won only because the Sox threw the Series. He knew in his heart that the Reds were the better team.[16]

After 85 years, it is time to give the Cincinnati Reds of 1919 the respect they deserve. They have suffered the humiliation of being "synthetic champions" long enough. The best team did win the 1919 World Series.

1 Author's Note: Although Roush called his radio a transistor, this is unlikely. He may have owned an "Operadio 2," which was a pre-transistor cordless model that was state of the art in 1928.

2 Steve Steinberg. SABR researcher.

3 Ibid. Urban Shocker was to die from heart disease in this same hospital later (September 9, 1928.)

4 For more detail on the Roush-McGraw wars, see 1916 chapter.

5 Recollections from one of many taped interviews from 1972-1985 with the author. Research of hospital records of the time have not succeeded in finding the "gangster's" name.

6 Author's Note: Although the description of Edd and his hospital mate in St. Louis is true, much of the specific language is hypothetical and is used to present dramatically this chance meeting that Edd remembered for the rest of his life.

7 Edd always pronounced Cicotte as "Sigh-Cot."

8 Sportswriter Fred Lieb, a personal friend of Edd Roush, identified Chase as the master fixer in *The Baseball Story*. 1950

9 Rothstein warned Johnson in a press release, "Ban Johnson needs to watch his step: the most peaceful of men can be driven too far."

10 Author's Note: Most of the men involved in the 1919 Series never talked about it afterward. When Hollywood was preparing to film *Eight Men Out*, author Eliot Asinof told director John Sayles, "A lot of the guys he talked to were still afraid of the gamblers, even though the gamblers were long in the grave. You simply didn't mess with these people." John Sayles. *Conversations with Filmmakers Series*. MSU. Press, 1999.

11 Ban Johnson received a telegram from Taylor Spink on October 24, 1924, informing him of the Pesch suicide. The telegram ended with an ominous note, "Zork still alive." HOF BSS/AL files.

12 Years later, Bill Rariden told friends at his gas station in Bedford, Indiana, that he was "stalked by some reporter or detective-type" for years after the 1919 Series. He claimed he was "finally cleared" and they left him alone. Interview with Tom Rariden, grandson. January, 2005.

13 Reference is to "Sleepy" Bill Burns, major witness for the prosecution in 1921 trial.

14 Edd refers here to Jimmy Widmeyer.

15 Source for majority of quotes listed: Gene Carney. *Burying the Black Sox*. (Chapter 2) Potomac Books, 2006.

16 After extensive statistical analyses, Harry Hollingsworth, SABR researcher, declared the 1919 Cincinnati Reds to be #26 in the "TOP 30 Baseball Teams of All Time." The 1919 White Sox came in at #115. Hollingsworth performed his analysis on pennant winning MLB teams

from 1901 to 2000. He then identified the "Best Team to ever play for each MLB Franchise." For the Chicago White Sox it was the 1901 team. For the Cincinnati franchise, the 1919 Reds were the #1 team of the 20th Century. …Hollingsworth Report, February, 2001. (Updated data supporting Hollingsworth's book, *The Best and Worst Baseball Teams of All-Time.* SPI, New York, 1994.)

Epilogue

The call came in at 11:45 a.m. The voice said, "We need an ambulance! A guy here is having a heart attack, or a stroke, or something! Come to McKechnie baseball field, and hurry! Come to the clubhouse. The guy's name is Roush. He's here in the press room."

The emergency men flew into action, jumped into the truck, and raced through the noon traffic. They made the two miles in six minutes flat. It took another four minutes to locate the squat, white building down the left field foul line and north of the grandstand. They pulled to a stop behind the building where a half-dozen men were motioning to them. One of the EMTs grabbed a defibrillator, the airway kit, and the meds bag, while the other followed with the stretcher.

In the small room, they found a little group of people hovering over an old man whose head was lying in the hands of another man. His bright red baseball cap with the Cincinnati Reds insignia on the front had fallen off his head onto the floor. There was a half-eaten hot dog and a beer sitting on the table in front of the old guy. His false teeth had been spit out on the table next to the food. The man holding his head was the first to speak.

"He asked me to hold his head. It's really hot. I think he's having a stroke." Then he said to the old man, "Edd, can you hear me? The ambulance is here. They're taking you to the hospital now." He looked at the young EMT and said, "He's ninety-four years old. This is Edd Roush."

The young man showed no sign of recogition.

"He's a Hall of Famer, for Chrissake," the man said. "He's had a few strokes and always pulled through. Hasn't been to the ballpark for three years. He wanted to come today, for some reason."

The young man hooked up the EKG. His partner handled the oxygen mask and took the vitals. Just as they feared—the heart was racing at 280, he was in V-Tac (Ventricular Tachycardia). They pushed back the group of onlookers, and put the electrical shock plates on the old man's chest. The shock jolted the body up and off he floor. Nothing. They tried again. Okay, the heart was beating, but they had to work fast now.

As they moved him onto the stretcher, several firemen joined them. The young EMT administered CPR, while his partner operated the ventilator and the firemen carried the stretcher. When they slid the old man into the back of the vehicle, the man who had held his head asked if they thought the old guy would make it. He introduced himself as Kent Chetlain, Manatee County Commissioner, former sports editor for the *Bradenton Herald* and longtime friend of the Roush family.

The young paramedic answered by shaking his head and said, "You'd better call his family."

With the old man in back, the paramedic jumped behind the wheel of the ambulance. He swung the vehicle around and headed straight for the baseball diamond. If he drove directly through the center of the field, he could catch the dirt road on the north side that would dump them out faster onto Highway 301. From there he could race directly to the hospital. He clicked off the radio and pushed down on the gas pedal.

Young athletes wearing Pirates and Rangers uniforms were warming up on the field.

They jumped out of the way as the ambulance screeched past. They must have wondered who was important enough to delay their game that day. All were far too young to remember when the old man, their fellow ballplayer, roamed the field and terrorized pitchers.

At Bradenton Memorial Hospital, Edd Roush was pronounced dead at 1 p.m., just as the game was beginning at the ball field. The next day, his obituary ran in all the major newspapers in the country, the details of his long life summed up neatly:

- born 1893 in Oakland City, Indiana
- died six weeks short of his 95th Birthday
- longtime winter resident of Bradenton, Florida
- died of a heart attack one month after death of his twin brother, Fred Roush
- oldest living member of Baseball Hall of Fame
- 18 years in major league baseball
- lifetime batting average of .325
- famous as stubborn salary holdout (held out entire year of 1930)
- star center fielder for Cincinnati Reds and New York Giants
- voted by fans as "Greatest Red Who Ever Lived" in 1969 at Cincinnati Reds Centennial Celebration
- last living participant in the 1919 "Black Sox" World Series

Columnist Howard Hall described it this way:

Roush died yesterday in an old-fashioned ball-park, Bradenton's McKechnie Field, a place where Wee Willie Keeler and Ty Cobb would have felt at home.

He went out in the blaze of noon.

It was later determined that Edd Roush died in the ambulance as it sped across the diamond into the outfield. Edd had died where he wanted to be—in center field.

EDD ROUSH (FAR LEFT) WITH JACKIE ROBINSON, BOB FELLER, AND BILL MCKECHNIE AT THE 1962 BASEBALL HALL OF FAME INDUCTION CEREMONY

Appendix

CIN	AB	R	H	2B	3B	RBI	SB	ER	AVG
Ruether	6	2	4	1	2	4	0	0	.667
Wingo	7	1	4	0	0	1	0	0	.571
Fisher	2	0	1	0	0	0	1	1	.500
Magee	2	0	1	0	0	0	0	0	.500
Neale	28	3	10	1	1	4	1	1	.357
Eller	7	2	2	1	0	0	0	0	.286
Duncan	26	3	7	1	0	8	0	0	.269
Daubert	29	4	7	0	1	1	2	2	.241
Rath	31	5	7	1	0	2	2	2	.226
Kopf	27	3	6	0	2	2	1	1	.222
Roush	28	6	6	2	1	7	2	2	.214
Rariden	19	0	4	0	0	2	1	1	.211
Groh	29	6	5	2	0	2	2	2	.172

Pitching:	W	L	ERA
Eller	2	0	2.00
Ring	1	1	0.64
Ruether	1	0	2.57
Sallee	1	1	1.35
Fisher	0	1	2.35
Luque	0	0	0.00

CHI	AB	R	H	2B	3B	RBI	SB	ER	AVG
McMullin	2	0	1	0	0	0	0	0	.500
Jackson	32	5	12	3	0	6	0	0	.375
Weaver	34	4	11	4	1	0	0	0	.324
Schalk	23	1	7	0	0	2	1	1	.304
S.Collins	16	2	4	1	0	0	0	0	.250
Gandil	30	1	7	0	1	5	1	1	.233
E.Collins	31	2	7	1	0	1	1	2	.226
Williams	5	0	1	0	0	0	0	0	.200
Felsch	26	2	5	1	0	3	0	2	.192
Kerr	6	0	1	0	0	0	0	0	.167
Risberg	25	3	2	0	1	0	1	4	.080
Liebold	18	0	1	0	0	0	1	0	.056
Cicotte	8	0	0	0	0	0	0	2	.000

Pitching:	W	L	ERA
Cicotte	1	2	2.91
Kerr	2	0	1.42
Williams	0	3	6.61
Wilkinson	0	0	3.68
James	0	0	5.79
Loudermilk	0	0	9.00
Mayer	0	0	0.00

TEAM	AB	R	H	2B	3B	HR	RBI	SB	ER	AVG
CIN	251	35	64	10	7	0	33	12	12	.255
CHI	263	20	59	10	3	1	17	5	12	.224

---

[1] Information provided by Jim Sandoval, SABR historian and 1919 World Series expert.

Books of Interest

Each book in the **Baseball Behind the Seams** series focuses on a single position, exploring it with the kind of depth serious fans crave. Through extensive research, including interviews with hundreds of players past and present, the authors have brought together the most original and informative series ever published on the game.

Each book in the series covers

- The physical and mental qualities of the position
- The position's history
- The plays, and how to make them
- Profiles of the position's top all-time players
- The best defenders of the position
- A day in the life of one player, from arriving at the ball park to the final out
- Lists of Gold Glovers, MVPs, and Rookies of the Year
- Fun and quirky facts about the position

   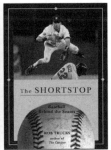

The Catcher	The Starting Pitcher	The First Baseman	The Shortstop
By Rob Trucks	By Rob Trucks	By Tom Keegan	By Rob Trucks
$14.99 Paperback	$14.99 Paperback	$14.95 Paperback	$14.95 Paperback
ISBN: 1-57860-164-9	ISBN: 1-57860-163-0	ISBN: 1-57860-261-0	ISBN: 1-57860-262-9

Available at local and online booksellers or at www.emmisbooks.com.
Emmis Books, 1700 Madison Road, Cincinnati, Ohio 45206

Books of Interest

The Baseball Uncyclopedia:
A Highly Opinionated, Myth-Busting Guide to the Great American Game

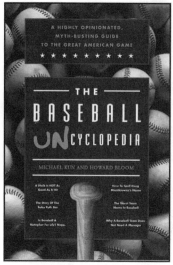